International Institute for Strategic Studies IISS

STRATEGIC SURVEY 1979

The International Institute for Strategic Studies
23 Tavistock Street London WC2E 7NQ

The International Institute for Strategic Studies

The Institute is an international centre. The IISS was originally founded in 1958 by a group of British analysts, academics, politicians, journalists and men of the Church to study the growing complexity of security in the nuclear age. However, it soon became clear that this could not be done from a national perspective, and since 1964 the Institute, which had in any case had an international membership from the outset, has become fully international. Its Council includes members from a variety of countries and its membership now extends over some sixty countries, with its publications being sold to many more. The Institute's staff is international, its researchers come from a variety of different countries every year, and its foundation support (its primary source of finance) comes from a number of countries in America, Europe and Asia.

The Institute has three major functions. It is a research institute (but not a teaching centre), an information centre and a place for discussion and debate on international security problems. The assumption underlying all its work is that rationality makes a major contribution to security — and this is what its research, the information it provides and the discussion forum it offers are all aimed at achieving.

Research: The Institute sees as its prime responsibilities the analysis of the complexities of international security and conflict and the injection of new thinking into the debate. Its research will thus always be policy-orientated. The major part of IISS research is carried out by a team of research associates, complemented by the Directing Staff. Up to eight Research Associates, from a variety of national and professional backgrounds, normally stay for one year, working on a specific project.

Information: The Institute is an independent source of information on military forces and security developments, and as such is widely used by journalists, analysts and students. The two major instruments of information are the Institute's libraries and its publications — *The Military Balance, Strategic Survey,* Adelphi Papers and *Survival*. For details of these see the back cover; for subscription arrangements see the cards between pages 60 and 61.

Debate: As an international centre for research and information, the Institute has become, over the years, a forum of discussion for the international constituency concerned with security, military and political conflict and arms control. Among its members, who include politicians, scholars, military men, officials and journalists, are a growing number from third-world countries. A variety of meetings and seminars are organized throughout the year in addition to the Annual Conference and the Alastair Buchan Memorial Lecture.

STRATEGIC SURVEY 1979

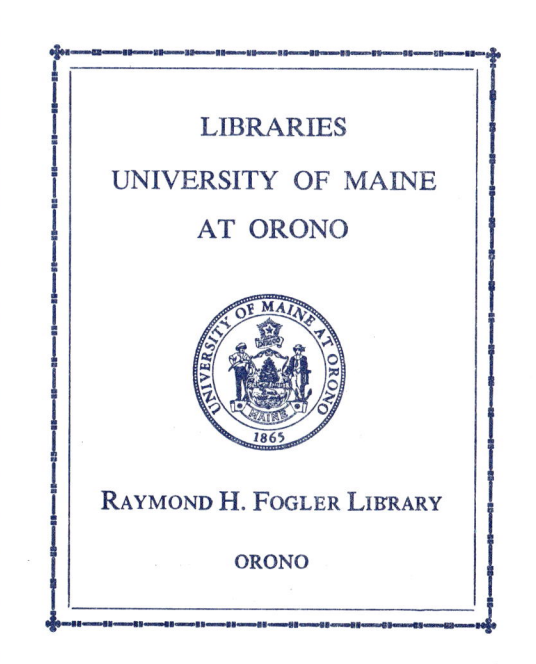

The International Institute for Strategic Studies
23 Tavistock Street London WC2E 7NQ

Published by
The International Institute for Strategic Studies
23 Tavistock Street, London WC2E 7NQ

This publication has been prepared by the Director of the Institute and his Staff, who accept full responsibility for its contents. These do not, and indeed cannot, represent a consensus of views among the world-wide membership of the Institute as a whole.

First published Spring 1980

ISBN 0 86079 037 1
ISSN 0459-7230

© The International Institute for Strategic Studies

All rights reserved. No part of this publication may be reproduced, stored in a retrieval system, or transmitted in any form or by any means, electronic, mechanical, photo-copying, recording or otherwise, without the prior permission of the International Institute for Strategic Studies

Printed in Great Britain by Neil Moore Associates, London

CONTENTS

PERSPECTIVES 1

NEW FACTORS IN SECURITY
Strategic Command and Control 11
Nuclear Proliferation in South Asia . . . 15
The Soviet Navy as a Political Instrument . . 20
Oil and Security 24

THE SUPER-POWERS
An End to Detente? 29
The United States: Concern Over Security . . 33
The Soviet Union: Arms and the Economy . . 39

SOUTH-WEST ASIA
Iran after the Revolution 41
Crisis over Afghanistan 48

EAST ASIA
War in Indochina 56
Co-operation in South-East Asia . . . 61
The Defence Debate in Japan 65
China's Defence Industries 67

THE MIDDLE EAST
Israel and the Palestinian Issue 73
Egypt and the Arab States 78

AFRICA
Southern Africa 84
The Maghreb: Implications of the Saharan War . 93

EUROPE
Modernizing Theatre Nuclear Forces in NATO . 99
Developments in Warsaw Pact Forces . . 103

CENTRAL AMERICA
Revolution in Nicaragua 108

ARMS CONTROL
Strategic Arms Limitation Talks 113
Negotiating European Security 117
Other Arms-Control Negotiations . . . 120

CHRONOLOGIES
North America 124
Europe 126
The Soviet Union 128
Asia and Australia 129
Middle East and North Africa 131
Sub-Saharan Africa 134
Latin America and the Caribbean . . . 136
East-West Arms Control 138

PERSPECTIVES

1979 began with the overthrow of the Shah of Iran, a close ally of the United States for thirty years; it ended with the Soviet invasion of Afghanistan – which sought to crush growing revolt against an unpopular Soviet-backed regime with the first large-scale use of Soviet troops fighting outside Eastern Europe since the end of World War II.

These events illustrated many of the security problems of the new decade. They underlined that the industrialized world's dependence on secure oil supplies has turned threats to the stability of the Persian Gulf region into threats to international security as a whole. They demonstrated that, while the sources of conflict in what is conveniently (if incorrectly) called the Third World may be primarily internal, such conflicts affect the interests of outside powers, which inevitably brings into play considerations of East–West rivalry and competition. Finally, they illustrated that, while military force is by no means ineffective, its ability to cope with crises emerging in the developing world is nevertheless severely circumscribed. American military potential could not stop the revolution in Iran, nor could concentrating US naval power in the region force fanatical students in Tehran to release the 50 American diplomats they took hostage in November. And the use of Soviet divisions in Afghanistan, far from rapidly imposing the Soviet notion of law and order there, triggered powerful indigenous challenges that promised major problems for the invaders.

The Soviet action in this sensitive region was bound to have profound effects on international security as a whole. For one thing, it threatened to reverse the increasing tendency of the West to consider third-world crises in their specific local and regional setting, rather than press them into the matrix of global East–West competition. The US-sponsored Camp David Accord between Israel and Egypt, Britain's successful negotiation of a settlement in Rhodesia, and the change in American policy towards the Somoza regime in Nicaragua all reflected this trend.

After the invasion of Afghanistan, however, this conflict-specific approach seemed likely to be superseded once more. At least for the West's leading power, the traditional aim of containing Soviet military power again became the primary one. In May 1977 President Carter had argued: 'Being confident about our own future, we are now free of that inordinate fear of Communism which once led us to embrace any dictator who joined us in our fear. For too many years we have been willing to adopt the flawed principles and tactics of our adversaries, sometimes abandoning our values for theirs. We fought fire with fire, never thinking that fire is better fought with water.' Less than three years later, in January 1980, after the Soviet invasion, he said in his State of the Union Message: 'We must pay whatever price is required to remain the strongest nation in the world ... [The cost of the necessary defence facilities] has increased as the military power of our major adversary has grown, and its readiness to use that power has been made all too evident in Afghanistan.' In the same speech, he said: 'Any attempt by an outside force to gain control of the Persian Gulf region will be regarded as an assault on the vital interests of the United States. It will be repelled by use of any means necessary, including military force.'

The contrast between these statements indicated the change not only in the mind of the American President but in the international climate as a whole. But the main question at the beginning of the 1980s was how profound and durable that change would be. Was the United States returning to the policies of earlier decades with their emphasis on the containment of Soviet power world-wide? Was the Soviet action in Afghanistan a continuation of past policies, or did it indicate new directions? What would this action mean for the future of East–West relations, as well as for relations between the United States and her allies? In the past decade the West had viewed military power with growing scepticism; would it again become a major instrument in the policies of both great powers in the next decade?

The United States: A New Assertiveness
The change in American policy had not come overnight. It had been visible well before the world's leading power suffered the humiliating experience of watching fanatics in Iran holding 50 American diplomats hostage, and before the Soviet invasion in Afghanistan. These events

were not the cause but the catalyst of the changed mood. They crystallized a consensus that had been developing for some time.

No great nation can remain forever in the state of self-doubt that the war in South-east Asia and the constitutional crisis of Watergate had produced; and humiliation often breeds determination. This combined with a growing feeling that America's weakness was being exploited by others, particularly the Soviet Union, and led to a growing concern over Soviet military power. This was caused both by Soviet actions in the Third World – from Angola to Afghanistan – and by the relentless Soviet military effort, not least in the nuclear-strategic field. Even before 1979 those who claimed that the Soviet Union was behind the frustrations of American interests in the Third World had met with growing popular approval, and Soviet strategic efforts were seen by an increasing number of analysts as the clear expression of a search for strategic superiority over the United States. Both fears came to the fore in the American debate over the ratification of the second Strategic Arms Limitation Treaty (SALT II) which Presidents Carter and Brezhnev signed in June 1979. In contrast to the reaction to the 1972 SALT I Agreement, distrust of Soviet motives was marked. Why, Americans asked, should one trust a state that had repeatedly used military power to seek unilateral advantage in the Third World? Why agree limitations on strategic power with a country that not only had shown no serious readiness to restrain its own military effort but had indeed invested heavily and continuously in the accumulation of strategic forces? It was not difficult to recognize the strength of American concern. Not surprisingly, the SALT debate became one essentially about the need to increase American strategic power and not about the merits of arms control.

After an interval of several years, therefore, the future direction of American policy and the public consensus on the US role in the world seemed to become clearer. The ingredients were a deep distrust of the Soviet Union, a new emphasis on the need for military strength, and generally a greater assertiveness in American policies. Yet, despite the superficial similarities, these feelings were unlikely to presage a return to the pre-Vietnam period of undisputed American superiority and unquestioned American will for leadership. The thrust of the debate did not suggest an attempt to resurrect the *Pax Americana* of the 1950s and 60s; rather the new assertiveness pointed to a more forceful pursuit of national interests and the belief that the United States would have to fend for herself in a hostile world. Growing impatience with what was seen as foot-dragging by America's allies over the crises in Iran and Afghanistan was likely to reinforce this belief.

The Soviet Union: New Insecurities

The Soviet Union seemed to the US to be increasingly confident of her accumulated power, and it was possible that this view was shared by the Soviet leadership. And yet, as the new decade began, Soviet strategic prospects were by no means unambiguously favourable.

There had been a relative stagnation in Western military efforts during the 1970s, but this seemed certain to change in the 1980s. The Soviet Union's search for military advantage and her exploitation of opportunities to project Soviet power in the Third World had not only eroded support for detente in the West but had also prompted the beginning of major increases in Western (and particularly American) defence programmes. By refusing to exercise military restraint at a time of Western military contraction, the Soviet Union had prompted a Western response which, if implemented, could weaken seriously her own strategic position by the second half of the decade. New American strategic programmes – such as development of the MX ICBM, the strategic cruise missile and more accurate warheads on all US delivery systems – coupled with the existing American lead in anti-submarine warfare, were likely to reduce the strategic vulnerability of the United States, while increasing that of the Soviet Union. With some 75% of Soviet strategic warheads concentrated in potentially vulnerable fixed land-based ICBM (as opposed to 26% on the American side) and with submarine forces highly vulnerable, the trend of strategic weapons technology threatened to erode many of the advantages that the Soviet strategic programmes had sought to secure. Other Western programmes would add to this challenge. In Europe, Britain was preparing to modernize her strategic forces, France was upgrading hers, and in December the NATO countries adopted a programme for the deployment of a total of 572 long-range theatre nuclear missiles which, once in place, would reach Soviet territory. And Japan, increasingly concerned over growing Soviet military efforts in north-east

Asia, seemed to be moving slowly towards expressing these concerns in the form of new military programmes.

In addition, events in China were likely to reinforce the traditional Soviet fear of encirclement, which had surfaced again in recent years. China was gradually emerging from the paralysis of the past and moving in the direction of modernizing her industry and, in due course, her military base, though these would not be rapid developments. But as the Peking leadership around Deng Xiaoping consolidated its position (having, with its February 1979 invasion of Vietnam, shown that it was willing to play a decisive regional role), latent Soviet anxieties were again aroused. Chinese reactions to the Soviet incursion into Afghanistan were likely to confirm these fears. Not only did Chinese leaders openly advocate support to Afghans resisting Soviet forces, but the invasion also prompted a more flexible American attitude to military co-operation with China. During a visit in January 1980, US Secretary of Defense Harold Brown emphasized the two countries' shared security interests in the region, and Washington agreed to provide militarily useful civilian technology to Peking. The prospect of the world's most advanced technological power supporting the world's most populous country could only sharpen the fear of encirclement.

Another factor affecting the USSR's outlook was that the days of her self-sufficiency in energy supplies appeared to be numbered. While estimates varied widely as to when she would become a net importer of energy, they all agreed that sooner or later the Soviet Union would have to seek energy from world markets – markets which she does not control and where payments would have to be made in the hard currencies.

How would the Soviet Union react to these trends? While the old and inflexible Soviet leadership was unlikely to preside over a major shift in priorities near the end of its tenure, the invasion of Afghanistan and subsequent statements by the Soviet leaders did not exclude a change in the direction of Soviet policies. A working relationship with the United States implying a recognition of military and political parity had long been a priority for the Brezhnev Politburo. Yet since the Soviet Union's own actions had undermined support in the United States for detente, her policy had instead begun to emphasize relations with Western Europe and to indicate that the proximity and weight of her military power should incline Europe to respect Soviet interests. That the Soviet Union had been willing to accept some undermining of her standing in the Third World as a result of her invasion of Afghanistan suggested that, while she was continuing her military efforts to achieve global reach, the USSR was nevertheless giving priority to her security needs at home and on her periphery – a contraction not of means but of emphasis. Western concerns that the Afghan intervention might be the first step towards a military interference in the sensitive Gulf region might seem premature, but it was nonetheless likely that the Soviet Union would see her military weight as a useful lever against oil-producing countries if she were to seek preferential agreements for the supply of energy.

A Detente of Tensions

As the new decade began, detente – the attempt to find East–West accommodation despite continuing rivalry – entered a new and difficult phase. In the East there was a recognition of the trends working against the Soviet Union, disillusionment over the repeated delays to the ratification of the SALT II agreement, and a certain bewilderment at the unpredictability of US policies. Initially at least, these factors prompted a hardening of positions, renewed emphasis on ideological conformity in Eastern Europe and maintenance of the military effort, notwithstanding growing economic difficulties.

Western scepticism over detente, particularly in the United States, threatened to delay a return to serious Soviet–American negotiation until the US again felt confident that she could negotiate from a position of military strength. However, her allies, particularly West Germany, were conscious of the advantages which the improved climate of East–West relations had brought over the past decade and were reluctant to jeopardize them. But the Afghan crisis also reminded them, if a reminder was needed, that Western Europe could not conduct a detente relationship with the East without American support and direct involvement.

The events of the year confirmed as well that developments in the Third World, outside the traditional sphere of East–West policies, could increasingly undermine the basis of detente – if not directly, then indirectly through their effect on popular support for negotiation with the Soviet Union. The repeated Western insistence that 'detente is indivisible' had not effectively constrained Soviet interventions in the Third World in the past and was even less likely to do so in future. It could never be a substitute for counter-measures on the spot. There seemed to be little direct advantage, therefore, in jeopardizing detente's utility in the traditional East–West sphere by insisting that it should be indivisible. And yet, as the impact of successive Soviet interventions in third-world crises had shown, acceptance of the Soviet Union as a partner for negotiation and agreement in the traditional field of East-West relations could not be isolated from her behaviour elsewhere: events in Angola in 1974 had led directly to the decline in US support for Soviet–American co-operation, and the invasion of Afghanistan in 1979 seemed to have postponed for some time the ratification of SALT II.

The impact of these crises on East–West detente had been aggravated by the absence of any serious high-level dialogue between the major powers on the whole range of their relationship. When President Carter, in his third year in office, finally met his counterpart President Brezhnev in their only Summit meeting (in Vienna in June), the atmosphere had been steadily deteriorating, and neither established any real understanding of the concerns and objectives of the other.

What Prospects for Arms Control ?

The crisis in East–West relations that was so apparent at the end of the year did not imply a total collapse of detente – contacts between East and West would continue. But it did underline the need to reassess both the procedures and the substance of future co-operation. This applied in particular to the objectives of arms control, which for many represented the most concrete example of the ability of East and West to compromise by regulating military competition. Yet at no time in the past two decades had there been such uncertainty about how to do this.

One reason for this uncertainty undoubtedly lay in Soviet behaviour. Soviet lack of military restraint had undermined the respect for the spirit, and not just the letter, of agreements that is for Western public opinion a concomitant of arms control and detente. Another reason was the difficulty of convincing a sceptical public, particularly the American public, of the primary importance of the SALT negotiations. Signed by Presidents Carter and Brezhnev in June 1979, the SALT II Treaty was a serious agreement that was the result of almost seven years of negotiations. Yet the Administration was unable to insulate it against a spreading sense, both in the Congress and among the American public, that arms control was a concession to the Soviet Union. Only after the Treaty had been signed did President Carter launch his campaign to secure its ratification, and then the momentum faltered as disputes on marginal issues (most notably that about the Soviet brigade in Cuba) diverted attention from the central ones. Perhaps by then it was too late anyway; the length of the negotiations – often extended so as to allow the American negotiators to pre-empt possible criticisms of the Treaty – had dissipated much of the clarity of their purpose, and with it the sense of their importance.

All the same, neither Soviet disregard for the spirit of agreements, nor the Carter Administration's failure to stamp its authority on the domestic debate could fully explain the collapse of the SALT process which at the beginning of the 1970s had been seen by many as a promising instrument for regulating military competition. A major element in Western thinking had been the belief that arms control, besides subjecting certain sectors of the arms race to agreed rules, could somehow move beyond the mere setting of upper limits to genuine reductions. The most notable expression of this idealistic hope had been the passage in President Carter's 1977 inaugural address which looked forward to the banishment of nuclear weapons from the face of the earth. Both SALT I and SALT II, however, instead of reducing the existing high levels of nuclear forces had permitted both sides to build up their arsenals substantially. Moreover, European concern over the growing arsenal of Soviet medium-range missiles testified to the fact that quantitative restrictions on certain weapons categories could not check military programmes outside these categories, and indeed even tended to encourage them. Partly because of this, negotiators strove for comprehensive agreements, rather than limited ones, and so found themselves bogged down in prolonged negotiations. While these often achieved the desired results, those results tended to meet strategic concerns which had been prevalent at the outset but were no longer relevant by the time the agreements were finally reached.

SALT II thus coincided with, and confirmed, a more general crisis in the traditional approach to arms control; and as the instrument lost its promise, so political support for its results inevitably diminished. This applied not only to strategic arms control and to the Vienna negotiations on reducing conventional forces in Europe, which had been going on without result since 1973, but was just as relevant to the negotiations on theatre nuclear forces which NATO members proposed to the East in December, at the same time as they decided to modernize their longer-range nuclear systems. The West offered to seek arms-control agreements before deploying the modernized weapons (this offer had been an important element in securing political support for the modernization in many West European countries) and suggested that negotiations should be conducted between the United States and Soviet Union in the context of SALT III. But the uncertain fate of the SALT II agreement could not fail to affect this plan, as it also affected the prospect of future discussions about the limitation of strategic arms.

These procedural uncertainties only tended to hide more profound substantive ones. Debating which forum should provide the setting for the negotiations begged the other, more fundamental, questions of what the aim of those negotiations should be and how it could be achieved. As the new decade began the ingredients of a new form of arms control, more responsive to the requirements of the future, were slowly emerging. Among these were marked reservations about comprehensive agreements, with their inevitably protracted negotiations; a growing interest in confidence-building measures (agreements designed to limit the activities of military forces, rather than their size); and a recognition of the value of constant communication between East and West (as in the SALT Standing Consultative Committee) as a means of minimizing miscalculations over military programmes and monitoring military competition.

At the beginning of 1980 the immediate prospects for East–West arms control seemed bleak. The Soviet Union still categorically ruled out any negotiations on medium-range systems in Europe unless NATO cancelled its December decision; in the aftermath of Afghanistan ratification of the SALT II Treaty was postponed. Yet arms control was unlikely to disappear from the international agenda. In the United States, even some of those originally unimpressed by the achievements of SALT II gradually seemed to recognize that the absence of agreed constraints on Soviet military programmes would reduce US security, rather than enhance it. For the Soviet Union, the prospect of major new American strategic programmes, and new medium-range systems to be stationed in Europe from the mid-1980s, should equally spur the desire to limit the nuclear competition. West Europeans, too, generally preferred agreements on mutual military restraint to the risks and the costs of embarking on major new weapons programmes; indeed the economic difficulties encountered by all major countries provided an additional incentive for seeking an alternative to new and costly military efforts. Sooner or later, therefore, governments would again move towards negotiations. It was important to use the interval to lay a sounder basis on which to build the sort of arms control which would be able to meet the security concerns of the 1980s.

The Strategic Debate

For a new approach to the control of arms, there will be a need not just for new procedures and instruments but also for an understanding of the requirements for deterrence in the years ahead. But while the debate was perhaps more intense during 1979 than in previous years, the issues on which it concentrated seemed unlikely to be the ones that would be most relevant in the 1980s and 1990s.

Much of the American strategic debate focused on concern about the theoretical vulnerability of the *Minuteman* ICBM force to a disarming first strike – a situation expected to arise in the early 1980s. Some saw this as providing the Soviet Union with a 'window of opportunity' during which she would be able to exploit the American strategic shortcoming for political advantage until the US could deploy new and less vulnerable land-based missiles, in particular the MX, towards the second half of the 1980s.

Though no doubt a problem which strategic planners would have to take into account, this did not seem to merit quite the central attention it received in the debate. For one thing, the scenario lacked plausibility. Would any Soviet leadership feel sufficiently confident that its own missile force had the reliability needed for a successful limited disarming strike against American ICBM? Could it count on an American President, warned of the attack, being willing to ride it out, rather than launch his missiles before they were destroyed in their silos? And even in the unlikely event of the initial attack being fully effective, could it assume that the United States, with millions of lives lost, would accept this as a *fait accompli* and not respond with the air- and sea-launched systems which make up some 74% of her strategic arsenal? In any case, those who claimed that the Soviet Union would draw major political advantages from the 'window of opportunity' were hard-pressed to spell out what these were. It remains a central feature of the nuclear age that not all asymmetries in opposing forces lead to a breakdown of deterrence or to exploitable political advantage.

Another asymmetry, that between Soviet and Western medium-range missiles in Europe, gave rise to a similar argument. The Soviet Union had enjoyed a marked numerical superiority in this category since the late 1950s, but over the last few years the new SS-20 mobile missile, with multiple warheads and much-improved accuracy, had been introduced, and the medium-range *Backfire* bomber was entering service at a rapid rate. Since the Soviet–American SALT agreements constrained neither of these new weapons in their theatre role, European concern was understandable, and former US Secretary of State Henry Kissinger seemed to give additional strategic justification to this concern in a speech he made in September (reprinted in *Survival*, November/December 1979, pp.264-8), warning that in the 1980s the American deterrent would no longer be fully effective against Soviet theatre threats. In much of the European debate, therefore, an asymmetry in one part of the nuclear spectrum, medium-range delivery systems, came to be seen as endangering the credibility of nuclear deterrence as a whole. This was the primary official reason for NATO's decision in December to deploy new longer-range theatre nuclear missiles on European soil.

As with the 'window of opportunity' argument, however, the feared consequences of this partial asymmetry were not axiomatic. The Soviet Union had enjoyed numerical superiority in medium-range weapons for almost twenty years yet the American deterrent had been regarded as sufficient to prevent their use. Why should that deterrent now have become less credible? Admittedly, SALT now limited US and Soviet strategic nuclear forces on a basis of equality, whereas the United States had previously enjoyed numerical superiority. Nonetheless, so long as American security interests were clearly at stake in Europe, was it conceivable that the US would fail to respond to a Soviet nuclear attack which for Europe could scarcely be seen as anything but strategic? Moreover, if American nuclear deterrence had indeed lost its credibility, then the deployment of new American missiles in Europe agreed by NATO members could neither resurrect nor effectively replace it. In order to deter Soviet 'Eurostrategic' threats, there was no alternative to relying, as in the past, on the readiness of the United States to link her fate to that of Europe.

All the same, both the 'window of opportunity' debate and that on the asymmetry in medium-range missiles touched on a deeper concern: the problem of the vulnerability of nuclear delivery systems to a pre-emptive strike. As Soviet missile accuracy and anti-submarine warfare capabilities increased, the survivability of second-strike forces – a central element in the Western notion of deterrence stability – was bound to become gradually more questionable. The real need to modernize NATO's theatre nuclear forces stemmed essentially from the growing vulnerability of the existing systems (see 'The Balance of Theatre Nuclear Forces in Europe', *The Military Balance 1979-1980*, pp. 114-17). And even the United States' new and mobile MX ICBM was not likely to escape for long the same threat of vulnerability that now faced her *Minuteman* force. It was this general trend that would profoundly affect the condition of deterrence in the decades ahead, rather than today's partial asymmetries and the limited technological responses designed to remedy them. And its general implications for military programmes, for arms control and for alliance relations will all need to be addressed.

Clouds over the Alliance
Political interests and concerns are closely intertwined with nuclear issues, as thirty years of alliance relations have shown. This came to the fore again in the debate on the consequences for Western deterrence of the Soviet SS-20 IRBM programme. While no doubt the Soviet programme could not but deeply disturb Europeans, underlying much of the concern was political uneasiness about the general state of European–American relations. Viewed from Europe, the policy objectives of the Carter Administration seemed at times to display a serious lack of consistency and predictability; seen from Washington, the familiar European tendency to criticize American actions without offering constructive alternatives seemed at times to indicate a disturbing lack of solidarity

and support. In an alliance founded on the assumption that the United States will be prepared to risk her own survival for the survival of Western Europe, political uneasiness tends to be translated into nuclear issues – as was again the case in 1979. NATO's December decision to deploy new American medium-range nuclear missiles on European soil thus became as much a measure to dispel political anxieties as to strengthen deterrence. Many in Europe saw it as a symbol of American political commitment to Alliance security; for some in the United States, particularly those worried over a supposed European tendency to 'self-Finlandization', it became a symbol for Europe's (and especially West Germany's) commitment to the West.

The December decision was, however, unlikely to remove the anxieties which had helped to produce it. In fact, as the new decade began, it was clear that the maintenance of a close relationship of trust and mutual support within NATO would be severely tested during the course of the 1980s.

There were two related reasons for this. First, there was a risk that security challenges to the West over the next few years might emphasize the differences between the United States and her allies, rather than the communality of their interests. Secondly, and more fundamentally, changes of outlook within the United States and Europe would render the formulation and pursuit of common policies more difficult in the new decade than ever before in the history of the Alliance.

Differences of interest in detente with the Soviet Union could prove divisive. For the United States, relatively secure in her geographic position and her military power, the security interest in co-operating with the Soviet Union was essentially limited to removing the danger of nuclear war, by regulating strategic arms competition and by reducing the danger of direct military conflict between the super-powers. A breakdown in detente would not produce an immediate deterioriation in American security. For most US allies, though, (and particularly those whose territory bordered the Soviet empire, like Norway, West Germany, Turkey and Japan) a deterioriation in the East–West relationship would mean an increase in Soviet pressure and the loss of the advantages that detente had brought. This was especially clear in the case of West Germany –half of a divided country, with an isolated former capital, Berlin–for whom the improvement in East–West relations had brought the growth of contacts between the populations of the two German states and a reduction in the tensions over Berlin. Thus West European governments would in general be more concerned than the United States with maintaining a working relationship between East and West. This was underlined during 1979 by their support for the SALT II Agreement, their initial ambivalence over the introduction of new medium-range missiles into Western Europe, and their half-hearted support for the intense American reaction to the Soviet invasion of Afghanistan. As the risk of disaffection between Europe and the United States grew, the Soviet Union could well seek to exploit the rift by subtle appeals to transatlantic differences of interest.

Third-world conflict and the Western response to it pointed to other areas of potential transatlantic (and trans-pacific) dissent. There was a clear difference in approach, not so much over the security challenge such conflict posed as over how to respond to it. The United States, with her global outlook and global means, was more ready to see threats to Western interests as Soviet-initiated challenges and more ready to contemplate military responses. Europe and Japan, on the other hand, instinctively interpreted these conflicts as indigenous and – with the occasional exception of France – were reluctant to consider military solutions. European instincts tended to follow short-run European interests. By refusing to endorse wholeheartedly the Camp David Accord between Israel and Egypt, Europeans hoped to maintain their commercial and diplomatic influence with the Arab oil-producers who opposed the Accord, and their reluctance to join in American action against Iran during the hostage crisis reflected concern over energy supplies and commercial links as well as their traditional preference for a diplomacy based on incentives rather than threats. As East–West security considerations superseded regional concerns over third-world crises it would become increasingly difficult for the Western Alliance to accommodate these differences in outlook and method. The establishment of a US quick-reaction force to cope with threats to Western security in areas of primary strategic interest, like the Middle East, would also require greater American flexibility in the use of US military forces earmarked for threats in Europe and the Far East. Even more important, American support for the traditional security needs of the allies was bound to be weakened if Europe or Japan were unwilling to support American action in the Third World which was undertaken – at least in the US perspective – in defence of their interests as well.

More fundamental than these differences of interest was another development: the redefinition of the American and European roles in the Alliance. In the past, the United States had been the undisputed leader of the Alliance, both by her own will and because she commanded the respect of her allies. The United States that emerged from the experiences of the 1970s, however, was no longer always willing to provide this leadership and, even when she tried to do so, no longer able to command the immediate respect of her allies. And yet those allies were still unwilling and unable to fill the gap that the United States had left.

Since the alliance throughout its thirty-year existence had depended on American readiness to define and sustain the common framework, the effect of this metamorphosis was bound to be profound. The change had already been visible in such traditional alliance matters as nuclear decision-making (where the US had in recent years been increasingly reluctant to shoulder alone the political costs of unpopular military decisions fundamentally most relevant to Europe), but it was also manifest in the Western inability to respond collectively to crises in the Third World. Events in Afghanistan in early 1980 clearly demonstrated these shortcomings. The US government, though perhaps over-hasty in its response, did at least respond to the Soviet invasion. European governments, on the other hand, sceptical of the relevance of some American moves, only gradually and cautiously came forward with a position of their own to deal with what was, after all, a threat to Western security interests as a whole. The result was not a common policy but uneasy and half-hearted solidarity, breeding frustrations and resentment on both sides of the Atlantic. European complaints over inadequate consultation by the United States, while procedurally quite correct, only served to underline the lack of a constructive European contribution.

If the risks of division are to be reduced, and if Alliance solidarity is to work in the uncertain 1980s, what will be required above all will be a conscious effort not to allow differences over secondary interests to outweigh what continues to be the primary and common interest of the Western world: security against the Soviet threat. Detente, however important for crisis management and defusing tension, cannot be an alternative to alliance; and different outlooks on third-world crises cannot hide the fact that, in sensitive areas like the Middle East, the energy security of the West as a whole is at stake, and not just (and perhaps least of all) that of the United States.

Furthermore, the Iranian and Afghan crises underlined the need for the Alliance to develop new procedures to cope with third-world crises. This would not mean extending NATO's geographical boundaries, which would in any case be of doubtful military effectiveness. Rather, what would be required was procedures for jointly defining responses for future contingencies. It is true that the uncertainties inherent in third-world developments could easily frustrate all contingency planning. Nonetheless, such procedures would at least enable Alliance members to develop common approaches to common problems in advance of a crisis, instead of producing the sort of improvised and divisive *post hoc* reactions with which they responded to the invasion of Afghanistan.

In the longer run, however, a more fundamental change within the Alliance would be needed so as to meet the strains that 1979 had increasingly exposed. In the difficult 1980s it would no longer be enough for the United States' major allies to call for US leadership and, if it were not forthcoming, to pursue their own national interests. They would have to take a greater share in the common effort of maintaining the alliance and assuring its relevance. A disunited West would be incapable of responding effectively and imaginatively to the security threats of the 1980s.

Military Force in Third-World Crises
That Western security could no longer be defined exclusively in East–West terms had been clear since the oil shock of 1973, and 1979 confirmed it. Security no longer meant military and political security alone but also secure supplies of energy and raw materials, often from politically fragile countries in the Third World.

In the Gulf, the Iranian revolution had sharpened ethnic and religious divisions into political challenges, but elsewhere in the Third World, too, unpredictability and potential volatility remained prominent characteristics. Moreover, the events of the year – in Central America,

Africa and Asia – confirmed the growing potential for conflict in these regions. While each case had specific, local causes, they nevertheless revealed a number of disturbing pointers to international security in the 1980s: the fragility of political regimes in many parts of the Third World, the risk of local conflicts expanding into international ones, and an increasing willingness, on the part of local as well as outside powers, to resort to military force in the pursuit of their interests.

Against this background, and in the aftermath of Afghanistan, it was not surprising that the need for military capabilities to deal with third-world contingencies again became an issue in the Western debate, particularly the United States. Yet, as events in 1979 emphasized, military force is by no means an unambiguous instrument for influence. To incorporate it effectively into Western strategy it will be necessary to define, more stringently than was sometimes the case in the concern over Afghanistan, the conditions under which it could be used to strategic advantage in third-world crises.

The general utility of military force was not in doubt: to deter outside aggression against friendly countries; to demonstrate a vital interest to the Soviet Union; to protect national interests in case of upheaval and turbulence. But when translated into the specific conditions of third-world conflict, each of these tasks inevitably became less clear-cut and imbued with considerable risk. In regions such as South-west Asia, where the USSR enjoys the advantages of proximity, how could a Soviet invasion like that of Afghanistan be effectively deterred? The large concentration of US naval force, assembled in the Arabian Sea in early December to demonstrate American resolve in the Iranian hostage crisis, did not prevent Soviet divisions from marching into Afghanistan. A general threat to take countermeasures in other regions, where the Soviet Union might be more vulnerable, would not be really credible unless Western security were directly at stake, as in the event of a direct Soviet attack against Western oil supplies. And to increase the risk attending Soviet action by issuing a general threat to respond would entail an additional danger; if in the event the threat could not be substantiated by tangible military countermeasures, the loss of credibility might well be greater than that involved in taking no action at all. The more specific the threat of counter-action the greater that danger would be, given the unpredictability of internal upheavals in of the Third World.

Yet, could a general undertaking to protect Western friends at least serve to reassure governments in the affected region? Again, the ability to implement such an undertaking would have to be demonstrable. But even if it were possible to muster the conventional military force required, too visible a military connection with the West, and in particular the United States, might weaken domestically uncertain regimes, rather than strengthen them – this was the possible explanation for Saudi Arabia's reluctance to allow the US to establish military facilities on her soil. Moreover, was it military presence on the spot which would best serve to reassure allies, or the capability and the will to act in an emergency?

But what would be the effect of actually using military force? In Angola and Ethiopia the Soviet Union had demonstrated the utility of military force in supporting a local regime and strengthening it against internal opponents; and French military interventions in Zaire in 1977 and 1978 had helped to defeat local insurgencies against President Mobutu's government. But fighting continued in Angola and the Horn of Africa for all that, and doubts over the stability of the Mobutu regime remained. Military intervention had thus bought time in which to deal with the cause of unrest, but it could not ensure that the time would also be used effectively. As to the Soviet invasion into Afghanistan, it was still too early, at the beginning of the year, to pronounce it a success.

The other potential use of military intervention – raids to free hostages and protect national assets – was not demonstrated during the year. There were those who argued that this would have been the right response to the hostage drama in Tehran, but it would clearly have been a course fraught with considerable risks. But if the Iranian example were to spread, limited, surgical military operations by the major powers to protect their nationals might come to be considered a necessary option.

To point to the limits and risks involved in the use of outside military force in third-world crises is not to deny that force could be an important instrument. But it is clearly one that will be less readily applicable than public debate often tended to suggest. While there will be situations in which this option will be valuable, it does not offer a general answer to the problem of coping with instabilities in the Third World. Military means are most likely to serve the purpose of reassuring allies if they are not stationed in the region but held (credibly) in reserve, and they are most likely to impress opponents if applied in a sustainable way. Here lay the significance of American plans to create a rapid-deployment force and of a general emphasis on naval power – the least disruptive form of military presence. Here also might lie the role of outside support; perhaps the best way to counter Soviet action in Afghanistan, and so deter similar invasions in the future, might be to supply those actively opposing the Soviet invasion of the country.

1979 had started and ended with reminders that third-world crises would increasingly affect international security in the 1980s. This did not mean that the other, traditional problems of security – maintaining effective deterrence in a changing technological and political context, and the search for East–West military restraint where this served security – had disappeared. On the contrary, third-world uncertainties gained additional impact from the fact that they would both reinforce and interact with traditional East–West rivalries and security concerns.

In devising the strategies to meet these challenges, it will be important to concentrate on problems that can be solved, rather than those that cannot. In the traditional sphere of East–West security, the problems affecting the maintenance of deterrence can be solved, if not through arms control then through arms. The security challenges in the Third World, though, will be less clear-cut, both in their origin and in the responses they require. The clear limitations of military force for promoting influence and stability in the Third World generally favour those with other instruments at their disposal. The Soviet Union's reliance on military means was a reflection not so much of the utility of military power as of a lack of alternative instruments, for her influence, in contrast to that of the West, simply continues to rest primarily on military power. There will be little sense, therefore, in the West following the Soviet example.

Instead, it will be necessary, through negotiation, to remove some of those problems for regional security that promise to be soluble. Compromise over the Palestinian issue in the Middle East would do more to strengthen Gulf stability than even the most effective and credible display of military force, just as the successful negotiations to resolve Rhodesia's problems radically reduced the threat of outside military intervention in the conflict. Indeed, this latter event provided another, more general, lesson for the 1980s: that without the concurrence of the regional states security cannot be imposed, and stability will prove elusive.

NEW FACTORS IN SECURITY

STRATEGIC COMMAND AND CONTROL

Strategic thinking in the United States on how to deter the use of nuclear weapons in war has moved from reliance on the threat of massive destruction to consideration of limiting the damage, or even 'winning' such a war, by the exact application of various levels of controlled escalation. These doctrines of limited nuclear war presuppose that, even after the initial nuclear strikes, the commanders on both sides will be constantly and accurately informed of the extent of their opponent's actions and the status of their own forces, so that they can base their command decisions on accurate judgements. Also presupposed is that rapid and secure communications channels will continue to exist and operate, for without them selective military options will be impossible.

A prominent feature of the most recent debates about the balance of strategic forces in the 1980s is therefore a concern for the survivability and performance of the command, control and communications (C^3) systems which support these forces. Clearly the intelligence systems which supply indications and warning information are vital as well, and it is now recognized that the vulnerability of all these systems (collectively known as C^3I) is the weakest link in the capabilities for conducting a controlled nuclear war. Large resources are currently devoted to improving the survivability and wartime endurance of these systems, but the inherent vulnerability of many of them, and the fact that several critical nodal points in the network cannot be circumvented, suggests that this effort is unlikely to be as successful as the current strategic doctrines would require.

The US System
The system of command-and-control arrangements, communications links and data-processing facilities developed by the United States so as to enable her strategic nuclear forces to be used at the command of the National Command Authorities (NCA) is very large, complex and diverse, as well as highly technical. It is not possible to quantify precisely the resources devoted to this system, but the number of personnel involved cannot be less than some 25–30,000, and at least $2,250 million per year is now budgeted for strategic C^3.

Much of this system developed without any overall co-ordination. In the 1950s, when many of its elements were designed and built, the principal concerns were to ensure that the President had complete control over any decision to use his nuclear forces, and that safety procedures were adequate to prevent accidental or unauthorized use. Little consideration was given to the need for the system to remain operational throughout a strategic nuclear exchange, and many of its current elements are indeed quite unsuited to do so.

Overall control of the US armed forces is exercised by the NCA, which consists of the President and the Secretary of Defense or their duly deputized alternates or successors. Therefore, though ultimate authority for the release of nuclear weapons rests with the President, in practice he would exercise it jointly with the Secretary of Defense. The subsequent chain of command is through the Chairman of the Joint Chiefs of Staff to the executing commander.

The NCA and the subordinate commands direct the armed forces via the World Wide Military Command and Control System (WWMCCS). Formally established in October 1962, its principal missions were redefined in December 1971, to make it much more responsive to the needs of the NCA, after a number of incidents involving critical command and communications failures: the Israeli attack on the US spy ship *Liberty* in June 1967, North Korea's capture of the spy ship *Pueblo* in January 1968, and the shooting down of an EC-121 electronic intelligence aircraft by North Korea in April 1969. At the centre of the WWMCCS is the National Military Command System (NMCS), which consists of the national-level command centres and the communications which link them to intelligence systems and other subordinate command centres. This in turn is made up of three principal components. The first is the National Military Command Center in the Pentagon which, though it is the hub of both routine and crisis command capability, is not specifically protected against nuclear attack. The second is the Alternate National Military Command Center near Fort Ritchie, Maryland, which could immediately assume control of US forces if the Pentagon were destroyed; although it is located underground, this might not survive a direct attack either. The final element, the National Emergency Airborne Command Post (NEACP), consisting of several E-4 (specially-equipped Boeing 747) aircraft, is the most survivable component of the NMCS.

In addition to the NMCS, the commanders of Strategic Air Command and the US forces in Europe, the Atlantic and the Pacific all have both fixed and airborne command posts capable of communicating with the nuclear forces. Only the first of these, however, maintains an alternative command post on continuous, survivable airborne alert: a system of EC-135 aircraft, one of which is always airborne.

Effective and efficient command and control begins with the real-time surveillance, warning and assessment systems which provide intelligence to the national command centres. In the case of ballistic missile attack, the most important of the various systems is the Defense Support Program (DSP) early-warning system. This consists of three 647 satellites in geostationary orbit (one over the eastern hemisphere to give 25–30 minutes warning of Soviet land-based missile launches, and two over the western hemisphere to monitor sea-based missile launches off the east and west coasts of the US) controlled from ground stations in Australia and at Buckley Air Force Base, Colorado. The eastern-hemisphere satellite's warning of an ICBM attack would be verified after about 10 minutes by various ground-based radar systems including the Ballistic Missile Early Warning System (three sites, at Thule in Greenland, Clear in Alaska, and Fylingdales in Britain), two over-the-horizon radars, and two phased-array radars, (at Grand Forks, North Dakota, and Shemya Island, Alaska). The two satellites which warn of sea-launched attack are also complemented by a network of ground-based radars on the east, west and south coasts of the US. Inherently these ground-based radars cannot be protected from physical attack, and they are also susceptible to jamming.

From these satellites and radar sites, and from other sources, early-warning and attack assessment intelligence is relayed to the headquarters of North American Air Defense Command (NORAD), near Colorado Springs, and Strategic Air Command (SAC), near Omaha, Nebraska, to the component elements of the NMCS, and to other key sites, including the Situation Room in the White House.

The WWMCCS provides some 43 different communications systems between the NCA and the US military forces, including underwater cables, landlines, satellite systems and radio systems which range from very low frequency to extremely high frequency. The great majority of these systems, however, are not expected to survive in a nuclear war. The most survivable portion of the network is the Minimum Essential Emergency Communications Network (MEECN). Its major components are the NEACP E-4 aircraft, the Air Force Satellite Communications system, which provides communications between the NCA and Strategic Air Command's ICBM and bomber forces, and the radio facilities supporting ballistic missile submarines. The primary means of communication with these submarines is very-low-frequency (VLF) radio. There are three high-powered VLF stations (two in the continental US and one in Australia) and two lower powered stations in the US, but none of them is hardened sufficiently to provide any real protection against direct nuclear attack and they are not considered survivable. Survivable VLF communication is currently provided by the TACAMO system: two squadrons of C-130 aircraft, specially modified as airborne VLF relay platforms, rotated through a number of bases to provide nearly continuous communications with submarines in both Atlantic and Pacific.

The final element of the MEECN is the Emergency Rocket Communications System (ERCS), which consists of a number of *Minuteman* ICBM with ultra-high-frequency radio packages in place of warheads. These packages would be launched into extremely high ballistic trajectories from which they can transmit instructions to the strategic nuclear forces for about half an hour. At least two of these packages would need to be launched to achieve effective transmission coverage. This 'final back-up system' is based with the ICBM (which will soon become the most vulnerable part of the US nuclear forces) and, although capable of being used in controlled nuclear exchanges, seems more likely to be used to signal a massive retaliatory response.

Soviet Capabilities
Like the United States, the Soviet Union has a very extensive network of C^3 systems for the command, control and support of her strategic

nuclear forces. Indeed, its overall architecture is fairly similar to that of the US network.

However, since the 1950s the USSR has paid much greater attention than the United States to the protection of the national command authority in a nuclear war. Shelters have now been constructed for about 110,000 members of the leadership, including party and government officials from national down to city level, managers of key installations and members of civil defence staffs. The first-echelon C^3 centres for the government and armed forces at the national level, dispersed and hardened within an 80-mile radius of Moscow, include some 75 underground command posts within the Moscow ring road system alone. These ground-based centres are backed up by a fleet of airborne command posts, operated by the Soviet Air Forces, which are regularly used during exercises and in crisis situations. However, the Soviet airborne system, though more than simply a communications link, is not as capable of continuously keeping in the air fully-equipped battle staffs with comprehensive intelligence data links as are its US counterparts, the NEACP and SAC airborne systems.

Early warning of US ballistic missile attack is provided by satellites, three over-the-horizon back-scatter radar systems (one in the extreme eastern USSR, another near Kiev, and a third in the Caucasus near Nikolayev) and more than a dozen extremely large *Hen House* search-and-track radars which have a range of about 3,200 nautical miles.

The Soviet military communications system incorporates a degree of redundancy similar to, if not greater than, that of the United States. Links in the network are provided by land-line and various airborne, satellite, troposcatter, microwave and other radio systems, but the enormous distances and the inhospitable terrain of much of the USSR, have caused relatively greater dependence on long-range high- and very-low-frequency radio and on satellite communications systems.

Satellites now carry the great bulk of Soviet military communications, and three types of systems have been deployed. One involves large numbers of small (100-cm diameter) satellites, each with an operational life of 2-3 years, launched in groups of eight by a single rocket into circular orbits of about 1,400-1,500 km. At least 24 such satellites are needed to provide global coverage, but Soviet military chiefs evidently prefer to keep aloft 36 to 48, so as to complicate Western jamming of the system. The second system employs some 16 *Molniya* satellites, launched into highly elliptical orbits with apogees in the northern hemisphere of approximately 40,000 km which provide 8-10 hours of continuous communications throughout the USSR and associated countries on each orbit. (The Soviet contribution to the Moscow-Washington 'hot line' uses *Molniya* 2 satellites). The third type of system uses satellites in geostationary orbits, the first of which was launched on 29 July 1974. An extensive network of *Orbita* ground receiving terminals has been built through the USSR near the headquarters of most of the Military Districts and near naval bases and missile fields.

Overall, the Soviet C^3 system for the strategic nuclear forces is believed to be at least as good as that of the United States. Indeed, the former US Navy Secretary J. William Middendorf declared in 1975 that 'the Soviets have the best command and control one can imagine'. True, some elements, such as the airborne command posts and satellite early-warning and real-time intelligence systems, are technically much less capable than their US counterparts. On the other hand, protection of the political and military leadership is much more comprehensive, and the extensive and redundant communications links make it difficult for any US strike to isolate the Soviet national command authorities completely from the strategic forces or to destroy the whole strategic intelligence network.

Perhaps the greatest weakness in Soviet C^3 is its reliance on highly centralized command-and-control procedures which expose the whole system to disruption. Observation of Soviet military exercises gives the impression that ships, aircraft and commands have carefully and specially planned roles, and that operational communications flow directly between headquarters in Moscow and the individual units in the field. Local commanders seem to have relatively little scope to adapt general orders to field conditions or to use their own initiative if they do not receive central orders. This tendency could be even more pronounced in the strategic forces, since Soviet leaders would be particularly loth to allow lower commands much room for initiative where nuclear weapons were concerned.

Threats to C^3 Systems

As well as being vulnerable to all the threats to which the strategic forces are subject, C^3 systems are also open to others more specific to command structures and telecommunications systems. Indeed, the strategic forces are relatively a good deal easier to protect, since they can be dispersed, buried underground in hardened silos or deployed in some mobile mode. These measures are generally not applicable to C^3 systems, many of which (early-warning radars, VLF communications for missile submarines, and satellite ground-control facilities, for example) may be large, immobile, above ground and inherently unprotectable. Some elements (such as underground command posts) can be hardened but, as ICBM accuracy improves, even their survivability becomes problematical – and in any case the cables and antennae with which they communicate can never be hardened to anywhere near the same extent as the rest of these underground facilities. Some elements of the system can be duplicated, but the national command authority will remain one of the weakest links in the chain, since assuring its survivability and communications links is particularly demanding. Indeed, since command centres in general are considerably fewer in number than the strategic systems they support, they will be priority targets for nuclear attack.

Where exchanges of large numbers of nuclear weapons are involved, C^3 facilities, both fixed command centres and communications facilities, would be the targets of a significant proportion of the attack. In an effort to make communications more secure, the United States now routes over 70% of her military communications through satellites, and early warning, too, depends very heavily upon satellite observation for its effectiveness. But satellites are not invulnerable, and the Soviet Union has been conducting an anti-satellite test programme since 1976. To date this has been limited to satellites on orbits lower than 1,000 km – which would include the US 'spy' satellites but not the early-warning and communications satellites, which are generally in geo-synchronous orbits at 36,000 km – but satellites in higher orbits cannot be regarded as indefinitely immune from attack. In any case, the ground stations on which the effectiveness of satellites depends are few in number and consequently very prone to attack.

Another difficulty is that communications links and the electronic and electrical components of command-and-control systems are also vulnerable to nuclear effects, even when not attacked directly. Atmospheric nuclear explosions cause ionization of the upper atmosphere which can degrade some radio communications, particularly high-frequency transmissions, at considerable distances from the point of detonation. For example, a one-megaton burst at an altitude of 200 miles in daylight hours would disrupt HF systems up to a radius of 1,500 miles and even further, and the blackout could persist for several hours. After a detonation at a height of 48 miles on 1 August 1958, HF radio communication was degraded over a region several thousand miles in diameter from shortly after midnight until sunrise. In addition, electronic and electrical components and devices are very susceptible to electromagnetic pulse (EMP), a short, intense electrical burst generated in the region of a nuclear detonation. The EMP effects of explosions at high altitudes can disrupt electronic systems at distances of a thousand miles, with computers, power supplies, antenna, radio stations and some telephone equipment being particularly vulnerable if not specifically hardened. (A US test in 1962, involving a one-megaton detonation some 248 miles above Johnston Island in the Pacific, caused street lights to fail and burglar alarms to ring in Honolulu, some 800 miles away.) A wide range of protective measures has been developed since the EMP problem was recognized in the early 1960s. However, since the Partial Test Ban of 1963 precludes nuclear explosions in the atmosphere, the testing of such measures is limited to simulations, and much uncertainty remains over their effectiveness.

Communications systems and their supporting electronic sensors are vulnerable not only to physical attack and the side-effects of nuclear explosions but also to various kinds of electronic attack. Most strategic communications systems depend to a considerable extent on radio (it provides the only means of communicating with missile submarines and aircraft), but all radio systems are in some degree vulnerable to electronic jamming or deception. The Soviet Union has long experience of electronic warfare, and her current emphasis on 'radio-electronic combat' emphasizes the important impact of electronic warfare on strategic C^3.

The most obvious kind of electronic weapon against communications systems is electronic noise jamming, like that used against radio broadcasts. This involves transmitting an interfering signal (often simply noise) on the same frequency as the signal to be jammed, which causes the receiver to hear a combination of the valid signal and the jamming signal. The effectiveness of noise jamming depends on the relative power of the competing transmitters, their distance relative to each other and the recipient, and the kind of signal being transmitted (morse code, for instance, can be heard in the presence of noise which would easily obliterate a voice signal). Automatic communications equipment, such as standard teletypes, are often more easily jammed than voice or manual morse links – and it is not always possible to determine if some automatic equipment is being jammed or not.

For every electronic interference technique a number of countermeasures are possible. Obvious choices to counteract voice jamming are to increase the power of the transmitter, or to use several frequencies to transmit the same message simultaneously, hoping that not all of them can be jammed. Most of the other possible approaches are based on spreading the signal over a wider than normal band width so as to 'dilute' the jamming signal, in some cases by a factor of a thousand or more. Since such countermeasures are generally quite expensive, few general-purpose communications systems are so protected, but some components of the American MEECN do incorporate extensive anti-jamming protection, particularly the VLF system for communicating with missile submarines and the satellite communication systems.

Strategic Implications

Dramatic developments are taking place in many areas of C^3 technology. Improvements in various types of sensor systems are greatly increasing the information available to the national command authorities, while developments in communications (such as 'packet switching', in which computers fragment a message, then interleave the fragments with those of other messages and transmit them all individually by a multiplicity of different routes for reassembly at the receiving end) and data processing are greatly improving the speed and security with which it can be delivered to them. On the other hand, the means for ensuring the survival of these systems in a nuclear war have not advanced to the same extent. Some developments may diminish certain threats. For example, developments in anti-jamming techniques, cryptography and packet switching seem to reduce the vulnerability of communications to some forms of electronic disruption, and new communications technologies using fibre optics or blue-green lasers (at a wavelength of about 5,000 angstroms) will permit even greater security. However, there is an obstacle to efforts to devise fully secure and survivable command and control systems: there is no way to test them. Neither the United States nor the Soviet Union can be sure that their elaborate procedures and links will be fully effective until they have to be put to use in the nuclear exchange for which they were designed.

On balance, the survivability and endurance of C^3 systems is likely to remain no better, and often worse, than those of the strategic forces they support. While it should be possible to maintain a minimum degree of communication between the national command authorities and the strategic forces, it is unlikely that political and military leaders would receive sufficient information to enable them to exercise full control over events once a nuclear exchange had escalated beyond 50–100 nuclear detonations.

This has profound implications for current strategic doctrines. If the threat of massive retaliation is no longer a credible means of deterring attack in an era of strategic parity, the doctrines which replace it envisage a limited and gradually escalating nuclear exchange directed against an array of specific targets. Without the certainty that the command-and-control mechanisms will work as planned during such an exchange, however, it is questionable whether those in command will be willing, or able, to follow the course the new doctrine prescribes. Despite all the resources now being devoted to C^3, therefore, the uncertainties that inevitably remain make the use of nuclear weapons for controlled escalation no less difficult to envisage than their use for massive retaliation.

NUCLEAR PROLIFERATION IN SOUTH ASIA

Throughout 1979 the prospects of avoiding the spread of nuclear weapons to South Asia appeared to grow steadily slimmer. Pakistan moved closer to completing a uranium enrichment facility and acquiring the capability to match India's 1974 nuclear test, while the United States, with partial support from other countries, tried unsuccessfully to pressure her into halting her nuclear programme. The resignation of India's Prime Minister, Morarji Desai, in July removed an influential opponent of that country's acquisition of nuclear weapons just at a time when pressures for response to Pakistan's activities started to grow. But as 1980 began, the United States Administration, responding to the Soviet invasion of Afghanistan, offered unconditional support for Pakistan's security, and former Prime Minister Indira Gandhi was returned to power in India. Both developments created new uncertainties to complicate efforts to avoid the dangers of nuclear competition on the subcontinent.

Pakistan's Quest for the Bomb

Soon after India detonated a nuclear explosive device in May 1974, the Pakistani government of Prime Minister Bhutto initiated a dual strategy for acquiring the fissile material necessary for making nuclear weapons. One part of this strategy was an attempt to buy a reprocessing plant from France; this would have permitted separation of the plutonium necessary for an atomic bomb from the spent nuclear fuel derived from Pakistan's one operating nuclear power reactor. But France, possibly more concerned about the sale's proliferation implications than she had been initially, and under consistent prodding from the United States, decided in the summer of 1978 to cancel the sale. These French concerns were clearly justified, for in a statement at his trial by the Zia ul-Haq military regime former Prime Minister Bhutto made clear what had been his government's ultimate intentions:

> We all know that Israel and South Africa have full nuclear capability. The Christian, Jewish and Hindu civilizations have this capability. The Communist powers also possess it. Only the Islamic civilization was without it, but that position was about to change.

Pakistan was simultaneously proceeding along a second route towards a nuclear device. By late 1978 and early 1979 it became evident that she was building a uranium enrichment facility using the gas centrifuge process to produce weapons-grade uranium. This programme had been assisted by lax security at the Dutch centrifuge facility of United Reprocessors (URENCO) at Almelo, and by loopholes in the network of nuclear export controls created after India's test and encapsulated in the 1978 London Nuclear Suppliers Guidelines. URENCO is a British-German-Dutch consortium, established in 1970 to pool the three countries' work on gas centrifuge technology in order to find a cheaper way of enriching uranium for nuclear fuel. It has plants in all three countries.

Pakistan's centrifuge enrichment programme is headed by Dr Abdul Qadar Khan, a metallurgist who had been employed at the Almelo centrifuge facility in 1974 and 1975 translating technical documents from German into Dutch. There he had had access to secret documents and reports, as well as blueprints of the facility, and before returning to Pakistan he also acquired information on the subcontractors and suppliers of equipment to the plant. It was on the basis of this information that Pakistan was then able to make clandestine purchases of components and materials for a centrifuge facility of her own. Nuclear export controls were circumvented in several ways. For some components with a legitimate civilian use, as well as a possible military one, Pakistan sought to hide the actual use to which they would be put. For others, ranging from electrical frequency inverters with characteristics comparable to those used in the British nuclear centrifuge facility to special extremely hard martensite steel, front companies were set up to act as purchasing agents.

These activities were fully uncovered in early 1978, but it took between six months and a year for key supplier countries, such as Britain and the United States, to tighten their controls. By the time they had done so, the foundations of the Pakistani centrifuge programme were well established. Although technical difficulties in implementing and engineering the centrifuge designs still could slow the programme, in early 1980 most informed observers were assuming that within one to four years Pakistan would have enough highly enriched uranium for five to seven bombs per year.

There have been periodic suggestions that Libya or another Arab country was financing Pakistan's centrifuge programme, and though General Zia denied such a connection, rumours of an 'Islamic bomb' cannot be dismissed out of hand. With rapidly dwindling foreign exchange reserves, a mounting foreign debt and domestic economic difficulties, Pakistan will have found it extremely difficult to finance the nuclear centrifuge project – estimated to cost several hundred million dollars – and Libya, which already has an extensive range of political, military and economic contacts with Pakistan, could be a logical source of financial support. While it was difficult to see Pakistan putting a nuclear device at the disposal of so amorphous a cause as Islamic unity, the possibility of a transfer of Pakistani nuclear weapons as a *quid pro quo* for financial help in acquiring them could not be completely discounted.

Security, prestige and internal political calculation seem to have been the driving forces behind the Pakistani quest for nuclear explosive material. At the core of the security incentive has been concern about possible blackmail by a nuclear-armed and regionally predominant India; in addition, the possession of nuclear weapons has sometimes been seen as a means of balancing the superiority of Indian conventional forces. There may also have been a belief that moving towards a nuclear-weapon capability would buttress Pakistan's ability to bargain for US conventional arms sales. Prime Minister Bhutto's warnings in 1974 and 1975, that without advanced arms Pakistan could be forced to 'go nuclear', clearly fit with that interpretation.

Prestige and internal political pressures reinforced these security motivations. The desire to prove that, if she chose, Pakistan could also detonate a nuclear explosive device continues to be a strongly held sentiment, particularly in the light of the scepticism India has expressed in the past. Members of the Pakistani high command appear to have begun pushing for a matching test soon after India's 1974 explosion. Under both the Bhutto and Zia governments, completion of the nuclear programme in the face of outside opposition acquired a nationalistic appeal within the country, and both governments feared that halting the programme would lead to a loss of domestic popular support.

Non-proliferation Efforts

The developments outlined above drove the United States in the first half of 1979 to a search for new means to arrest Pakistan's nuclear programme. But in contrast to the situation immediately after India's test, when renewed security assurances and conventional arms sales along the lines sought by Prime Minister Bhutto just might have significantly affected Pakistan, there were few compelling economic, military or political tools now available.

Neither the April 1979 decision to cut off economic assistance to Pakistan, as mandated by the Symington Amendment to the Foreign Assistance Act of 1976, nor US unwillingness in June 1979 to reschedule the Pakistani debt had much impact on Pakistan's centrifuge programme. More stringent economic sanctions were not adopted, because they might actually strengthen Pakistani resolve and because it was thought they would harm the Pakistani people more than they would affect the government.

In an attempt to reduce the security motive, the United States in early 1979 had offered to sell Pakistan 50 F-5E fighters if she would agree to place the centrifuge facility under international safeguards. President Zia's government, however, turned down the offer. The sale of more advanced aircraft was rejected by the US Administration because of concern over possible Indian reaction and out of a reluctance to 'reward' Pakistan for her past nuclear weapon programme. A proposal to create a South Asian nuclear-free zone (involving Indian and Pakistani acceptance of full-scope safeguards, backed by guarantees from the USSR, the US and China not to threaten either India or Pakistan with nuclear attack) was turned down by the governments in both Islamabad and New Delhi. Pakistan felt that there was only a tenuous relationship between such a zone and her security problems, and judged that the guarantee clause had only limited relevance and little credibility. From India's point of view, not only did the proposal fail to deal with the military threat she saw from China but it also appeared to be just one more American attempt to force her to adhere to full-scope safeguards.

Throughout the last months of 1979 President Zia responded to the growing international criticism by denying that his country intended to build a bomb, asserting that the controversial facility at Kahuta was an integral part of Pakistan's legitimate nuclear energy plans and offering to accept safeguards on all Pakistani nuclear facilities if India did likewise. Pakistani actions involving the construction site at Kahuta, about 25 miles south of Islamabad, lent no credibility to these protestations, however, and it seems clear that something beyond a commercial nuclear plant is being built there. At the end of June, the French Ambassador and a senior French diplomat, who had driven out along the road to the site, were stopped by a lorry driven across the road as a blockade and severely beaten by a number of Pakistanis who had followed them from Islamabad. In August, after some wild reports had circulated that India or the United States might try to destroy the site, a cordon of troops was deployed there and anti-aircraft guns and ground-to-air missiles were placed around it.

Although Zia refused to rule out a nuclear test, it is unlikely that a decision to test a nuclear explosive device as soon as sufficient fissile material is at hand has been taken. The drive behind Pakistan's search for the bomb need not be inconsistent with future decisions either to stop short of actual detonation – much as Israel may have done – or, failing that, merely to match India's original 'peaceful nuclear explosion'. Much will depend on the still uncertain repercussions of the Soviet invasion of Afghanistan on 27 December 1979 and of Indira Gandhi's return to the Indian premiership in January 1980.

The Impact of Afghanistan

One of the immediate casualties of the Soviet invasion of Afghanistan was the US policy of using economic and military leverage to try to induce Pakistan to shelve her centrifuge enrichment programme. Fearful that a militarily weak and politically isolated Pakistan would provide a tempting opportunity for further Soviet political – if not military – gains, President Carter indicated in January 1980 that he would ask Congress to waive its restrictions on aid to Pakistan. Though the details had yet to be worked out, a figure of $400 million in economic and military aid over the next two years was mentioned. Sales of air-defence and anti-tank missiles and possibly even A-7 attack aircraft were expected to be part of a renewed arms-sales package. (Ironically, in 1977 Carter had refused to sell Pakistan the A-7, which, with suitable radar, has all-weather, day-and-night capability against armour and other targets.) In addition, the US reaffirmed her 1959 security agreement with Pakistan and encouraged China and other countries to provide further support to that country. General Zia's initial reaction to these moves was cautious, for he was concerned about the longer-term reliability of the United States and wary of possible 'strings'. In March 1980 he turned down the $400 million as inadequate.

Yet the strong American reaction to the Soviet invasion of Afghanistan may have increased, rather than decreased, the chances of preventing a Pakistani nuclear test. Former Prime Minister Bhutto's initial decision to acquire nuclear explosive material, and Zia's follow-up action were both motivated by their concerns over Pakistan's security, and renewed and reinforced security ties with the United States might neutralize that particular incentive. Moreover, the prospect of a long-term Soviet military presence in Afghanistan and Mrs Gandhi's return to power in India may enhance the value of a restored security connection with the US. As a consequence, Pakistan may come to think it too costly to detonate a nuclear device and thus risk losing American support and aid.

Indian Reactions

Much to the surprise of many outside observers, India's detonation of a nuclear device in May 1974 was not followed by further testing and deployment of nuclear weapons. Pressures from the scientific-atomic establishment to go ahead with a full-fledged programme were resisted, first by Mrs Gandhi, and then, after 1977, by her successor as Prime Minister, Morarji Desai. By the late 1970s the Indian nuclear weapon 'programme' had effectively been shelved.

During the first half of 1979, however, the Indian government found itself under increasing pressure to reassess its nuclear-weapon activities, as the evidence mounted that Pakistan was building a uranium enrichment plant. Official Indian statements at first emphasized that there was no need for 'panic' and that India would stand by her past policy of nuclear abstinence. But those statements were quite soon followed by others expressing 'great concern' at Pakistani activities and reassuring the Indian Parliament that 'the government's policies are being constantly reviewed in light of this development.' Nevertheless, a combination of Prime Minister Desai's continued opposition to acquiring nuclear weapons and scepticism about the seriousness of Pakistani nuclear efforts dampened the Indian concern and response. But by the autumn of 1979 both these constraints had been eroded: a caretaker government under Charan Singh had replaced that of Morarji Desai, and India began to take Pakistan's intentions and ability to build a bomb more seriously. Rumours circulating at this time in New Delhi went so far as to talk of an imminent nuclear test by Pakistan, and official Indian statements began increasingly to warn that Pakistan's continued nuclear programme could lead to a reassessment of Indian policy, if not to an eventual decision to step up India's own nuclear weapon capability.

This shift towards a harder line was likely to be accentuated by Mrs Gandhi's return to power in January 1980. Unlike her predecessor, Mrs

Gandhi (who took the original decision to test a nuclear device) was not opposed in principle to an eventual Indian nuclear-weapons programme (although in an interview given just before the election she maintained that her government would not develop nuclear bombs), and, had there been a less hostile foreign reaction to the first test, she well might have authorized more testing in 1975 and 1976. Moreover, her past political record was one of greater toughness towards Pakistan. Her government was thus likely to be more sceptical of President Zia's reassurances about Pakistani intentions concerning nuclear weapons and more ready to respond to Pakistani stockpiling of weapon-grade uranium – even without a test – by revitalizing India's programme. In addition, her past foreign policy outlook had been marked by far greater cautiousness, if not outright hostility, towards the United States. This could incline her to react strongly to renewed American-Pakistani ties and to distrust US efforts to reassure India about the limits of those ties. The 1974 detonation was intended partly to demonstrate India's claim to a regional pre-eminence and a global role, and limited resumption of a nuclear weapon programme might eventually be thought necessary to serve the same purpose again. Moreover, pressures for such a resumption would be even greater if Pakistan's centrifuge programme continued unabated (as seemed likely) and if it were feared that Pakistan would detonate a nuclear weapon once she had received the proffered American arms and assistance.

Though perhaps more disposed than her predecessor to a resumption of Indian nuclear-weapon activities, Mrs Gandhi was nonetheless likely to adopt a cautious attitude in the months ahead. Much would depend on the detailed contours of the new regional relationships taking shape, on Pakistani actions, and on US policies of reassurance. For that reason President Carter's reported intention to exercise his right to waive Congressional restrictions and permit shipments of nuclear fuel to India, even though she had not accepted the full-scope safeguards required by the 1978 Nuclear Non-proliferation Act, was especially important. Such a decision could avoid a bitter dispute with the new Gandhi government just when the United States was trying to gain its acceptance of renewed US ties with Pakistan and when she was trying to prevent the resumption of the Indian nuclear-weapons programme.

Possible Outcomes

In this changed regional and international milieu any projection of the most likely proliferation outcome in South Asia would be fraught with uncertainty. At best some possible alternatives can be described briefly.

Latent Proliferation: Pakistan might complete development of her centrifuge facility, begin to stockpile highly-enriched uranium, but stop short of testing a nuclear explosive device. She might or might not go so far as to assemble weapons which had been only partially tested. India, having by this time been separating and stockpiling plutonium for several years, might then decide that this precaution alone would suffice, and would take no decision to resume testing, develop weapons or deploy a nuclear force. But a future Indo-Pakistani crisis could easily trigger a race to the bomb.

A Pakistani Test, followed by the shelving of Pakistan's programme and continued Indian restraint: Pakistan might detonate a 'peaceful nuclear explosion' in the early 1980s but then announce that she does not intend to go further. She would call on India to accept her proposal for mutual inspection of each other's critical facilities and non-deployment of nuclear forces. Assuming that it could be confirmed that Pakistan had stopped with that single test, the Indian government might choose to continue modernizing its conventional forces, rather than respond by choosing to deploy a nuclear force. Even so, it probably would step up its preparations for such a deployment.

Limited Indian and Pakistani testing and stockpiling of nuclear weapons, but without creation of a dedicated nuclear force: This would entail decisions in the early 1980s by India and Pakistan to test a series of nuclear weapons so as to master more advanced design techniques and gain confidence in their weapons. New designs would be stockpiled under close guard and central control, but there would be only limited preparations and training for the actual use of the nuclear weapons, whether in a first strike, on the battlefield, or in a second strike. That is to say, no equivalent to the US Strategic Air Command – with specified missions, training, equipment, bases, and so on – would be created. Inertia, limited threats, emphasis on the political sybolism of testing – all could contribute to this outcome. It might well be only a stage on the way towards the military deployment of nuclear weapons. However, there would be incentives for Pakistan to refrain from going beyond this stage. Given the economic, technical and industrial disparities between the two countries, any Indian nuclear force is likely to be larger, more versatile, more technically sophisticated and more capable of either supporting military operations or inflicting damage. Moreover, because of the greater dispersion of the Indian population, trained elite, industry and infrastructure, Pakistan could be significantly more vulnerable to any sort of homeland nuclear exchange.

Lessons for the Future

The Carter Administration relied basically on economic leverage and political pressure to restrain the nuclear-weapon-related activities of India and Pakistan. Regardless of its merits, that approach was shown to be inadequate in the light of the developments in the region. The United States and other powers wishing to curb the dangers of nuclear proliferation will have to learn from this experience. The new steps would require different types of actions by all outside parties concerned, particularly the US.

Any country which, like Pakistan, is bent on acquiring a nuclear-weapons capability cannot be stopped, and at best can only be delayed. Security guarantees by an outside power may alleviate some security concerns but not all. In the aftermath of Afghanistan, American military support may reduce Pakistan's concerns about Soviet ambitions but not those about Indian ambitions; similarly, reassuring India about Pakistan's intentions will not affect traditional Indian concern about the threat posed by China. Since the security of third-world countries cannot be defined adequately in East-West terms, Western military support intended to deter an Eastern threat (as in the case of Pakistan) will not always provide reassurance enough to make a third-world country's nuclear effort expendable.

A policy that attacks both nuclear and conventional weapons proliferation simultaneously is unlikely to be effective. Conventional military weakness tends to accelerate the quest for nuclear weapons in countries concerned about their security; conventional military assistance, on the other hand, could reduce it.

Pressure by nuclear suppliers may be less powerful in deterring a country from acquiring a nuclear weapon than the recognition of the regional consequences of that acquisition. This could help to arrest the dynamics of nuclear proliferation at a stage below that of fully-fledged nuclear forces. Future non-proliferation policies must therefore encourage regional dialogue and consultation. The key to keeping South Asian nuclear proliferation limited will lie in finding means to alleviate the uncertainty felt by both India and Pakistan and to verify that each had stopped her programme at a level which does not require an escalation by the other. Without such a means of verifying each other's capabilities and plans, pressures within both countries to move up the nuclear-weapons ladder would be difficult to resist.

THE SOVIET NAVY AS A POLITICAL INSTRUMENT

The Soviet Navy has become a powerful instrument of military force in recent years. Not only have its capabilities increased, but it has also been used more actively and more directly in support of Soviet foreign policy. Nevertheless, although these changes are real, the primary reason for the Soviet Navy's enhanced 'visibility' is increased Western and international attention to the role and place of the navy in the Soviet military establishment and an increased awareness of its impact in the international arena.

The Soviet Union has been exploiting her naval forces for political purposes for the last decade and a half. Two crucial preconditions for this exploitation were plainly the decision to develop the requisite capabilities and the evolution of a doctrine for their use. The creation of capabilities would have been the consequence of a long-term development strategy, presumably formalized in ten- and twenty-year plans. The most direct testimony about this comes from the Commander-in-Chief of the Soviet Navy, Admiral Gorshkov. In his 1967 article 'The Development of the Soviet Art of Naval Warfare', in *Morskoi sbornik*, he wrote that the reorientation of the Navy in the mid-1950s had aimed at generating capabilities not only for a nuclear war between the coalitions, but also for 'the support of state interests' abroad in peacetime and participating in conventional (local) wars involving interests which were, by Soviet definition, less than vital.

The decision to reorient Soviet development strategy coincided with a time when the USSR was showing a new and more positive attitude towards third-world nationalism and searching for influence with non-Communist countries. In the early 1950s she was already using all the instruments of third-world policy she uses today (trade, cultural exchanges, diplomatic support, economic and military aid, even naval goodwill visits) with the sole and significant exception of coercive naval diplomacy. It seems unlikely that she would have overlooked the compatibility of a diplomacy of force with her new foreign-policy orientation, or failed to consider that the security of some of her chosen policy instruments (e.g., arms aid) depended on being able to operate substantial naval forces in distant areas. Moreover, all the expensive investments she might make in favoured foreign regimes would be in jeopardy without a Soviet presence to deter domestic coups and to ward off foreign intervention.

The evidence suggests that if the Soviet Union did not adopt a diplomacy of force in the 1950s it was because she lacked a credible capability for it. Krushchev, in his memoirs, recalls that he proposed a naval demonstration in connection with an unspecified crisis but was talked out of it by his Minister of Defence, Marshal Malinovsky, among other reasons because it would have been 'ineffective'. Krushchev agreed, conceding that the USSR had to rely on her nuclear deterrent and should not take on her adversaries in areas 'where they are ahead of us'.

Soviet doctrine throughout the first half of the 1960s was consistent with that appraisal, emphasizing that any war involving the super-powers would inevitably escalate into a nuclear war. At the same time care was taken to imply that the USSR would go to war only if vital interests were involved – and in the Third World such interests were scarce. In short, the Soviet Union had no doctrine for a third-world diplomacy of force, and there were no instances of its practice.

Since the mid-1960s, however, this situation has altered, and the emerging capabilities generated by the decade-old decision to reorient naval development, explain the timing of the change. In early 1966 the 'international duty' of the Soviet armed forces was expanded to include conventional military action in the Third World. Even before this, in late 1965, there had been a subtle change in military doctrine. Whereas it had hitherto been stressed that even local wars would 'inevitably' escalate if the super-powers became involved, it was now said that escalation was only 'possible'. Even a direct military clash with the United States might therefore well remain at the conventional level. The Soviet Union now had a doctrine in which costs and risks were more adequately tailored to the less-than-vital interests at stake in third-world contests.

The development of capabilities and the recasting of doctrine was immediately followed by a marked expansion in forward deployments – an almost fourteen-fold increase between 1964 and 1976. SAM-defended Soviet surface combatants, present in the Mediterranean from 1964, were reinforced with cruise-missile submarines between 1966 and 1967, and their stationing declared 'permanent'. In 1968 Soviet warships moved into the Indian Ocean; in 1969 the practice of periodic sorties to the Caribbean was introduced; and in 1970 the nucleus was established in the eastern Atlantic for what was to prove a permanent West Africa patrol. Moreover, the Soviet Union has a large and continuing naval building programme. This is partly because of the need to replace obsolescent vessels, partly in order to update existing ones, and only partly to introduce new classes. Nonetheless, its effect is to provide a greater potential for distant-water operations. Though it may not have radically increased the number of its vessels, the Soviet Navy has become much more than the force designed primarily for coastal defence that it was in the 1950s.

Having established a presence, the Soviet Union immediately began to practice naval diplomacy in both its co-operative and coercive forms. In crises her concern has been indicated through fleet augmentations and movements, and when her interests seemed in jeopardy, she has demonstrated resolve by changes in fleet posture. On a number of occasions she has gone further, authorizing politico-military interventions in areas of actual or potential armed combat, when she felt that the need to protect and further her interests outweighed the risks (and these risks could be minimized by prudent behaviour and by the careful selection of occasions for confrontation). Since the first case of coercive military diplomacy during the Middle East War of 1967, not a single year has passed without at least one repeat performance.

In short, the Soviet Navy's forward presence has become a significant peace-time tool of national policy. To be sure, the Navy is not the USSR's only such politico-military instrument, nor does she regard these instruments as the only, or even the primary, tools of diplomacy – but simply as the 'ultimate' ones.

Specific Tasks

Of course, naval diplomacy – 'the support of state interests' – is not the Navy's main task. This is its 'national-defence task', which includes both peace-time and intra-war deterrence, and involves protecting the Soviet submarine-based nuclear deterrent with general-purpose forces and countering US sea-based deterrent forces. However, there is no obvious contradiction between the postures needed for wartime and peace-time missions, particularly where the object for the Soviet presence in forward areas is to cover US carrier task forces. So long as Soviet forces are in the vicinity of their targets, they are well placed to execute either mission.

The peacetime political mission has involved four distinct tasks: maintaining forces in important theatres, both on a routine basis and in crisis periods; augmenting forward forces (especially those types most appropriate for countering the US Navy); supporting Soviet air and sea lines of communication to the Third World; and delivering or evacuating high-priority materiel and influencing events ashore. Surface ships and general-purpose submarines have so far carried the brunt of these assignments. Strike aircraft of Soviet Naval Aviation have never deployed to the Third World (the Tu-16s deployed to Egypt in 1971 were meant for Egyptian use and, save on ferry missions, never flew over water). With the obvious exceptions of airborne troops and Military Transport Aviation, none of the other branches of the Soviet armed forces has so far played a significant role in her policy towards the Third World, except on the immediate periphery of the Soviet Union. (The single exception to this was the deployment of 25,000 Air Defence Troops in Egypt between 1970 and 1972.)

The deployments of Soviet naval units reflect a keen political awareness, as the transfer of the carrier *Minsk* from the Black Sea to the Pacific Ocean Fleet in 1979 indicated. The *Minsk* avoided the expert scrutiny and opprobrium that visiting the Mediterranean might have produced, preferring the more congenial receptions provided by Soviet clients in Angola, Mozambique and Aden. While she was in Aden, from 26 May to 2 June, her Ka-25 *Hormone* helicopters and Yak-36 *Forger* vertical take-off aircraft flew demonstration sorties, and the accompanying amphibious warfare transport *Ivan Rogov* flooded her well-deck and launched her amphibious air-cushioned vehicles and conventional landing craft. Since support for amphibious operations probably ranks quite low among the *Minsk*'s actual missions (both in war and in peace), the display of capabilities during this 'official friendly visit' were primarily related to the political purposes of her voyage.

The routine deployments of the Soviet Navy differ radically from the continuous, steady-state deployments of the US Navy. Normally, about 10% of the Soviet fleet is deployed at sea in forward areas, but this figure masks striking variations in the size and level of activity of the units deployed. As a rule, a core force of minimum size is maintained in the forward area, spending roughly two-thirds of its time at anchor or in port and being joined intermittently by units from home waters for medium-sized exercises. Once or twice a year large-scale augmenting forces are deployed for major exercises, among which are the quinquennial displays that the West has come to refer to as the *Okean* series.

Since observers are more sensitive to change than to continuity, one effect of this style of operation is that Western and other commentators have tended to focus on the 'big' Soviet Navy, which is seen only on occasion, rather than on the smaller force most commonly encountered in a particular area. As a result, the Soviet Navy has achieved a reputation for global reach and capability with a relatively small operational effort. All the same, this reputation reflects more than just symbolic behaviour, for in crises the Soviet Union has carried out major augmentations of forces in forward areas.

In such augmentations the Soviet Navy never loses sight of its potential wartime tasks. Soviet actions have been shaped predominantly by the Western posture and the actions of the immediate parties to the crisis, and in each major confrontation since 1967 specially tailored anti-carrier groups have deployed in numbers that generally exactly match the Western carrier task groups responding to the crisis. (For example, in February 1980 the Soviet Union deployed two missile cruiser task forces into the Arabian Sea in answer to the dispatch of two US carrier task forces). The Soviet forces mark the positions of Western carriers and, in periods of extreme tension, as at the climax of the Arab-Israeli war of October 1973, engage in exercises that use US carriers as simulated targets (activities which Western observers recognize because, since 1968, the Soviet Union has repeatedly demonstrated them in routine exercises in non-crisis conditions). This suggests that one of the purposes of routine Soviet activity is essentially political: to widen the vocabulary of signals available to Soviet leaders in crises.

The structure and pattern of operational use of the Soviet Navy indicates that its main task is countering Western naval power, predominantly that of the US. If the need arises for the rapid intervention of ground forces beyond contiguous territory, the Soviet Union must resort to her airborne and airlift forces. But the use of such interventionary forces tends to be supported by other means, and the Soviet Navy can help with this. For example, when Soviet airborne intervention was threatened during the 1973 Middle East war, the potential cost to the United States of interdicting it, had she wanted to, was increased to imponderable levels by the presence of the 96-ship Fifth *Eskadra* in the Mediterranean.

Soviet naval units in forward areas also have other tasks in crises, including protection and navigational support for airlift and sealift units. These were demonstrated during the October 1973 Middle East War, the Angola crisis, and most recently in the 1977-8 Ogaden war in the Horn of Africa. Soviet amphibious ships participated in each of these operations, in some cases taking on or landing materiel over the beach. There is no firm evidence, however, that Soviet ships have provided gunfire support or engaged in other combat operations directed against the shore (although there were reports of their giving gunfire support to the Ethiopian garrison surrounded by Eritrean forces at Masawa in early 1978). The existing balance of the Soviet Navy's tasks therefore gives first priority to countering US naval power, and puts the projection of power ashore, in the Western sense, well down the list. These priorities are likely to persist, at least until a significant number of *Kiev*-class carriers and *Ivan Rogov*-class amphibious warfare transports (and their successors) become available.

Naval Facilities Ashore
The maintenance of naval forces in distant waters is a complex undertaking, expensive in military, economic and political terms. Here the level of support from the shore, and the conditions of access to it, are important. Since the late 1950s the Soviet Union has gained access to shore support in several third-world countries. But this access has been not to bases, which the USSR could use as she pleased, but to facilities, which can be used only at the discretion of the host nation. While a number of states have granted her varying degrees of access to their port facilities, only a few have allowed her the use of facilities ashore (usually airfields for maritime surveillance operations). Major cases include Egypt (from 1967 to 1976), Somalia (from 1972 to 1977), Cuba, South Yemen and Vietnam.

The Soviet Navy does not in fact need much shore-based support to maintain a forward presence. By providing logistic support at sea, by careful servicing of equipment and by maintaining remarkably low operating tempos, the needs of deployed combatants for shore-based support have been kept to a minimum. This was demonstrated in 1977, during the Ogaden war. The Soviet Indian Ocean Squadron was augmented by 50% and then used extensively for six months after Somalia withdrew the use of its Berbera base and probably before its support element could be shifted to Aden. All the same, access to local ports has been very useful. It has made it easier and cheaper to keep warships deployed for long periods in areas often several weeks sailing time from home waters. This has meant proportionately less time wasted in transit and has enabled the Soviet Navy to support deployments with a higher ratio of combat to support vessels. In addition, the use of facilities ashore (e.g. long-range communication stations and airfields for reconnaissance aircraft) has enhanced the combat capabilities of the forces deployed.

Access to such facilities has involved costs and conditions that have varied from case to case. More often than not, access has been the product not of bribery or 'arm-twisting' but the 'natural' outcome of convergent state interests. Typically, the host country has had a direct stake in supporting the Soviet Navy, and the political costs of giving support were limited. Egypt, for example, recognized that Soviet use of her facilities served her own security needs after the débâcle of the June 1967 War, and economic considerations influenced Yugoslavia's decision to grant the Soviet Union limited use of her naval repair facilities in the mid-1970s. In other cases access was granted in return for supplies of Soviet arms. Occasionally the ultimate cost to the USSR turned out to be far more than the initial outlays suggested. For example, modernization of Somalia's armed forces in the early 1970s, in exchange for access to her facilities, enabled Somalia in 1977 to unleash an irredentist war in the Ogaden that proved both economically and politically costly when she cut her links with the Soviet Union.

On balance, access to support ashore has been a complicating but secondary consideration in Soviet policy. The quest for improved access has given additional impetus to the cultivation of relations with various regimes, but has not in the end altered the fundamental thrust of Soviet foreign policy. Neither has concern for the preservation of already established access. The threatened loss of important facilities, first in Albania (1961) and later in Egypt (1972 and 1976) and Somalia (1977) did not prevent the Soviet Union from taking actions that diverged significantly from the interests of those host nations. Thus, while access has been an objective of Soviet policy in the Third World, it has not been the determining factor.

Implications

The effect of the Soviet Navy's use in a coercive diplomatic role on international relations, particularly on the behaviour of the super-powers, is difficult to assess. Other factors, especially the shift in the balance of strategic forces and the emergence of new centres of power, have clearly had greater and more widespread impact. Equally clearly, however, the Soviet effort has meant that both super-powers – not, as in the past, only the United States – can now field credible naval forces in most regions of the world.

An overall assessment must be a balanced one. There are dangers in both overestimating and underestimating the worth of today's Soviet Navy as a political instrument. To be sure, it has vastly increased its capability for the forward projection of power, but considerable constraints of geography and operational capability still limit its overall flexibility. Now a powerful force in absolute terms, it does not yet match the West's greatly superior capacity for operating in distant waters.

If the Soviet Navy's new capabilities pose a problem for the West it is the same problem that all Soviet military forces pose: the fact that the Soviet Union has the will to project these forces into forward positions. It should be possible for the West to contain this threat – always provided that it shows the will to honour its basic commitments to the freedom of the seas and to the sovereignty of states with respect to their domestic affairs and established boundaries. The major danger is that, at a time when third-world conflicts are on the increase, greater Soviet naval strength creates a higher risk of clashes, accidental or deliberate, arising out of the super-powers' pursuit of their respective interests.

OIL AND SECURITY

In the international oil market 1979 was a year of instability and disintegration. After four years of relative calm and sufficient, or even abundant, supplies the interruption of oil exports from Iran, the drastic change of oil export policies by the new regime there, and a series of major price increases revealed the underlying fragility of the oil market. That there was an energy crisis was hardly a new idea, but thinking had hitherto focused too much on the abstract problem of intersecting supply and demand curves, and too little on the political forces and pressures that kept the market in equilibrium, or threatened to tilt it into instability.

For the industrialized countries growing concern about East–West imbalances had tended to obscure the fact that many of the security challenges of the 1980s are likely to come from the Third World, arising out of indigenous pressures and developments largely beyond the reach of great-power manipulation and control. These challenges will reflect problems stemming from instability in developing countries and regions, principally through interruptions of supplies of vital resources. They will also reflect the politicization of resource issues, as a result of the central role of these issues as a lever for the 'South' in 'North–South' negotiations between the industrialized and the non-industrialized nations.

The Eastern Bloc

For much of the 1980s the Soviet Union is likely to remain self-sufficient in energy and most other raw materials. Indeed, she is a major exporter of

Table 1: Development of Major OPEC Crude Prices in 1979 ($US per barrel)

	Saudi Arabian light (34°)	Saudi Arabian heavy (27°)	Iranian light (34°)	Kuwaiti (31°)	Iraqi Kirkuk (36°)	Libyan Brega (40°)	Nigerian Bonny (37°)	Venezuelan Tia Juana (31°)
1 January 1979	13.34	12.51	13.45	12.83	13.52	14.69	14.82	14.22
April 1979	14.55	13.64	16.57	15.80	16.28	18.25	18.52	16.70
July 1979	18.00	17.17	22.00	19.49	21.25	23.45	23.49	20.90
November 1979	18.00	17.17	23.50	25.50	22.18	26.22	26.26	20.90
20 December 1979	24.00	23.17	28.50	25.50	26.18	n.a.	26.26	24.90
1 January 1980	26.00	25.00	28.50	25.50	26.18	34.67	34.50	26.90 (provisional)

SOURCE: from *Petroleum Economist* and *Financial Times*

oil, as well as of a range of other resources. Yet it would be misleading to assume that the USSR could isolate herself and her empire from the impact of resource shortages. Western predictions about a pending Soviet energy shortage were confirmed by revelations at the meeting of the Supreme Soviet at the end of the year which dealt specifically with problems encountered in Soviet oil and coal production. Even if the USSR maintained her present level of oil exports to the countries of Eastern Europe (running at about 80 million tons per year), this would not prevent their energy supply falling short of demand. But financing additional world market imports will be difficult for them, and each price increase increases a problem already compounded by the severe impact of Western economic recession on Eastern European countries.

The growing dependence of the Council for Mutual Economic Assistance (COMECON) as a group on oil imports via international markets poses a dilemma for the Soviet Union. Obtaining preferential supplies from a client state in the Middle East, if this were possible, would be tempting economically but would probably not be without political risks, as past experience (with Iraq, for instance) has shown. Yet purely commercial transactions would be not only difficult to finance but also subject to the same uncertainties that the Western industrialized world has to face. This was vividly illustrated during the Iranian crisis. The temporary closure of the pipeline carrying gas from Iran to the southern Soviet Union, and the subsequent energy shortages there, underlined that not even the USSR at the height of her energy autonomy, let alone Eastern Europe, could be totally isolated from the reverberations of energy problems created by political instability in producing countries.

For the Soviet Union this posed a difficult choice, which transcended the Iranian crisis, between exploiting political opportunities to the disadvantage of the West and concern for her own security of energy supplies. Should she seek to aggravate turbulence in the oil-producing regions, and thus weaken not only the West's energy supplies but her own as well? Should she work for stability, or should she promote change and a social upheaval that she believed to be inevitable by providing political and even military support to the regimes emerging from that upheaval, in order to secure, if not preferential energy supplies, then at least ideological conformity? That the Soviet Union, faced with the undeniable need to secure additional supplies of energy sometime in the 1980s, would prefer to do so on the basis of special relationships not subject to international market conditions was obvious. But the question remained as to whether she would have that choice.

The Break-up of the Old Order

The evolution of international oil prices during 1979 provided a clear indicator of the growing fragmentation of the unity of the Organization of Petroleum Exporting Countries (OPEC), as Table 1 shows. The price increases, the growing differentials between different types of crudes, and the movement of spot-market prices can none of them be explained solely in terms of market forces. In the first nine months of 1979 OPEC production rose 4% above 1978 levels, while oil demand outside the centrally planned Eastern economies expanded only marginally. In addition, oil supplies from non-OPEC sources were growing, and stocks in the consuming countries reached an all-time high. Nevertheless, prices continued to move up. The explanation is simple: buyers were reacting not to the actual market situation, but to the underlying insecurity and uncertainty about the future. Prices thus came to reflect the state of affairs in the international order.

The relative calm in the oil market and the decline of prices in real terms between 1976 and 1978 had also fundamentally reflected political forces and arrangements. The persistence of adequate, and sometimes even abundant, supplies was in itself based on political decisions, particularly by Saudi Arabia. The special relationship between Saudi Arabia and the United States was central to the 1975-8 oil order: the former used her influence and leverage within OPEC to secure price stability and ensure adequate supply levels, while the latter undertook to protect Saudi Arabia and her present regime against external threats and to support a settlement of the Israeli-Arab conflict along lines acceptable to the majority of the Arab world and to the Palestinians. This relationship was supported by a number of additional pillars: the close co-operation between the US and the Shah of Iran; the predominance of moderate and pro-Western forces in the Arab world, headed by the Saudi-Egyptian alliance; and a general climate of optimism in the producer states, induced by the vast windfall of oil revenue which seemed to open dramatic new opportunities for rapid economic development. This atmosphere of stability focused political attention on domestic issues and led to a remarkable improvement in co-operation between Middle Eastern countries, particularly in the Gulf region.

The twin shocks of the Camp David agreement and the fall of the Shah brought a rapid disintegration of this structure, though fissures in it had become visible before then. The failure of industrialized countries, particularly the US, to check the growth of their oil imports had already made the Saudi position more and more difficult. If Saudi Arabia wanted to maintain her leverage over OPEC and world oil prices, she had to enlarge installed capacity and expand exports in line with growing Western oil demand; this, however, was less and less justifiable from a purely national point of view, and would only encourage the US and other industrial countries to continue to depend on oil as their primary energy source. Her decision not to expand installed capacity (partly as a result of her growing concern about the remaining life of her oil reserves) and technical problems with existing production facilities had effectively eroded Saudi freedom of manoeuvre as early as 1978, and the option of 'flooding the market' – the ultimate threat that Saudi Arabia held over the head of OPEC – had become less and less credible. In addition, developments in Iran during 1978 underlined the potentially destabilizing impact of massive oil revenues on Middle Eastern societies.

The Iranian revolution and the Israeli-Egyptian peace treaty thus combined to accentuate the inherent weaknesses in the previous order. The change of government in Iran removed an important underpinning of this order, and the new Iranian oil policy (reducing production in the name of conservation, maximizing oil revenues through price increases and shifting exports to the lucrative spot market) reinforced similar thinking among other oil producers. The Egyptian-Israeli peace treaty deeply split the Arab world, eliminating Egypt and weakening Saudi Arabia as factors of moderation in intra-Arab affairs and strengthening the radicals. This, in turn, reduced Saudi Arabia's leverage in Arab politics: while the previous arrangement had provided the best possible environment for the effective use of her political assets (oil money and mediation), the new situation in the Arab world underlined her vulnerabilities by demonstrating the weakness of the US security link. Saudi Arabia had already been worried by US inability or unwillingness to prevent Somalia's defeat in the war with Ethiopia and her Cuban and Soviet allies, and by the establishment in 1978 of a Marxist, pro-Soviet regime in Afghanistan. Now, it seemed to her, Washington had failed two more crucial tests: it had been unable to secure an acceptable Israeli-Arab settlement, and it could not maintain a friendly regime in power in Iran.

Challenges to the West

Thus, by the end of 1979 there were few elements of stability left in the international oil market. OPEC governments were no longer able to muster sufficient strength to bring prices under control, as the organization's January 1980 meeting in Venezuela showed. The oil companies had again managed a fair distribution of the shortfall in the first months of 1979, thus reducing its impact, but this ability to react flexibly was undermined by changes in the market structure – up to 25%

of OPEC oil exports were now being sold on the spot market or through bilateral deals at special prices.

During 1979 there was once again speculation about military intervention, ostensibly as a response to the seizure of the hostages at the American Embassy in Tehran. In fact the speculation was more an expression of the growing frustration and exasperation, felt particularly in the United States, over the limited means available to the West to deal with the evolution of internal politics in Iran and the other oil-producing countries of the Middle East, and the high vulnerability this entailed.

Yet military intervention hardly seemed a solution. Even if the formidable logistic and practical problems could be overcome, the political repercussions would still make the option an unattractive one, to be reserved for the last resort. It would unify the Middle East into a violent anti-Westernism, unless the intervention were seen as protecting not only Western interests but the Gulf's own security as well – an unlikely conjunction except in the event of a direct military threat from elsewhere against the countries of the region.

The Western oil supply problem would therefore have to be tackled politically. The ultimate solution to energy dependence problems must come from restructuring energy supply and demand, and the issue of readjusting the OECD countries' energy consumption has so far generated more questions than answers. What sort of savings could realistically be expected from more stringent energy conservation by oil-consuming countries? How much of the time needed for this readjustment will actually be available (the less time there is, the more painful the process will be)? Could the period be prolonged if the West adopted the right policies towards the producing countries? And to what extent might energy policies be co-ordinated within the group of industrialized countries, so as to avoid a direct conflict over available energy supplies?

Such efforts as were made between 1974 and 1978 were clearly insufficient, and this failure of Western policy contributed significantly to the difficulties of 1979. There are major uncertainties over both the willingness and the ability of the Gulf oil-producing countries to supply sufficient quantities, and, according to CIA estimates, a 'worst-case' projection could imply the loss of up to 8 million barrels per day (b/d) from the Gulf area. (See Table 2.) The resulting shortfall

Table 2: Gulf Oil Production (million b/d)

Country	Present	'Worst-case' in 1982
Saudi Arabia	8.5	2.5
Iran	4	3
Kuwait	2	1.5
United Arab Emirates	1.9	1.4
TOTAL	16.4	8.4

SOURCE: National Foreign Assessment Center, *The World Oil Market in the Years Ahead*, (Washington DC: NFAC/CIA, ER 79-10327U, August 1979).

would be about 10% of assumed needs of the OECD countries in 1982 (79.3 million b/d) or about 11% of their 1978 levels of energy consumption (75.2 million b/d). Supply cuts of this order should be theoretically assimilable, but the process would be extremely painful politically: the areas where savings could most easily be made are road transport, which alone now accounts for about 14% of the total OECD energy consumption, and residential/commercial uses, which account for another 24%. Means would have to be found to manage the scarcity which distributed the burden 'fairly' both within and between the consumer countries, and political systems and structures of intra-OECD co-operation would come under severe strain if it were necessary to react quickly to such shortages.

The response of Western industrialized countries to the 1979 supply crisis at least pointed in the right direction. In March 1979 the International Energy Agency (IEA) members decided on a reduction of oil demand levels of 5% of projected 1979 consumption, and this decision was supported by a parallel target set for the EEC, thus effectively bringing France into the framework of Western co-operation on energy. In June the EEC members agreed on an import ceiling for the period 1980-5 of 470 million tons per year, and this ceiling was confirmed at the Tokyo summit and at the follow-up meeting in September in Paris; the US set her import ceiling at 425 million tons for 1985, and Japan set hers at 315 million tons. A further IEA meeting in December set the 1980 import target for its members at a level roughly corresponding to that of 1979, and lowered the objective for 1985 by 1.4 million b/d to 24.6 million b/d. Admirable though these objectives were, there were two problems with them: they were not always met, and were therefore of limited credibility (for instance, the IEA as a group had not achieved the 5% reduction in oil consumption by the end of 1979), and they did not go far enough. A detailed analysis of the Tokyo summit targets, for example, makes it hard to avoid the conclusion that the 'sacrifices' could be accommodated comfortably without much additional effort, given the changes in previous assumptions about economic growth and energy prices during 1979. Thus, while the strategy was right, the political will to take it beyond mere reluctant acceptance of inevitable demand curtailments was lacking. Overall, the efforts were clearly an insufficient response to the challenge they had to meet.

Serious attempts to put co-operation between producers and consumers on a broader basis were conspicuously absent throughout the year. Western consumer countries seemed to rely on what was left of the American-Saudi special relationship and on the fact that if OPEC hurt the West too much it would hurt itself as well – not much of an answer when OPEC was failing as a cohesive organization and when individual OPEC governments proved too short-sighted to resist the temptations and domestic pressures to play leapfrog with the price of their oil. Both producers and consumers essentially agreed on a desirable solution (a gradual and phased increase of oil prices over the next few years), but they seemed unable to implement it. This led to a renewed interest in bilateral arrangements between individual producer and consumer countries in spite of the problems and dangers of this course – which were underlined in early December 1979, when Saudi Arabia cancelled an oil agreement with Italy over alleged irregularities in the payment of the 7% commission involved. The revival of bilateralism only contributed to the process of fragmentation in the market, without making any contribution to the longer-term objectives of the consumers.

The challenge of the coming years therefore remains the building of a viable political structure for the international oil market. The threat to the West lies not so much in the effect of sharply reduced oil supplies on its economies, but rather in the damage that could be done to political cohesion both within individual countries and between the members of the Western Alliance. The ability of the West's political systems to manage severe oil shortages without damaging existing structures of co-operation among the industrialized countries and without serious domestic upheavals will doubtless be tested to the full.

In the longer term, it seems essential that new structures of co-operation should be developed between producers and consumers. If the present instability and fragmentation of the oil market continues, the strain on co-operation between OPEC governments, particularly in the Gulf region, could lead to the final collapse of OPEC's common pricing system. The best strategy for enabling the industrialized countries to cope with those challenges would consist of two elements: oil import reductions (coupled with preparations to cope with the 'worst-case' if it happens), and taking steps to initiate a serious producer–consumer dialogue to deal with the questions of future oil supplies and prices. Here the creation of the atmosphere of greater political trust between the West and the oil-producing nations in the Gulf that would support such a dialogue is essential. Yet this atmosphere would depend on the governments in the region being able to control events. As 1979 showed, it was uncertainty about precisely this that underlay much of the uncertainty about oil supplies.

THE SUPER-POWERS

AN END TO DETENTE?

Relations between the United States and the Soviet Union had been marked by ups and downs during 1977 and 1978, but 1979 was a year of unambiguous deterioration. Although one event took place during the year which the two sides had been working for since 1977 – the signing of a SALT II agreement at the first summit meeting between Presidents Carter and Brezhnev – this stood out in sharp contrast to the increasingly tense mood. At the year-end the atmosphere was grim: Soviet troops were in Afghanistan, the SALT II agreement was languishing unratified in the US Senate, and the United States had sharply curtailed what little remained of super-power detente by embargoing grain sales to the Soviet Union, limiting transfers of technology and calling for a boycott of the 1980 Olympic Games in Moscow.

The problems were real and persistent. From very different perspectives, both Moscow and Washington appeared to have concluded that detente between them amounted to little. That feeling was obvious in the United States, but there were hints of a similar perception in the Soviet decision to invade Afghanistan. In these strained circumstances, the central core of the relationship – SALT – simply could not support detente by itself, and conflicts outside Europe, such as those in Afghanistan and Iran, were bound to become major issues between the two. The invasion of Afghanistan thus seemed to mark the end of the East–West detente that had begun a decade earlier. What would follow was unclear, but it was hardly likely that there would be a return to the presumptions, or the expectations, of the 1970s.

As differences of interest between the US and the USSR became sharper, the reality of super-power relations was more and more difficult to manage. But miscalculation and mishap also played a role. An aging Soviet leadership was confronted by deepening economic and demographic problems, as well as unrest around its borders. In the United States, as another election campaign began, President Carter seemed to be less the architect of the increasingly truculent public mood than to be swept along by it. The response to the invasion of Afghanistan gave some new vigour and coherence to his Administration, but the President continued to find it difficult to frame and implement a consistent long-term approach to the Soviet Union.

The China Aspect

The year opened with difficulties between the super-powers as a result of the normalization of Sino-American relations, which had been announced at the end of 1978 but took effect from 1 January 1979. The nearly completed SALT II accords were held up by the Soviet Union in consequence, as was the long-awaited summit between Presidents Carter and Brezhnev, originally planned for mid-January. The Soviet leadership was clearly upset that the American Administration apparently was giving priority to the relationship with China and was worried about the growth of Sino-American ties and their implications. Although President Brezhnev stressed a 'wait-and-see' attitude, calling normalization 'the proper relationship between sovereign states', *Pravda* warned that only time would show whether 'practical deeds and political actions' would confirm President Carter's assurances that the ties with China would not be used to the detriment of the Soviet Union.

In the event, Vice-Premier Deng Xiaoping's visit to the United States in late January was seen by the Soviet Union as the true reflection of American intentions. The Administration had carefully tried to assuage Soviet fears about the visit. Emphasis that Soviet-American relations would not suffer in consequence was bolstered by renewed commitments to a quick signing of SALT, a promise not to grant Most Favoured Nation (MFN) trading status to China without doing the same for the Soviet Union, and an unwillingness to condemn any Soviet role in the Vietnamese invasion of Cambodia. Deng, however, used his visit to denounce Soviet hegemonism, stressed the identity of views between Washington and Peking, called publicly for a Sino-American-Japanese Alliance, and proclaimed that China would find it necessary to 'punish' Vietnam for her actions in Cambodia. The Carter Administration tried to distance itself from these sentiments; the final communiqué, while expressing opposition to hegemonism, was followed by assurance that 'the security concerns of the United States do not coincide completely with those of China'. But Deng's visit was clearly a popular one in the US, and Moscow's bitterness that the host country had not disciplined the guest was only partly lessened by firm assurances that Washington would not sell military equipment to China (though it would not obstruct such sales by its allies). Soviet statements alleged American acquiescence, if not outright collusion, in China's subsequent invasion of Vietnam, and this perception was reinforced when the US sought to remain aloof from the 'conflict between Asian Communist states'. but was willing to proceed with trade negotiations with China during the hostilities.

The Carter Administration's previous balancing act over trade relations was soon abandoned. The Soviet Union allowed more Jews to emigrate than before (some 50,000 in 1979, compared to 29,000 in 1978 and 16,700 in 1977) but still refused to make any explicit commitment that would meet the provisions of the 1974 Jackson-Vanik amendment (which linked the granting of MFN status to the USSR with the easing of Soviet restrictions on Jewish emigration). By contrast, the Sino-American MFN agreement was submitted to Congress and passed in January 1980, immediately after the invasion of Afghanistan. Soviet fears of a *de facto* Sino-American Alliance were increased by China's explicit support for NATO's proposals for modernizing its long-range theatre nuclear forces, and by the emergence of 'parallel' strategies in regard to Afghanistan after Defense Secretary Brown's January 1980 visit to Peking. The Kremlin also reacted with deep suspicion to announcements that the US planned to move away from her previous line on arms sales by selling 'non-lethal' military equipment to China.

The Vienna Summit
The summit meeting postponed as a result of the opening to China finally took place in Vienna on 15–18 June, the first direct meeting between the American and Soviet Presidents since Mr Carter had come to power. Although the SALT II treaty was duly signed, this brief hiatus in a steadily deteriorating relationship was anti-climactic, if not counter-productive. The United States had hoped for substantial results on a range of arms reductions for the next decade, and hoped that an agreement limiting anti-satellite weapons, and perhaps a Comprehensive Test Ban (CTB) agreement, could also be ready for the summit. In addition, she aimed for some statement of principles on regional conflicts, and also hoped that the USSR might agree to guarantees on Jewish emigration that would fulfil the Jackson-Vanik Amendment, thus enabling the US to grant her MFN status.

However, because of the Soviet President's weak health, the Soviet Union treated the summit merely as the occasion for signing the SALT treaty. Apart from this the only concrete result was a commitment to regular meetings between the two leaders, of which little was heard later.

Soviet Brigade in Cuba
The 'discovery' in late August of a Soviet combat brigade in Cuba, and the crisis this provoked, exemplified the perils of mismanagement in a situation where facts are ambiguous and emotions strained. For both super-powers, it was the wrong crisis at the wrong time, played out to damaging effect. The way in which it was handled by the Carter Administration could only generate doubts in the Soviet Union and elsewhere about the constancy of American foreign policy, and about whether any value could be gained from dealing with the US during a Presidential election campaign.

Early in its tenure, the Carter Administration, as a goodwill gesture, had stopped intelligence overflights of Cuba. But a number of factors subsequently increased intelligence interest in Soviet activities in Cuba, including the discovery in 1978 that MiG-23 aircraft were stationed there, and suspicion of Cuban involvement in the Nicaraguan revolution. The resumed overflights and intensified intelligence gathering undertaken as a result yielded apparent proof that the USSR was maintaining in Cuba a 'combat brigade' – a very unusual formation in Soviet military organization. Instead of quietly defusing matters as it had done with the MiG-23 issue, the Carter Administration agreed to let Democratic Senator Frank Church of the Foreign Relations Committee release the story. Church, facing a tough re-election battle against conservative sentiment in Idaho, linked the withdrawal of the Soviet unit to the ratification of the SALT II treaty by the Senate. Senator Richard Stone of Florida, whose constituency included the anti-Castro Cuban refugee community in Miami, then accused the Administration of hiding the truth during the previous summer's debate on the ratification of the Panama Canal Treaty, when Secretaries Vance and Brown had assured Congress that no significant increase in Soviet activity had taken place in Cuba.

Although they asserted that ratification of the SALT II treaty would not suffer, the Administration, and the President personally, compounded their difficulties by echoing Congressional sentiments about the seriousness of the matter. The President went so far as to insist that 'the *status quo* was unacceptable'. The Soviet Union, on the other hand, stood firm, asserting that 'it is perfectly obvious that they [the troops] cannot either in their numbers or in their functions constitute a threat to the United States or to any other countries'. The Carter Administration soon found it necessary to admit that the troops might have been in Cuba since 1976, or even earlier, and that they constituted no offensive threat, given their small numbers and lack of sea and air support. It seemed likely that the troops were, as the Soviet Union insisted, in Cuba to train Cuban troops, guard Soviet intelligence facilities and meet obligations undertaken at the time Cuba became involved in Africa.

In the end, President Carter was reduced to announcing on 1 October a series of modest steps which somewhat increased military and economic aid and intelligence activity in the Caribbean and speeded up plans for a US rapid-deployment force; in return, the Soviet Union promised not to alter the *status quo*. The 'unacceptable' had become acceptable. Although the episode seemed to be a storm in a teacup, its effect was considerable; SALT ratification was dealt a blow from which it never recovered, and the Soviet incentive for dealing with an Administration so much a prey to the vagaries of senatorial politics must have been much reduced.

SALT and NATO

Soviet interests in SALT II were also affected by other developments: the Carter Administration's decision to move ahead with development of the MX missile; the firm undertaking to continue to provide nuclear assistance to America's allies, in particular Britain; and especially NATO's plan to meet the growth of Soviet medium-range missile capabilities by introducing new American missiles on European soil. On 6 October in East Berlin, in a speech clearly aimed at Western Europe and West Germany in particular, President Brezhnev offered to discuss reductions in the Soviet missiles targeted on Western Europe – but only if NATO deferred a decision on its modernization proposals. This offer was accompanied by an unconditional pledge to withdraw 20,000 troops and 1,000 Soviet tanks from East Germany. If the Soviet offer were ignored, however, Brezhnev threatened that any country that accepted the new missiles would find its position 'considerably worse'. But the speech contained too little and came too late to change the NATO decision. For the Alliance now to defer its modernization would have been a sign of weakness in the face of Soviet pressure, and President Carter immediately characterized the Soviet proposals as an effort 'designed to disarm the willingness of our Allies to adequately defend themselves'. The more positive aspects of Brezhnev's proposals were welcomed more openly in Western Europe, but there was an equal determination to negotiate only after a positive decision to develop and deploy the NATO missiles had been taken (see pp. 99–103).

Conflict Outside Europe

As in previous years, however, the main strains on US-Soviet relations arose not so much from the traditional issues of arms and arms control as from developments in the Third World, outside the regions of clear super-power control. The first major crack in the political support for East–West co-operation in the United States had been caused by the Soviet intervention in Angola in 1975, which had raised the image of an expansionist Soviet Union disregarding the rules of detente as the US saw them. Throughout 1979 the old pattern persisted. The Soviet Union was hostile to the Egyptian–Israeli peace accords, and, although actions to undermine the Camp David Accords remained muted, she continued to give military support to the confrontation states – particularly Libya, Iraq and Syria. And Soviet support for the Vietnamese invasion of Cambodia, the resulting military threat to Thailand, and the obstruction of aid destined for the Cambodian refugees were new sources of friction during the year. But the most serious conflicts emerged around the Persian Gulf, beginning with a relatively minor confrontation between North and South Yemen, and concluding with the Soviet invasion of Afghanistan.

Iran

Super-power relations during the Iranian crisis reflected the difficulty each had in influencing events in the region (see pp. 45–6). It also exposed the ambivalence with which the Soviet Union regarded the chaos in Iran, for revolutionary Islamic change presented the Soviet Union with the prospect of unpredictability on her borders and Muslim alienation within them. Although encouraging the Iranian revolution through radio broadcasts, she was reluctant officially to attack the Shah or support Khomeini until it was absolutely clear which of them would come out on top. Once in power, however, Khomeini in general received vocal backing from the USSR. She vigorously condemned the role of the United States in supporting the Shah and officially welcomed Iranian efforts to secure the return of the Shah for trial.

Concerned about the danger of American military intervention, the Soviet Union also warned of the dangers of the naval build-up in the Persian Gulf and invoked the clauses of her 1921 Treaty with Iran which provided a pretext for possible Soviet retaliation in such an event. Her concern about this possibility was reinforced by the crisis caused when the American diplomats were taken hostage in Tehran in November. The Soviet Union was unwilling publicly to condone this violation of international law or to provoke American military intervention. Thus, after some initial radio broadcasts encouraging the Iranian radicals, she quietly supported the early US efforts to have the hostages released. Nevertheless – despite the fact that the Ayatollah Khomeini's attitude to Moscow (criticizing the Soviet role in Afghanistan and cancelling agreements to export large quantities of gas to the USSR) indicated that there was little prospect of amicable Soviet–Iranian relations during his reign – the Soviet Union deliberately exploited anti-Western sentiments within Iran. This was seen as tantamount to condoning an act of international terrorism and was thought to be incompatible with the behaviour expected of a power with a stake in the international order.

Afghanistan
Given the deteriorating relations between the super-powers, perhaps neither the USSR's invasion of Afghanistan nor the American reaction to it were as surprising as they seemed. American impotence in the Iranian crisis may have led the USSR to underestimate the intensity of the response that her action in Afghanistan was likely to provoke. What the Soviet leadership apparently failed to understand was the cumulative effect of its actions on the West – and particularly on the United States, which was more and more concerned about Soviet intentions and capabilities. For American public opinion Afghanistan was the final straw.

All the same, better Soviet assessments – or even the ratification of SALT II – would not necessarily have forestalled the decision to invade. Seen from the Kremlin, events in Afghanistan increasingly pointed to the necessity of drastic action, and arguments for caution must have seemed weaker and weaker. Already troubled by Iran, the Soviet Union was clearly unwilling to be faced with the possibility of another radical Muslim regime on her southern border. More important, she had willy-nilly become increasingly involved with her Afghan client regime after the coup of April 1978. With this regime failing, despite the presence of large numbers of Soviet advisers, the USSR faced the spectre of defeat for a client to whom she was tied by a treaty of friendship. The choice must thus have seemed to lie between making a humiliating withdrawal or greatly increasing her military presence in Afghanistan – and the external signs suggested that the costs of strong action would be manageable.

American reaction was swift. Within two days of the invasion President Carter labelled the action a 'threat to world peace' which would 'severely and adversely affect relations between the two countries' and said that his opinion of the USSR had 'changed more drastically in the last week than even the previous two and a half years'. On 4 January, rejecting Moscow's crude and unconvincing rationalizations for its actions, he imposed an array of sanctions on the Soviet Union. These included suspending licenses for high-technology exports, cutting grain sales by 17 million tons down to the 8 million tons the US was committed to sell to the USSR by agreement, curtailing Soviet fishing rights in US waters, delaying the expansion of Soviet consular facilities in the US, and threatening to boycott the Moscow Olympics. Ratification of SALT II was suspended, efforts to establish military facilities in East Africa and the Gulf were stepped up, and, notwithstanding previous sour relations, Pakistan was offered $400 million a year for two years (half in economic and half in military aid). Even-handedness as between Moscow and Peking was forgotten as the United States and China found that the invasion gave them additional parallel interests in opposing the Soviet Union. American resolve was indicated in President

Carter's State of the Union address, in which a firm but ambiguous line was drawn on further Soviet advances in the area ('an attempt by any outside force to gain control of the Persian Gulf will be regarded as an assault on the vital interests of the United States') and the possibility of military conscription was raised with a plan to reintroduce registration.

The Soviet Union refused to bow to these pressures. Instead she took several steps designed to show that Western pressure would not succeed, vetoing the UN resolution on economic sanctions against Iran, expanding her military presence in Afghanistan, and stepping up her campaign against dissidents by imposing internal exile on Andrei Sakharov. Repeating the Soviet justification for intervention, President Brezhnev turned on the United States, accusing her of trying to poison detente. The USSR was clearly seeking to drive a wedge between the US and her allies. Meanwhile in Afghanistan itself, the Soviet forces seemed to be settling in for a prolonged occupation.

At the beginning of 1980, it was clear that the Soviet Union had been surprised by the depth and the breadth of the reaction to the invasion. Unprecedented protest from the Third World was expressed in the support of 104 nations for a UN resolution condemning the invasion and in a similar statement supported by 36 members of the Islamic Conference, meeting in Islamabad in January. And the detente with the United States, which the Soviet Union had made a priority of her policy since the mid-1960s, seemed severely impaired if not at an end.

Nonetheless, both super-powers recognized that points of co-operation must be redeveloped if a very dangerous turn in international relations was to be avoided. This consideration was likely to affect Soviet assessments, as the Moscow leadership took stock of the difficult situation that its own actions had created. For his part, President Carter, in his State of the Union address stressed that efforts to control nuclear weapons 'would not be abandoned', and that the door was not shut fully on future negotiations.

THE UNITED STATES: CONCERN OVER SECURITY

Trends within the United States which had been discernible for several years were focused by events in 1979 towards a consensus in favour of increased military spending and a more assertive American presence abroad. To some extent the immediate pressure for increased defence expenditure reflected specific phenomena: the onset of the 1980 presidential campaign; some senators' use of the threat to vote against the ratification of SALT II for leverage on an administration they regarded as reluctant to support major new strategic weapons programmes; and the Soviet invasion of Afghanistan. Yet, since the new defence programmes were for the most part in train before the Soviet move into Afghanistan, it was wrong to regard them as a reaction to it (or indeed to see the US response to the invasion as little more than a Washington election gimmick). Moreover, the mood underlying them was quite broadly based and liable to endure. A Gallup poll conducted in late September showed that 60% of the electorate supported increased defence expenditure, with only 9% favouring reduction (whereas an identical poll in 1971 had produced figures of 11% and 49% respectively).

The most important reason for this change was straightforward: a greater appreciation of the magnitude of Soviet military efforts over the past decade. Concern over Soviet capabilities and intentions had already been evident as early as 1976, when Governor Reagan compelled President Ford to drop the word 'detente' from his political lexicon. But it took until 1979 for the Carter Administration and the Congress to develop the same degree of concern over the steady build-up of Soviet military strength that was agitating critics of US defence policies. The SALT debates then concentrated Congressional and public attention on the relative decline of American military power. Demands for increased military spending were in these circumstances inevitable.

Iran and Afghanistan underlined a resurgent sense of American vulnerability to events in the Middle East and Persian Gulf. Public concern dated back to 1973, but it was only fully crystallized by the overthrow of the Shah and the resulting fuel shortages in the United States, by the occupation of the US Embassy in Iran and the taking of American citizens as hostages, and, still more strikingly, by the invasion of Afghanistan. These events generated overwhelming support for a build-up of American naval and interventionary capabilities. In their frustration, many viewed the taking of the hostages as a result of US military weakness (for example, believing that the Iranian students would not have dared seize the Soviet Embassy), and the invasion of Afghanistan was seen as an even starker sign of the need for American strength.

In the first instance, the announcements of new military measures were symbols of the United States' commitment to her friends in the region and signals of her resolve to the Soviet Union. However, there was a risk in signalling intentions that could not be fulfilled if need be, and there were obvious problems in obtaining military power in the region and then using it effectively. Even with the Shah in power, the Soviet Union had held an overwhelming advantage in conventional power in south-west Asia. Equally, the American search for staging rights and military facilities, might, by identifying friendly governments too closely with the United States, expose them more than it protected them. The United States negotiated such rights with Oman, Kenya and Somalia in early 1980, but Saudi Arabia refused them to her for precisely this reason. Finally, as the hostages in Teheran illustrated, it is difficult to apply military power when there is no clear military threat; the presence of a US carrier task force in the Arabian Sea from early December did not help obtain the release of American diplomats from their unlawful captivity in Iran.

Strategic Forces
Clear signs of evolution in American strategic doctrine appeared in 1979. 'Counterforce', the rallying cry of its critics on the right, was no longer a concept to be avoided by the Administration. The findings of the review of nuclear war plans which Defense Secretary Harold Brown had ordered in 1978 began to be translated into policy, and his Defense Report for the Fiscal Year 1980 differed sharply in tone from the FY 1979 version. Brown argued that a true 'countervailing' strategy required a capacity to cover Soviet military targets, including hardened missile silos, and that in the current environment a deterrent strategy based solely on an assured destruction capability was no longer 'wholly credible'. There were press reports of efforts to devise targeting options designed, for example, to undermine Great Russian ethnic ascendency or Communist Party political control in wartime. And Administration interest in American command and control, air and anti-missile defence, and civil defence was also a reflection of these shifts in doctrine.

In the countervailing strategy, unlike earlier US doctrines, there was a place for the capability to destroy hard targets with a great degree of urgency – i.e. to destroy Soviet missiles in their silos. This was reflected in the Administration's decision, after much hesitation, to procure the MX mobile ICBM, which, after languishing in engineering development for several years, moved into full-scale development in the spring. President Carter opted for the 190,000-lb, 92-inch diameter model, rather than a smaller 86-inch version, and this in effect excluded the possibilities of a common programme for both the MX and the *Trident* II sea-launched missile and of an air-mobile or air-launched MX. The new missile would be tipped with ten Mk 12A warheads, each with an estimated yield of 300–350 KT. Its initial operational capability (IOC), originally scheduled for FY 1982, was unlikely to be achieved before 1986, with full operational capability (FOC) not likely until the end of the decade. (The Administration, supported by the Joint Chiefs of Staff, resisted efforts to accelerate the FOC to FY 1985-6 on the ground that this would not justify its enormous extra cost).

While the missile itself therefore seemed firmly on the way to procurement, its basing mode remained uncertain. Resolution of this issue was dictated less by operational necessity than by the desire to assure Congress that the Administration seriously intended to deploy the new missile, rather than to sacrifice it as a bargaining chip in SALT negotiations. In September, Secretary Brown announced that a horizontal multiple protective shelter basing mode for MX had been selected – a choice largely dictated by arms-control considerations.

This called for each missile to be mounted on a transporter-erector-launcher vehicle which would be driven around an elliptical track studded with 23 dispersed shelters. The planned 200 missiles would therefore have 4,600 separate potential launch points, but the provision of movable 'sun roofs' atop each shelter would assure Soviet reconnaisance that only 200 missiles were in fact deployed at any one time.

There was concern over the extent to which arms-control considerations had inflated the cost of this option, and the Administration's $30–40-billion estimate of MX's final cost was regarded by many as over-optimistic. As 1980 began, doubts were increasing as to whether the 'racetrack' system would ever be built as planned. Constructing it in the American south-west, as early plans suggested, would be an enormous task, and a myriad lawsuits and problems with federal and state environmental legislation had already begun. The system depended on the extent of the Soviet threat continuing to be subject to the limitations imposed by SALT II, particularly the limitation on the number of warheads that each type of Soviet missile was permitted to carry. Moreover, there was the formidable technical difficulty of giving a massive missile launcher the 'dash' speed needed to relocate a missile from one silo to another in the period of 30 minutes or so between early warning of a Soviet ICBM launch and the missiles' arrival. These practical problems and the delay in ratifying SALT II combined to give impetus to a reopening of the debate over other basing alternatives, some of which involved active defence of silos by anti-ballistic-missile missiles, which would require modification of the ABM Treaty.

The MX issue was closely related to concern over the theoretical vulnerability of America's 1,000 *Minuteman* ICBM to a pre-emptive strike by the Soviet Union. Unexpectedly accurate test performances by Soviet SS-18 and SS-19 ICBM compelled the government to revise estimates of the date at which US ICBM would become vulnerable to a Soviet first strike from the mid-1980s to 1983. Efforts to increase American missile accuracy also continued. Silo upgrades and the refitting of the *Minuteman* force with the NS-20 guidance system were completed during the year, and deployment of the new Mk 12A warhead (scheduled to equip 300 *Minuteman* III) begun. With improved yield and accuracy, *Minuteman*'s single-shot kill probability against Soviet silos would double to between 66% and 80% or more, depending on the hardness of the silo.

The *Francis Scott Key*, the first *Poseidon*-equipped missile submarine to be refitted to carry the new *Trident* I missile, went out on operational patrol in the Atlantic in October. Eleven other *Lafayette*-class boats will be similarly refitted by 1982. The *Trident* I missile carries eight 100-KT Mk 4 re-entry vehicles and is as accurate as *Poseidon* over twice the range. The *Ohio*, the first submarine designed from the outset to carry *Trident*, was launched in April but will not join the operational fleet until 1981. To be fitted with 24 *Trident* I missiles, she will be based at Bangor, Washington, and deployed in the Pacific. An Atlantic base for *Trident* boats was under construction at King's Bay, Georgia. But this submarine-building programme was still plagued with difficulties; in 1976, it had been hoped that ten *Ohio*-class boats would be deployed by 1981, but it now appeared that only one or two would be available by that date. Spiralling programme costs had made it necessary to extend the service lives of *Polaris*- and *Poseidon*-equipped boats so as to avert a sharp drop in US SLBM strength in the mid-1980s.

Efforts to improve the strategic bomber force intensified in 1979. In the FY 1980 budget $440 million was allocated to extend the service life, and to some extent to increase the penetration capability, of the B-52 bomber. At the year-end a 'fly-off' competition between the General Dynamics AGM-109 (*Tomahawk*) and the Boeing AGM-86B cruise missiles was under way. The victor was to be selected in 1980 as the Air Force's new air-launched cruise missile (ALCM), the first of which were planned to be deployed aboard a B-52G in September 1981. While it was not yet clear what form the ALCM force would ultimately take, one-third of these weapons was likely to be deployed on board B-52Gs. The remaining two-thirds would be carried by a specialized type – a modification of either a large transport plane, such as the Boeing 747, DC-10 or C-5, or a smaller transport, such as the YC-14 or YC-15. However, it was reported that the Air Force was also considering development of an austere, fixed-wing version of the previously cancelled B-1 bomber, designed to carry some 30 ALCM. This, by virtue of its rapid take-off and fly-out capabilities, would be more likely to survive an attack on American airfields by Soviet sea-launched ballistic missiles.

Manpower Problems
President Carter announced in January 1980 that the United States was considering re-instituting registration for the draft, to include women. In its timing this was primarily a signal of the seriousness with which the US regarded the Soviet invasion of Afghanistan, but it also reflected real and enduring manpower problems within the American military. The President referred to these several times during 1979, and at the year-end they were highlighted by press reports of an internal memorandum from the Chief of Naval Operations detailing the Navy's problems in retaining skilled enlisted personnel.

The most obvious problem was recruiting enough people to fill service requirements. Manpower needs in 1980 would rise by 20% over 1979, but the number of males in the 17–21 age group had been declining since 1978. In 1979, for the first time since America moved to an all-volunteer army in 1973, all four military services failed to meet their recruiting quotas. Similarly, it was harder and harder to recruit people with sufficient education: the proportion of army recruits with a secondary school diploma fell from 74% in 1978 to 64% in 1979.

Even more serious than recruitment was the problem of retaining skilled personnel. This had hit hardest in the Navy – where the career re-enlistment rate fell from 90% in 1971 to 62% in 1979 – but every service had been affected. In a number of skilled jobs, such as pilots, physicians, engineers and a variety of technical non-commissioned officers, the services faced increasing competition from the private sector. The military instituted a number of incentives to improve retention, and in January 1980 the Joint Chiefs of Staff requested pay increases of over 10%, well above 7% granted to government employees.

Another effect of abolishing the draft had been a dramatic reduction in the level of reserves, which was causing growing concern about the United States' ability to respond to military threats outside Europe. Her ready reserve, which had declined from a peak of 1.5 million in 1972 to a low of 356,000 in 1978, numbered about 400,000 in 1979. The absence of the draft necessarily meant that the United States had a smaller pool of people with recent military experience – and hence a lesser capacity to mobilize – than the Soviet Union.

Forward Deployments
By the middle of the year the President had retreated on another front. In 1977 he had honoured a campaign promise by announcing his intention to withdraw US combat troops from South Korea. Small withdrawals were made in 1978, but late in that year an intelligence review indicated that North Korean military forces had been underestimated by as much as 25%, so that the parity of forces on which American withdrawal had been premised no longer existed. In January 1979 a special Senate study group chaired by Senator Sam Nunn urged cancellation of the troop withdrawal plans. The cost of repatriating and reconfiguring the Second Division was expected to be $1.5-2.4 billion, and there were fears that the withdrawals might undermine deterrence on the peninsula without reducing American obligations in the event of war, since some 16,000 US Air Force personnel and support troops were to remain in any case. In July 1979, after visiting Seoul and touring the de-militarized zone, the President decided to postpone US withdrawal until 1981 at the earliest.

Amid growing concern about American ability to project military power, Washington renegotiated several agreements on basing rights. Rights to the Subic Bay and Clark Air Force Base facilities in the Philippines, both critical to American capabilities in the Pacific and Indian Oceans, were renewed in 1979. President Marcos had originally hoped to receive $1 billion in military assistance alone in exchange for agreeing to the renewal. However, partly in response to pressure from his colleagues in the Association of South East Asian Nations (ASEAN), he settled for a mixed economic and military aid package worth $500 million, to be spread over five years. The new agreement, which emphasized Filipino sovereignty, with Filipino officers nominally commanding the bases, was to remain in force until 1999. Agreement was also reached with Portugal to extend the 1951 arrangement permitting American forces to use Lajes Air Base in the Azores. The United States had been permitted to return to her bases in Turkey on an interim basis in October 1978, after the lifting of the 1975 embargo on certain military sales which Congress had imposed after the Turkish intervention in Cyprus. In October 1979 a three-month extension was arranged, and in early 1980, the two countries finally repaired their defence relationship, by initialling a co-operation agreement which provided a status for American forces in Turkey and a framework for US aid. With the new agreement, only details remained to be settled to give the United States continued access to some 26 installations in Turkey.

Rapid-deployment Force
The succession of third-world crises – Iran, the Yemens, and Afghanistan – focused attention on the task of projecting military power beyond the United States' traditional deployment areas, a task long advocated by National Security Adviser Brzezinski.

The American military presence in the Middle East and Persian Gulf area increased sharply in 1979. In response to instability in Iran, the carrier *Constellation* sailed from Subic Bay for the Gulf in early January. This plan was cancelled, however, and *Constellation* was left hovering in the South China Sea, while a squadron of unarmed F-15 air-defence fighters was temporarily sent to Saudi Arabia in a somewhat hollow demonstration of military reassurance. In late February, war broke out between the two Yemeni Republics. The US Administration, prompted by Saudi Arabia, responded swiftly, and it was a testimony to the changing American mood that when the President used his discretion to short-circuit the Congressional arms sales review processes (instituted as recently as 1978) Congress made no protest. North Yemen was supplied, at Saudi Arabia's expense, with some $300 million worth of US equipment, including M-60 tanks, two C-130 transports and a dozen F-5E fighters. (However, there were later indications that Saudi Arabia, ambivalent in her attitude to North Yemen, had held up the transfer of much of the arms.) *Constellation*, supported ultimately by ten surface combatants drawn from the Sixth and Seventh Fleets, was again dispatched to the Arabian Sea, and a squadron of armed F-15s and two Airborne Warning and Control System (AWACS) aircraft were sent to Saudi Arabia. By the autumn, however, fighting along the Yemeni border had diminished, the North Yemen Government looked stronger than it had six months before, and spasmodic unification talks between the two Yemens were reportedly under way. That suggested to some that US efforts had been timely; to others, that they had been unnecessary.

Throughout 1979 the American naval deployment in the Indian Ocean, particularly of aircraft carriers, dwarfed the efforts of previous years. *Constellation* was relieved in April by the USS *Midway*, which left in early June but returned in October for joint exercises with the British Navy in the northwest quadrant of the Indian Ocean and stayed on when the Iranian hostage crisis broke on 4 November. On 16 November *Midway* was ordered to close on the straits of Hormuz and was later joined by the carrier *Kitty Hawk* and a substantial number of surface combatants. At one point in early 1980 the United States had a total of about 30 ships in the Indian Ocean, including three carriers, and in February 1980 a force of 1,800 Marines with equipment was dispatched to join this force.

The idea of a 'quick strike' or 'rapid-deployment' force had been under study for some time, but in 1979 the plans became more concrete, and money was allocated for carrying them out. In the wake of the 1973 Middle East war many observers had felt that American interventionary capabilities in and around the Persian Gulf were dangerously weak in relation to both the importance of American interests there and the range of potential threats in the region. Although the United States still had some intervention capability (see *Strategic Survey 1978* pp. 14–15), she no longer had either strong allies or access to bases in the region. Moreover, the level of possible turmoil and of armaments in the region suggested that any intervention would take place in a hostile environment, and that the forces would have to be 'heavier' and more self-supporting than those currently available.

The five-year defence plan announced in December 1979 included $9 billion worth of equipment for a newly-formed rapid-deployment force. The Army would earmark approximately 110,000 US-based troops for this force, including the 82nd Airborne Division, while the Marine Corps would contribute another 40–45,000 men. The Administration expected to spend $6 billion on developing and procuring a projected long-range wide-body transport (CX) with a projected IOC in 1986-7, and $80 million was earmarked for initial development in FY 1981. It remained unclear whether CX would be an entirely new aircraft or a modification of existing designs like the Boeing 747 or the C-5 *Galaxy*.

The newest element of the defence plan, the allocation of $3 billion for the procurement of fifteen specialized multi-purpose cargo vessels, reflected the difficulty of obtaining permanent bases in third-world regions. Stocked with tanks, artillery, vehicles, ammunition and supplies, these ships would be deployed at sea in the vicinity of potential trouble spots. In the event of a crisis (and a foreign request for assistance, for these plans presumed little or no local opposition), Marines would be flown in and fitted out with the seaborne equipment. The proposed FY 1981 budget included $220 million to fund construction of the first two cargo ships, and by 1983 the Marines hoped to be able to move 16,500 men, with armour and air support, to virtually anywhere within six days and sustain them in combat for thirty days. The Marine Corps, in recent years uncertain of its future role, now faced new tasks. And, since these tasks were seen to complement Marine missions on NATO's northern and southern flanks, some of the new cargo ships would also be deployed in the eastern Mediterranean.

Defence Spending

The Administration presented its FY 1980 defence budget to Congress in January 1979. Current outlays of $122.7 billion were requested, on the assumption that this approximately represented the 3% real increase over the FY 1979 budget which had been promised to NATO in 1977. However, the use of an extremely optimistic 6.4% inflation estimate meant that by the middle of the year the Administration was compelled to request a $4-billion supplemental appropriation in order to meet the growth target. Despite the clamour for increased defence spending, this request was initially obstructed in both the Senate and the House of Representatives. However, late in the year Congress finally approved an FY 1980 budget authorizing outlays of $127.4 billion and a total obligational authority of some $138 billion.

The FY 1980 budget was criticized in Congress and elsewhere as being 'Eurocentric' and neglecting third-world contingencies. Air- and sea-lift deficiencies were not addressed and, although funds for a 62,000-ton 'midi' carrier were requested, development of the AV-8B *Harrier* V/STOL aircraft for use from carriers was cancelled. These decisions satisfied neither those who believed in 'super-carriers' able to steam into harm's way nor those favouring smaller V/STOL-equipped ships.

The President had vetoed the FY 1979 budget since it included funds for a 90,000-ton *Nimitz*-class nuclear-powered carrier, but had promised to earmark funds for a new carrier in the FY 1980 budget. The resultant request for the 62,000-ton vessel came over the objections of the Defense Department, which favoured a 90,000 *Kennedy*-class conventional-powered carrier. The House of Representatives held firm for a nuclear carrier, arguing that rising conventional fuel costs made it cost-effective. In October the White House yielded – reportedly as part of a deal to prevent Senator Helms' threat to sponsor lifting sanctions against Rhodesia and thus disrupt the Lancaster House talks on a Rhodesian settlement – and $2.36 billion was appropriated for a *Nimitz*-class vessel in the FY 1980 budget.

The five-year plan announced by the Administration in December called for an average 4.5% real increase in defence appropriations during each of the next five years. The President promised to seek supplementary appropriations to maintain this level, even if actual inflation rates exceeded government estimates. For FY 1981

US Defence Outlays 1960-81

	Indices (1970=100)		$ billion (Current prices)
	Constant prices	Current prices	
1960	76.5	59.3	45.4
1965	82.1	66.5	51.8
1966	97.6	81.6	63.6
1967	112.7	96.8	75.4
1968	115.7	103.6	80.7
1969	110.8	104.5	81.4
1970	100.0	100.0	77.9
1971	92.3	96.1	74.9
1972	92.6	99.6	77.6
1973	88.1	100.8	78.5
1974	86.9	108.2	84.3
1975	84.3	119.1	92.8
1976	79.7	116.8	91.0
1977	83.0	129.5	100.9
1978	80.4	134.9	105.1
1979*	81.8	147.6	115.0
1980*(projected)	83.4	163.5	127.4
1981*(projected)	86.1	183.2	142.7

* Based on US-estimated military inflation rates (successively 7.5%, 8.6% and 8.4%).

the Administration requested appropriations totalling $157 billion (a full 5% in real terms above the FY 1980 figure of $138 billion). However, actual outlays requested amounted only to $142 billion, an inconsistency which evoked criticism from both ends of the political spectrum on Capitol Hill and raised doubts as to whether the Administration, faced with increasing inflation at home, would follow up its own strong words.

Still, it was clear that the centre of gravity in defence debates had shifted radically. Jimmy Carter, who had advocated major defence reductions in 1976, now presided over the first substantial real increase in the US defence budget since the height of the Vietnam War in 1968. Over the previous ten years defence outlays had moved steadily downwards, and in real terms the United States spent less on defence in 1976 than in any year since 1960 (see table above). As the table shows, US defence outlays in real terms have gone through rising and falling cycles lasting for a number of years. The increases announced by the Carter Administration followed the historical low point of 1976. Though at first glance a reaction to what was seen as an increasingly hostile international environment, they might therefore mark the start of a rising trend which, like the underlying public mood, could persist.

THE SOVIET UNION: ARMS AND THE ECONOMY

Like the United States, the Soviet Union gave a high priority to her defence effort during 1979. Unlike the United States, though, she was not accelerating that effort after years at a slackening tempo; Soviet military expenditures had been continually rising. But that defence effort came from an increasingly troubled economy that fared worse in 1979 than it had in 1978. The defence burden grew, the economy declined, Soviet leaders aged, and the year brought little hint of the shape of the leadership after Brezhnev.

The Momentum of Military Build-up

The relentless pace of Soviet military expansion continued in 1979, and defence expenditure again rose by 4–5% in real terms. The American Central Intelligence Agency increased its estimate of the defence burden on the Soviet economy, putting it at 15% of GNP in 1975, and expecting it to rise to 18% in 1980.

In the strategic forces category, SS-17, SS-18 and SS-19 ICBM continued to be deployed at a rate of about 125 launchers a year. At the year's end, there were more than 200 SS-18s in converted SS-9 silos, and about 150 SS-17s and over 200 SS-19s in converted SS-11 silos. Deployment of the SS-20 mobile intermediate-range missile continued at about 50 per year. Versions of this missile can carry a variety of warheads, ranging from a single giant 18–25-MT warhead to several 150-KT multiple, independently targetable re-entry vehicles (MIRV). More important, Soviet missile accuracy seemed to outpace earlier US estimates, as the Soviet Union tested missiles to accuracies as good as a 600-ft CEP (circular error probable).

Modernization of the Soviet submarine-launched missile force also moved ahead. At the year-end, there was a total of 20 *Delta*-I- and II-class submarines operational, each carrying 12–16 SS-N-8, single-warhead ballistic missiles with a range of about 8,000 kilometres. An additional 12 *Delta*-III-class boats were armed with 16 SS-N-18 missiles, each capable of carrying 3–7 MIRV. The building of a new large *Typhoon*-class missile submarine also continued. The new long-range Soviet bomber which Western analysts had been expecting did not appear in 1979, but the total number of Soviet strategic nuclear warheads deployed increased during the year by about 1,000, to 6,000.

In conventional forces, the pattern of previous years persisted, with newer generations of improved weaponry coming into service. Since 1965, the Soviet Union had increased the total number of her divisions, from 148 to over 170, and added about 1,400 aircraft and 31 regiments to her tactical air armies. Much of the numerical expansion had resulted from the military build-up in the Far East, but qualitative improvements had spread across the entire range of Soviet forces. For instance, in 1979 a new version of the Mi-24 *Hind* helicopter gunship was seen operating in East Germany, and there was increased evidence of development of a 'look down, shoot down' capability, effective against low-flying intruders, in new versions of the MiG-25 air defence fighter. The Soviet tactical air forces continued to be modernized with the introduction of late-model MiG-21s, MiG-23s, MiG-27s, Su-17s and Su-24s. By the end of the year about 80% of the frontal aviation fighter force consisted of these types, giving the Soviet Union for the first time the capability to attempt long-range air-superiority and interdiction missions.

There was no significant change in the overall number of conventional naval units during 1979, as total additions to the inventory broadly balanced deletions, but deployment patterns and capabilities continued to develop. By the year-end, as a reaction to the US naval build-up in the area, the Soviet contingent in the Indian Ocean had been increased to 26–30 ships, including mine-sweepers. Just as important, the ships under construction appeared to reflect a change in the mission priorities of the Soviet Navy, as the ocean-going warship force continued to expand. A third *Kiev*-class guided missile carrier was fitting out, as was a 27–30,000-ton nuclear-powered warship in Leningrad. First detected in 1978, the latter could be in service by 1981, and there was a sister ship under construction. Overall, about ten ocean-going surface warships a year continued to be produced.

The Soviet Union's ability to project power far from her borders continued to increase in 1979. New cruisers were entering the fleet, and roll-on/roll-off ships, like the 13,000-ton *Ivan Rogov*, assigned to the Pacific fleet in 1978, gave her the ability to deploy wheeled and tracked vehicles rapidly, even in less-developed areas. (She did in fact make extensive use of naval resupply in assisting Ethiopia during the conflict with Somalia.) The expanding Soviet ability to project power, already evident in the Indian Ocean, was emphasized by the use of newly-acquired access to air and naval facilities in Vietnam.

Economic Problems

The momentum of the Soviet defence effort stood in stark contrast to the growing troubles of the Soviet economy. In his speech to the Central Committee of the Party on 28 November President Brezhnev himself catalogued the weaknesses – a growing shortage of oil, poor returns on agricultural investment, chaos on the railways – and he did so in terms more direct and specific than ever before. The situation gave all the more cause for concern because of the uncertainties of Soviet economic interaction with the West, especially with the United States, in the wake of the Afghanistan invasion.

Short-term factors accounted for some of 1979's sorry results, but they were hardly the cause of the bleak longer-term picture. The severe winter reduced the 1979 grain harvest to 179 million tons (compared to 237 million tons in 1978) and had some effect on industrial production as well. Yet, as a result of the slow population growth of the last decade, the population of working age would increase by only 0.5% a year during the next decade. That, coupled with the effects of recent low rates of new investment and the continuing low productivity of the work force (55% of the American figure in 1977), boded ill for industrial growth in the 1980s. Indeed, overall economic growth, having peaked at 7.7% per year in the 1966–70 period, was down to around 3.9% in 1976–9, and rates of 2% or even less were expected to be seen during the early 1980s.

As the defence effort continued to grow at about 4–5% per year, faster than the economy, it threatened to consume an ever larger portion of GNP. That would mean more sacrifice for Soviet consumers but would probably be seen as no more than an unhappy fact of life by Soviet leaders. Indeed, in the light of the degree of separation between the defence and civilian sectors of the Soviet economy, one recent Western computer model suggested that freezing defence expenditure would add only 0.1% to an assumed basic GNP growth of 4%. Thus, whatever their political interests, Soviet leaders would have little economic reason to reduce defence spending, at least in the medium term.

Energy remained the key imponderable in the economy, and especially in the Soviet Union's foreign economic relations. Brezhnev announced that oil production in 1979 was 585 million tons, 8 million tons below the target figure. The CIA's now-famous 1977 study *Prospects for Soviet Oil Production* concluded that Soviet production would peak in 1980 and then decline, making the Soviet Union a net importer of oil by 1985. A 1979 update of world oil prospects (*The World Oil Market in the Years Ahead*), which included a section on the Soviet Union, hedged on imports but still predicted that Soviet production would peak in around 1980. Yet even a more conservative assessment would confront the Kremlin with hard choices. A diminished rate of increase in production – which virtually all analysts presuppose – would mean that the USSR must force her Eastern European partners to buy more of their oil on world markets (the USSR continued to supply some 80% of their needs, except in the case of Romania). That would mean more debt for the Eastern European countries, who had little prospect of finding the hard currency to pay for oil. Alternatively, the Soviet Union would find herself with less and less oil to sell to the West for hard currency – and oil exports produced about half her 1979 export earnings.

Grain was the other principal element of Soviet foreign trade. During the Brezhnev leadership the USSR had spent $16 billion on foreign grain – more than her entire current foreign indebtedness. Even before the United States cancelled 17 million tons of grain exports (largely destined for use as animal feed) in the wake of the Soviet invasion of Afghanistan, meat consumption in the Soviet Union was expected to fall below 1975 levels. In early 1980 there were indications that the Soviet Union might be able to make up for much of the reduction in American supplies, but meat would still be in even shorter supply.

Other implications of trends in East–West economics were still harder to identify. With a net hard-currency debt of about $15 billion, the Soviet Union remained a good credit risk, and the surge in the price of gold would give her more room for manoeuvre. However, she remained dependent in some measure on high-technology imports from the West, although no doubt she had scaled down her expectations. To ship oil and gas from new sites in Siberia the Soviet Union, by some estimates, needed to build the equivalent of the Alaska pipeline every two months; it was for this reason that she had had to buy some $10 billion worth of pipe and related machinery from the West. Only in oil-drilling technology did the Soviet dependence on Western technology impose a significant constraint on Soviet production. But even there the constraint might have stemmed as much from an unwillingness to involve Western technicians deeply in a sensitive area as from specific lacks of technology.

Succession

As a subject of speculation, the question of who would take up the leadership of the Soviet Union after Brezhnev had come to rival that of who will lead Yugoslavia after Tito. About the most that could be said at the end of 1979 was that the Soviet leadership became older and less flexible. President Brezhnev was 73 and Premier Kosygin 76, and both of them were ill (Kosygin, who was out of public view from October 1979 to February 1980, perhaps the more seriously so). There was no indication that younger leaders had any more success in reaching senior party or government posts than in years past. In part, that reflected the fact that the immediate post-Brezhnev generation – men in their fifties during the last decade – was both small and poorly educated, as a result of World War II and its aftermath. More important, however, it demonstrated the continuing grip of the Brezhnev generation, which had been the beneficiary of Stalin's purge and had been at or near the top of the leadership for forty years. Brezhnev, for example, was 45 when Stalin proposed him as candidate member of the Politburo in 1952; by contrast, recent promotions again went to the Brezhnev generation – Tikhonov (74) became Deputy Premier, and Brezhnev's confidant Chernenko (68) became a Party Secretary.

Nothing in 1979 suggested much change in the likely pattern of succession. If Brezhnev (who already limited his involvement in daily affairs) were to die, the senior members of the Politburo would function as a kind of board of directors. The nominal successor – perhaps Andrei Kirilenko, who at 74 was older than Brezhnev but in fair health, or Chernenko – would be no more than first among equals and would be unable to dominate a group that included Suslov, Ustinov, Andropov and Gromyko. And if developments during 1979 gave few pointers about immediate prospects for the leadership, they shed equally little light on the likely course of a new leadership once in place. Any new leaders would continue to face pressure for economic reform but would be unlikely to risk yielding to it, for the same ideological reasons as the Brezhnev regime. They would be tempted to look to the military budget for savings, but would yet want to sustain Soviet power, and might in any case find that there was little short-run domestic advantage in defence cuts.

Would new – or transitional – leaders be tempted to foreign adventures, perhaps as distractions from domestic failings? A post-Brezhnev leadership, once installed, would have experience neither of Western strength during World War II nor of pre-war Russian weakness. It might feel that neither the detente nor the defence policies of the Brezhnev era had given the Soviet Union her rightful place in the world. And yet its choices would be circumscribed by the new military efforts of those who saw the Soviet Union as a continuing threat, by the weakness of the economy and by the increasingly difficult task of maintaining control over the Soviet camp, not least in Eastern Europe.

SOUTH-WEST ASIA

The revolution in Iran, which led to the overthrow of the Shah in February 1979 and the emergence of a new regime under the religious leader, Ayatollah Khomeini, had profound consequences both in the Gulf region and beyond. At best, the new leaders of Iran would be preoccupied with recurrent internal conflicts. At worst, however, they might be intent on actively exporting their revolution to their neighbours, for whom Khomeini's fundamentalist Islamic challenge raised questions about the legitimacy of their regimes. For the Soviet Union, though, the fall of the Shah's regime brought the opportunities for exerting influence provided by the proximity of power in the absence of strong regional countervailing forces. For the United States it meant that she could no longer rely on the local states to ensure stability on their own and would now need to become more directly involved with maintaining security in the region. This could lead not only to a further weakening of the domestic authority of local regimes but also to increased risks of confrontation between the major powers, the Soviet Union and the US.

In a region which President Carter's January 1980 State of the Union message described as 'vital to US interests', the background of political developments was thus ominous. Internal strains merged with Islamic revivalism, oil with greatpower politics. Anti-Western sentiments did not, however, necessarily favour the Soviet Union, whose invasion of Afghanistan further antagonized Muslim governments in the region. Their response was impressive: in January 1980, at an Islamic summit in Islamabad, 36 governments condemned the Soviet invasion. But Western hopes that this demonstration of Soviet expansionism would lead to support for Western interests were premature at the least, if not illusory. In spite of Afghanistan, governments in the region emphasized their distance from both super-powers. The Arab world, wary of the US relationship with Israel, was reluctant to allow the Soviet invasion of Afghanistan to overshadow the Palestinian question and the Arab-Israeli conflict, a dispute which they feared had now become a threat to their own internal stability as well as to the stability of the region as a whole.

IRAN AFTER THE REVOLUTION

Politics in Iran in 1979 were conditioned by the continuing uncertainties accompanying the collapse of a regime which had been in power for 37 years. The new regime under Khomeini inherited neither a political consensus nor a monopoly of armed force within the country. There had been consensus over the removal of the Shah, but this did not extend to the policies to be followed after his departure, and the removal of the unifying symbol of the monarchy revealed a fissiparous trend towards the reassertion of local nationalisms and particularist loyalties among Iran's many minorities. This and the collapse of the national army led to the emergence of new competing authorities, especially in the more remote parts of the country, for the writ of the new government, insofar as it ran at all, ran only in a few major cities such as Tehran, Isfahan and Abadan.

Even at the seat of government there was a continuing power struggle. A major division existed between those who sought to limit the revolution and those who sought to extend it. The former wished to establish order, consolidate the gains the revolution had brought, build a new army and buckle down to the challenges of economic growth and social equity. The latter sought to continue the revolution, which they saw only as the first of several stages which would end in a totally transformed and classless society. Straddling the two was Khomeini, now 78, who personified the authority of the revolution, but whose own preferences and priorities were at the least ambivalent and at the most unclear. The charismatic Ayatollah was in fact as much the echo as the voice of the crowds, as much their captive as their leader. And while he sought, through an Islamic constitution, to prepare new structures of government to perpetuate his visions of a future Iran, it was by no means certain that the revolution would survive his departure from the scene.

After a year of confusion and uncertainty, in which the hard-line Moslem clergy who seized power after the collapse of the Bakhtiar Government in February attempted to consolidate their position, some predictions could be made with greater certainty than before. For all its inherent instabilities, the fundamentalist Shi'ite regime under Ayatollah Khomeini was not likely to be quickly overthrown by some combination of internal and external forces. Nevertheless, the challenge posed by the mainly Sunni ethnic minorities – notably the Kurds – proved more durable than many expected, and overcoming the minorities' resistance to participation in the kind of Islamic republic that might emerge would not be easy. The sudden and total collapse of the Imperial armed forces in mid-February had been startling, and they were left at about half strength, with their morale broken, lacking an officer corps, plagued by desertions and hampered by both political restraints and material shortages.

Much of the year was spent by the pro-Khomeini clergy in trying to gather back into their own hands again the power that had drained away earlier in the year: to the local security committees (or 'Komitehs'); to the armed guerrillas; to the strike committees which had agitated against the Shah in every major public and private institution; to powerful provincial figures, whether tribal leaders, clergymen or old-style landlords; and to those who spoke up for the demands of the ethnic and Sunni minorities, the Kurds, the Baluchs, the Arabs and the Turkomans. The administrative arrangements set up in the aftermath of the revolution were inevitably *ad hoc*, and the new administrators were uncertain of their power and how to use it. Mehdi Bazargan, leader of the small Iran Liberation Movement and a member of the secret Revolutionary Council which effectively exercised power throughout 1979, was appointed Prime Minister in February for the transitional period. However, his authority, derived directly and solely from his mandate from Khomeini, was crippled both by the apolitical notions of the Ayatollah and by the way in which other groups, also claiming to act in the leader's name, followed their own impulses. His administration had to struggle continuously to assert its authority over other revolutionary and Islamic bodies – notably the new courts which ordered the execution of over 700 people, including former Prime Minister Howeida and many prominent members of the former regime. Initially, though, Mr Bazargan's task was greatly aided by the fact that the left-wing and middle-class nationalist elements of the grand anti-Shah coalition decided either to co-operate with the new authorities, or at least not actively to oppose them. But soon conflict on the streets of Tehran erupted between opponents of the drift towards clerical authoritarianism and hard-line Khomeini zealots. In August, the clergy-dominated Revolutionary Council (increasingly apparent as the real rulers in Iran) ordered a crackdown, driving the Marxist left and their associates, the radical Moslem *Mujaheddin-e-Khalq*,(or'Holy Worriors for the People'), underground.

Constitutional Changes

Mr Bazargan had been charged with carrying through lengthy and time-consuming constitutional changes. These were a referendum on the abolition of the monarchy (the requirement on the voting slip for concomitant approval of an as yet undefined Islamic republic was the first cause of concern to liberals and uncommitted Iranians); the drafting of a new constitution; creation of a Constituent Assembly and a referendum on the outcome of its deliberations; the election of a President as head of state; and, finally, election of a national legislative assembly.

The first referendum was held at the end of March, recording a somewhat unreal majority of over 99% in favour of the change. Deciding the shape of Iran's new republican constitution, however, was a crucial and prolonged battle between supporters of a plural society and Khomeini's lieutenants. The victory of the fundamentalists proved to be a watershed; thereafter any challenges to Khomeini's authority, from whatever direction, could be stigmatized as opposition to the future of the revolution.

A draft constitution was drawn up in secret by Khomeini supporters, after going through several versions. It emerged for public discussion, before going to the Constituent Assembly, as a liberal charter drawing on many features of the American and French systems and specifically guarding against abuses remembered from the Shah's day. However, Khomeini's insistence that it must be a thoroughgoing 'Islamic' constitution, freed of any Western taint, ensured that it would not emerge from the Assembly in this form. To make sure of compliance with his wishes, the Assembly – an 80-member body ostensibly elected by a national poll – was filled with known Khomeini supporters among the clergy. A prominent part in the election was played by the newly formed Islamic Republican Party (headed by Ayatollah Beheshti, a senior member of the Revolutionary Council), which was to become both the largest and the best organized in the country, enjoying widespread provincial support.

During the two months of debates the draft constitution was considerably amended. The most significant change was the introduction of the new concept of a *Velayat-e-Faghih* (roughly, 'Trustee of the Faith') as the country's supreme leader. Although Khomeini was not named to the post the description of the attributes its incumbent would need made it clear there could be only one candidate. The sweeping powers granted to him included the approval and dismissal of the President and the supreme command of the armed forces.

Internal Dissent

The controversial nature of the constitution confirmed the Sunni minorities and the numerous followers of the rival Ayatollah Shariat-Madari – mainly the Turkish-speaking Azerbaijanis – in their opposition to the central authorities in Tehran and Qom. The most serious opposition to the new institution came from Shariat-Madari, a moderate and pragmatic religious leader, considered by many to be senior to Khomeini in terms of learning, who was supported by the Moslem People's Republican Party. His supporters in Azerbaijan, in the north-west, were upset at the constitution's failure to even take into account Iran's multi-racial make-up, and a series of confrontations between the two religious leaders and their followers ensued, culminating in serious rioting in Tabriz, the capital of the Azerbaijan province, in December. But the outcome was never in doubt, partly because Shariat-Madari did not seek a total confrontation. Azerbaijan's proximity to the Soviet Union, historical memories of its brief period of Soviet-backed 'independence' in 1946, and its large population (9–11 million) did, however, combine to make any threat of autonomy or secession from this quarter the most serious that could be imagined for the future of the Iranian state.

The same considerations did not apply in the Kurdish region further south, where an autonomous state in all but name had been in existence since the breakdown of government authority in 1978. Its nebulous frontiers ebbed and flowed according to the relative strengths of the Kurdish irregulars, on the one hand, and the central government's Revolutionary Guards and regular forces, on the other, as well as according to the state of negotiations between the two sides. In this area, centred on the city of Mahabad, Khomeini's writ did not run (unlike anywhere else in the country, alcohol was readily available), and the socialist-inclined Kurdish Democratic Party (KDP) and the Sunni religious leader Sheikh Ezzedin Husseini commanded most allegiance. Throughout the summer and autumn Iran's 3½–4½ million Kurds engaged in a series of bloody confrontations with the government. In September they were swept out of their main urban strongholds, but within six weeks were back in control. The KDP was officially banned, and its leader, Dr Abdirrahman Qassemlou, along with Sheikh Husseini, were condemned by Khomeini in terms that allowed little room for compromise, and negotiations to solve the crisis proved inconclusive throughout the year. The central authorities realized that they could not hope to crush the Kurds militarily, given the poor state of the armed forces. This in turn encouraged the Kurds to stick to their position: full-scale autonomy within a newly designated Kurdish region along the western border with Iraq and Turkey.

The worry, particularly in Turkey, of a 'Greater Kurdistan' embracing the 14 million Kurds who inhabit contiguous areas in Iran, Iraq, Turkey and the Soviet Union remained unrealistic, since the divisions between the different groups once again seemed to be stronger than the bonds. However, as relations between Iran and Iraq reached their lowest level since the 1975 Algiers agreement had ended a decade of regional rivalry and border clashes, Iraq may have provided discreet aid to the opponents of the Khomeini regime, especially in Arab-populated Khuzestan.

At the end of the year, therefore, Iran's internal cohesion remained uncertain. The economy was severely affected, with over 30% unemployment in a total work-force of some 10 million, and over 50% of the population under the age of 20. Prime Minister Bazargan resigned in November, and under the new constitutional arrangements Abolhassan Bani Sadr, former Finance Minister and a close aide to the Ayatollah, was elected President in early 1980. But the new form of government did not guarantee accepted and effective authority. Only the departure of Khomeini would ultimately reveal the strength of both the institutions created by him and the forces which were opposed to the clerical authority of his rule.

Relations with the United States

The attitude of Iran's new government towards the super-powers was bound to be influenced by perceptions of their recent roles in the country. In this comparison, the United States inevitably suffered; as the supporter of the Shah, his armourer and the beneficiary of Iran's previous policies, now considered traitorous, she stood condemned. This bitter historical legacy alone made it manifestly impossible for Iran's new leadership to maintain close ties with her, but Iran's new religious leaders also held her responsible for the corrupting influence of the American style of culture which had been adopted, if not encouraged, by the Shah. Ayatollah Khomeini's oft-repeated rejection of the influence of both East and West thus became in practice a singular obsession with that of the West. The confrontation with the United States over Iranian demands that the Shah should be returned to stand trial and the resultant seizure of hostages at the US Embassy on 4 November therefore received his full backing, and at the end of 1979 and the beginning of the new year this crisis overshadowed all other issues.

Given the burden of the past, the US early in the year had been careful not to alienate the new regime further. She offered negotiations on arms, put the best construction possible on domestic developments, avoided comments or criticisms and waited for time to heal the past legacy. More concretely she offered military spare parts and lubricating oil in the summer when Iran needed them, hoping Iran's needs would translate into business-like ties. For its part, the Iranian regime under Prime Minister Bazargan and Foreign Minister Yazdi sought a 'correct' relationship, but Iranian domestic politics prevented this.

On 4 November – two weeks after Mr Bazargan and Mr Yazdi had met President Carter's National Security Adviser, Zbigniew Brzezinski, in Algiers, and after the Shah had entered the US for medical reasons – a group of student radicals took over the American Embassy in Tehran and seized 63 hostages (13 of whom were later released). This played into the hands of those who sought to prevent a normalization with the US and to continue the 'radicalization' of the revolution. The United States was outraged that the Iranian government condoned this act of terrorism, but was uncertain how to respond. A military riposte would not only not save the hostages, it would strengthen elements in Iran opposed to reconciliation with the US, increase Tehran's reliance on the Soviet Union, jeopardize Western nationals in Iran, inflame Islamic opinion, and force regional states to oppose the United States. At the same time, the lack of a visible American reaction courted other dangers, since a muted response of restraint, calm and patience would leave the United States open to accusations of timidity or impotence. In a sensitive and vulnerable region her credibility as a great power and ally was put to such a test that virtually any response involved long-term costs for US interests in the region.

Rather than force an immediate, dramatic and dangerous show-down, the American Administration chose to increase pressure on Iran by sending two carrier forces to the Arabian Sea in December, and by using such economic levers as were at its disposal, including the freezing of Iranian assets in US banks. While there were indications from Tehran that the diplomatic hostages might be released in connection with an investigation into the Shah's regime by some international commission, American efforts were hampered by the fact that there was no functioning government in Iran to which either pressure or incentives could be applied. Hopes that the Soviet invasion of neighbouring Afghanistan would lead such Iranian authorities as there were to realize their ultimate need for American support, and thus to seek a rapid resolution to the hostage crisis, were not rewarded. As the year ended, the humiliation of the United States, which had been borne with impressive restraint by the Carter Administration, seemed to be far from over.

Relations with the Soviet Union

Although the Soviet Union worked pragmatically with the Shah, she did not suffer from identification with the old regime as did the United States. Although she made no direct criticisms of the Shah until his departure from Iran on 15 January 1979, throughout the remainder of the year, she nonetheless posed as the 'protector of the revolution', and often referred to President Brezhnev's November 1978 warning that 'any interference' in Iran would affect Soviet security interests, as having deterred US military intervention.

Initially the Khomeini regime treated the Soviet Union with marked aversion. It announced its decision to denounce the 1921 treaty with the USSR – a symmetrical move to balance the renunciation of formal ties with the West expressed in CENTO membership and in the 1959 Executive Agreement with the US. It also cancelled plans to build a second gas pipeline to the USSR as part of a gas exchange agreement with the USSR and Western Europe. In addition, at a time of impending energy shortage in the eastern bloc, it started negotiations to increase the price of gas already being piped to the USSR under a 1966 agreement and, by reducing oil production, also decreased the amount of gas that was made available under that agreement.

In other respects, too, Iran's policies were not in line with Soviet interests. The emphasis on Shi'a militance that was weakening the Sunni regime in neighbouring Iraq was of no benefit to Soviet interests, and in the long run Islamic rhetoric could have a negative effect on the Soviet Union as well as on the West. This rhetoric was manifest in the statements of various Iranian clerics throughout the first part of 1979, denouncing the Soviet Union's assistance to the Afghan government against the Muslim rebels. But in practice the new regime's denunciations of the Soviet Union lacked conviction. The focus of internal hostility was the West, and particularly the United States. And, as domestic problems piled up, more moderate personalities were isolated and freedom came to be stifled, it became clear that opposition to the West could serve to unify the fraying coalition in support of the revolution.

The last half of 1979 demonstrated clearly that the focus of Iran's militancy had shifted against the West, largely as a result of the ebb and flow of the power struggle itself. Soviet policy could be gauged quite clearly from the actions of the *Tudeh* (Communist) party. Initially forced underground with other leftist groups in August, the *Tudeh* was the only non-Islamic party tolerated after October, because it had aligned itself fully and unconditionally behind Ayatollah Khomeini. This appeared to reflect a tactical decision by the USSR not to repeat the error made in the 1950s when the *Tudeh* had failed to support Mohammad Mossadeqh. The calculation was straightforward: if Khomeini were to die soon, the *Tudeh* would be the least prepared of all the groupings to engage in the power struggle that would ensue; but if he lived for several years, it could use the time to organize without interference and harrassment. The *Tudeh* also calculated that in the current fluid situation it could influence the course of events better from within Khomeini's camp than from without.

As a result of *Tudeh* support for Khomeini and of the emphasis on anti-Americanism, criticisms of the Soviet Union were conspicuously absent in the latter part of 1979. Only in January 1980, when the USSR, through her ambassador in Mexico, appeared to be floating the idea of assisting in the defence of Iran against the US – a notion with obvious connotations for Iran's independence – was there a strong reaction by Khomeini, who repudiated any need for support. The Soviet invasion of Afghanistan was criticised first by the Government on 29 December, then by Presidential candidates Finance Minister Bani Sadr and Foreign Minister Gotbzadeh in January, and only in February by Khomeini himself. This somewhat reluctant denunciation, fully six weeks after the invasion itself, revealed an imbalance that had grown during 1979 and still persisted at the beginning of 1980.

What degree of balance in relations with the super-powers was ultimately to be embodied in Iran's future foreign policy would be determined by the struggle for power within Iran. Practical considerations would suggest that the armed forces would need to be reconstituted, and – being US-equipped – they would need American supplies. Any renewed interest in Iran's historic foreign-policy posture of seeking a diplomatic counterweight to Soviet proximity would also suggest the re-establishment of ties with the West. And events in Afghanistan were likely to increase these incentives. Yet, as long as the Revolution was insecure, unconsolidated and dependent on support from the Left, some in Iran were likely to see a greater threat from the United States than from Soviet imperialism, and others would seek to exploit this to move Iran closer to the Soviet Union.

Effects on the Region

Reverberations from the Iranian revolution echoed throughout the region in the course of the year. The Gulf states, and particularly Saudi Arabia, felt a deep sense of insecurity and shock at American inability to maintain the Shah in power, at the West's apparent willingness to come to terms with Khomeini, whose revolution it deeply suspected, and finally at the American impotence in the hostage crisis. If Iran under Khomeini was 'Islamic' it was an Islam whose appeal to populist militance and concentrated anti-Western emphasis threatened their security. This made it increasingly costly for them to take any pro-Western positions, whether in support of the Camp David agreement, in favour of moderate pricing policies in OPEC, or in providing access to friendly powers to assist in guaranteeing their security. Saudi Arabia's policy, in particular, had to take this into account, even though there were no alternatives to relying on the US for her ultimate security. The aftermath of Iran's revolution had made the appearance of alignment with the West even more dangerous, while at the same time significantly increasing its importance.

A harbinger of this difficulty came in March, when an incursion by South Yemen (PDRY) into North Yemen (YAR) revealed Saudi Arabia's military impotence even when her own borders were threatened. She welcomed the US response in rushing $400m in military goods and 75 advisers to the YAR (an arrangement rushed through without Congressional review), but the attendant publicity and the despatch to Saudi Arabia of a squadron of F-15s and a carrier, together with an offer of AWACS aircraft, embarrassed her by its very visibility. Since the aid was to be chanelled through Saudi Arabia, she in fact used her position to delay the delivery of weapons to the YAR, hoping thereby to increase her own influence over events between the two Yemens.

Iran's new foreign policy contributed to the regional instability. Reflecting the ambivalence at the top, Iranian leaders throughout the year alternately denied any intention of exporting their revolution and then indulged in revolutionary rhetoric containing elements of Pan-Shi'ism, Pan-Islam and revolutionary socialism. This impulse – to export the revolution, ignore the existence of national frontiers and call on oppressed peoples to rise up against non-representative elites supported by foreign bayonets – was particularly troubling to the region's many monarchic regimes, with their overlapping minorities susceptible to manipulation by their neighbours. Shi'a-inspired disturbances that took place in Iraq, Kuwait and Bahrain during September and October were put down firmly, but their recurrence, notably in Saudi Arabia's eastern (Hasa) province in November and December, provided a disturbing omen for the governments in these countries.

There was no evidence that the seizure of the Grand Mosque in Mecca in November 1979 was Shi'a-inspired. The attack was led by a religious zealot who had proclaimed himself the *Mahdi* (the awaited Messiah) and most of his 250 followers were Saudi Bedouins of the Otaiba tribe. Although there were a few students from other Arab states among the gunmen, the composition of the group suggests that support for the siege was limited and tribally based. The Saudi forces, mindful of the effect that heavy arms would have on the Mosque, took two weeks to defeat the rebels, killing 75 and capturing 170, who were later sentenced to death. During and after the seizure of the Mosque there were no reports of unrest in the major cities of Saudi Arabia. But the attack on the Mosque and the disturbances in Hasa led the ruling group in Saudi Arabia to institute a number of reforms which were directed at removing the grievances these actions symbolized, and it seemed likely that the unrest would be gradually reduced.

Iraq and Bahrain, however, with their much larger Shi'ite populations, seemed to be more vulnerable to efforts by the Iranian clergy to export their revolution in the interests of the Shi'ite faith. Nevertheless, despite the rhetoric it seemed doubtful in the light of her many domestic problems that Iran would have energy to spare to devote to a revolutionary foreign policy. But, as 1979 showed, domestic difficulties slid over into foreign problems. The Kurds were not solely an Iranian concern, the fate of the Turkic population in Iran interested Turkey, that of the Shi'a in Iraq concerned Iran, and the condition of the Arabs in Khuzestan was followed closely by the Arab world. The prospect of a weak, fragmenting Iran was therefore almost as frightening to her neighbours as the prospect of a strong, revolutionary Iran.

Iraq's continued shift back towards the mainstream of Arab politics in the Peninsula, particularly the growing understanding with Saudi Arabia, was one of the most notable developments of the year. It formed an important part of the closing of the ranks which characterized the Arab response to the Iranian revolution. The one exception to this trend was Oman, whose regional isolation was emphasized by her alignment with Egypt and, in Iranian eyes, her close connections with the Shah's regime. Her abortive effort to encourage joint defence arrangements among her Arab neighbours, served only to deepen her isolation. In view of her strategic position (the Mussandam Peninsula dominates the entrance to the Gulf), Oman argued that her naval and air forces should be built up with Western equipment, financed by other Gulf states, so as to be better able to counter any threat to the oil tanker traffic through the vital Straits of Hormuz. The scheme was rejected by Iraq as a cover for a Western presence, and in some Western quarters there was uncertainty about Oman's own stability in the light of the fast pace of her development and the resulting internal strains.

To the Arab states of the Gulf littoral, there were now threats from several directions to the security of what had been a region of calm and reasonable stability only eighteen months earlier. Powerful US naval forces were gathering in the Gulf of Oman in response to the crisis over the American hostages in Iran. At the same time the Soviet invasion of Afghanistan brought some 90,000 Soviet troops, with armour and air support, closer to the Gulf's oil fields and to within 500 miles of the narrow Straits of Hormuz. And all the indications were that the Soviet Union would stay in Afghanistan for some years to come to consolidate her position.

CRISIS OVER AFGHANISTAN

For hundreds of years Afghanistan – sharing borders with Russia and China, Iran and Pakistan – had been looked upon, and fought over, as a buffer state between Russia and the Persian Gulf. The importance of Persian Gulf oil, the revolutionary ferment in Iran and the resurgence of militant Muslim sentiment throughout the region, had given developments in Afghanistan an increasing significance and heightened the importance of control over this barren, landlocked country. This went far to explain the Soviet Union's willingness to break her self-imposed restriction on the use of her own forces outside the boundaries of Eastern Europe and invade the country on 27 December 1979.

Her swift and effective entry into Afghanistan must have been planned at least four months in advance. Like all moves fraught with as many risks and political implications as this, its motivation would have been complex, though a number of reasons for it can be suggested. The Soviet leaders, seeing the growing domestic opposition to an Afghan regime to which they were giving very heavy economic and military support, would have been deeply concerned over the instability they saw developing close to Soviet borders in 1979. They would also have wanted to prevent the unrest emanating from Iran from spreading throughout the region. Further, they undoubtedly believed that Afghanistan was now within the Soviet area of influence, and thought that this was tolerated, if not accepted by the West. They would thus have been unwilling to see the threatened imminent collapse of the Amin regime in Kabul lead to forces unfriendly to the USSR emerging in control of the country.

The Background

The April 1978 revolution in Afghanistan, which brought a distinctly leftist government to power, had taken almost everyone by surprise. Though under attack from right and left, the previous Republican government of Muhammad Daud, which had been in power since the overthrow of the monarchy in 1973, seemed in full control of the situation and on good terms with its Soviet neighbour. In the act of crushing left-wing opposition it was itself overthrown in a coup led by army and air force officers who released the imprisoned leftist leaders to form a government. The Soviet Union welcomed the new government, but there was little evidence that she had any hand in the coup which appeared to have been the work of a small group of discontented and frightened officers, mostly Soviet-trained. Most of the army held aloof until the result of the heavy fighting was known and Daud was dead.

The new government was dominated by civilians of the People's Democratic Party of Afghanistan (PDPA), formed by the amalgamation of two other parties in 1965, and its Secretary-General, Nur Muhammad Taraki, became Chairman of the Revolutionary Council and Prime Minister. The PDPA's basic membership was recruited mainly from the small professional class educated in a western style, and its greatest strength was in Kabul, where it found support from high school and university students. Outside Kabul it had very little following and had performed badly in elections before 1973. Judging from its publications, the party's programme was generally leftist, leaning heavily on Marxist concepts and analysing the Afghan situation along traditional Marxist lines which bore little relationship to reality. In particular the PDPA completely underestimated the nature of the hold of traditional leaders on popular loyalties. It appears to have become a prisoner of its own ideology, founding its policies upon a simple stereotype of a feudal society, rather than upon the complex realities of the Afghan social, economic and political structure, and thus condemning itself to an indefinite dependence upon force in order to retain power.

From its beginnings the PDPA had been consumed by internal struggles. Its two major groupings were the *Khalq* (Masses) and *Parcham* (Flag) factions – so-called after the publications they espoused during the 1930s – which corresponded to the parties that had amalgamated to form the PDPA in 1965. These two had split in 1969, but they reunited in 1977 and both entered the new government in April 1978. In July 1978, however, Hafizullah Amin replaced Taraki as party Secretary-General, some of the leading members of the Parcham faction were dismissed and some – including its leader, Deputy Prime Minister Babrak Karmal – sent to insignificant diplomatic posts abroad. (Mr Karmal became Afghan Ambassador to Prague; he soon left this post but still remained in exile in Eastern Europe until December 1979.) In August 1978 one of the April coup leaders, Colonel Abd al-Qadir, was arrested, and a succession of further purges in the party and the armed forces followed. At the end of March 1979 a major reorganization took place. More Parchamis were imprisoned, the Foreign Minister, Hafizullah Amin, became Prime Minister, and the Cabinet was reformed. Taraki, however, created a new lever of power, the Supreme Homelands Defence Council, with himself as President.

The March 1979 reorganization was partly a response to the deteriorating internal security situation, but it was also the result of a conflict which had been developing between Taraki and Amin. At the end of July, Prime Minister Amin apparently strengthened his position. He took over the Ministry of Defence from Col. Muhammad Aslam Watanyar, a 1978 coup leader (who became Minister of Interior) and promoted his most loyal follower, Dr Shah Wali, to Foreign Minister. In September 1979 the conflict between Taraki and Amin exploded: Amin dismissed Watanyar and two of his supporters from the Cabinet, and in turn Taraki, probably with Soviet encouragement, tried to arrest or kill Amin. In the ensuing struggle Amin emerged victorious. It was announced that Taraki had resigned because of ill-health (and, some weeks later, that he had died of 'an incurable illness') and Amin took over as Chairman of the Revolutionary Council and the Supreme Defence Council. Watanyar and his supporters apparently sought refuge in the Soviet Embassy. Amin further consolidated his position by purging his rivals, and in November he made a move to gain greater support by calling a constitutional conference.

In intellect, ability and determination the extrovert Amin was undoubtedly a more formidable figure than the rather naive Taraki. But his uncompromising pursuit of the party's unpopular policies made his regime dependent on ruthless coercion and awakened opposition more widespread than that which had already developed against the Taraki regime.

Land Reform

During 1978–9 the central feature of the PDPA programme, and the focus of much resentment in the country, was land reform. This comprised three related measures: the progressive abolition of peasant mortgage debt; the reduction or elimination of marriage dowries (a major cause of rural indebtedness); and a land distribution plan.

The government claimed that the abolition of mortgage debt freed 11 million peasants (i.e. the whole cultivating population of Afghanistan) from debt to big landowners. But it also left cultivators unable to get credit from their traditional sources in order to buy seeds, or pay for equipment. The abolition of dowries, which was in any case difficult to enforce, fared little better. It was regarded as a gross infringement of social custom as well as the loss of a capital asset by families with daughters.

The most important measure was the redistribution of land. The government produced statistics to demonstrate considerable inequalities in landholding – though other calculations and local studies suggested that large landowning was a feature of some provinces only, and notably not of eastern Afghanistan. By Decree 8 of November 1978 land was divided, according to its quality and water supply, into seven categories, ranging from the best orchards and vineyards to third-class dry land. All land in excess of 15 acres per family of best land, or 150 acres of the worst, was confiscated and given to sharecroppers, landless labourers and nomads (who were to be settled).

The redistribution began on 1 January 1979, and after six months the government announced that it had been a complete success, transferring land from large landowners to deserving and oppressed peasants. How much of the original programme was actually carried out, however, remained uncertain. Initially it had been stated that there were 1.9 million families of villagers in Afghanistan, one third of them landless, and that the programme aimed at making 3.4 million acres available for redistribution to 680,000 peasant families. At completion it was claimed that 1.5 million acres had been distributed to 285,000 families, although other sources gave lower figures. Even these figures were subject to considerable doubt. When the minister responsible for the programme, Saleh Muhammad Ziari, was transferred to another ministry in July, it was reasonable to conclude that the land distribution programme was at least a partial failure and had been brought to a premature end. In the absence of adequate data or trained administrators, and amid the disturbances which prevailed throughout large parts of Afghanistan, it was difficult to believe that so large and complicated a measure could have been carried out successfully, particularly within so short a period of time.

The objects of land reform were stated to be the destruction of feudalism, the formation of an alliance of workers and peasants, and the improvement of agricultural production. Despite government claims, the last objective was apparently unfulfilled; the upheaval, the uncertainty of ownership and the lack of credit combined with a severe drought to cause a general fall in production, leaving Afghanistan heavily dependent upon grain imports to feed herself. The first two objectives were political and ideological. Conscious of its own very narrow basis of support in an almost non-existent working class, the PDPA hoped to win the political allegiance of the peasants and to destroy the economic basis for the political power of the country's traditional leaders: landowners, tribal and religious leaders. Ideologically, it seems to have felt a compulsion to demonstrate its left-wing character by espousing policies with which left-wing parties identified elsewhere. These objectives, however, did not seem to have been attained, for the peasants were not won over.

Armed Opposition
Soon after the April 1978 coup there were reports of spasmodic risings in Afghanistan. From the beginning of 1979 such reports became more detailed, and in the course of the year opposition to the PDPA Government attained considerable dimensions. There were four main centres of organized opposition: in the eastern provinces of Paktia, Ningrahar and Nuristan; in Badakhshan in the north-east; in central Afghanistan in the Hazarajat; and in the west near the Iranian border. There were also outbreaks of armed resistance to the government in several other provinces and some army mutinies and desertions.

The size and character of the opposition was hard to gauge. In the strong tradition of independent and self-contained local communities in Afghanistan, it often manifested itself as local opposition under local leaders to government encroachment, rather than as a co-ordinated or national movement. In Badakhashan and in the Hazarajat it was primarily of an ethnic character, with the *Setem-i Milli* in Badakhshan apparently representing a Persian-speaking Tadjik opposition, and the Alliance of Islamic Warriors of Afghanistan in the Hazarajat seemingly made up of Persian-speaking Shi'ite Hazaras; in western Afghanistan, too, the Islamic Movement of Afghanistan included Persian-speaking Shi'ites. Although the PDPA professed a policy of raising the status of minorities in Afghanistan and of developing education and publication in their own languages, it remained a predominantly Pushtun party (particularly since the expulsion of the Parchamis). However, the principal opposition to the PDPA came from the predominantly Sunni Pushtuns many of whom had sought refuge in Pakistan. Some, including many from the Durrani tribal confederation, crossed into Baluchistan and neighbouring districts, while a larger number of the Durrani found shelter in the tribal areas of northern Pakistan, where Peshawar became their main centre. The Durrani Pushtuns – who included the former royal family and many of the present rebel clans – were historical rivals of the Ghilzay Pushtuns who dominated the PDPA, and their opposition was a reflection of the hostility between the two.

The tribal, ethnic, regional nature of this opposition was fortified by the use by the leaders of the various groups of religious sentiment to underpin the anti-government campaign. The PDPA regime was denounced as atheistic and upon her charity. By December 1979 the number of registered Afghan refugees in Pakistan had risen to 400,000, and there were believed to be many more unregistered ones. In fact, neither Afghanistan nor Pakistan could fully control the tribesmen on their borders. The Kabul government also complained of Iranian encouragement to its opponents and blamed Iranian intruders for the Herat disturbances of March 1979.

Unable to admit that the opposition was the consequence of its own policies the PDPA government was compelled to blame its trouble on Pakistan, Iran and on international powers acting through them, including China, the United States, West Germany and Egypt. Its relations with the United States steadily deteriorated. When the PDPA first came to power the US suspended judgement on the left-wing regime, but after US Ambassador Dubs was killed in a kidnap attempt in Kabul in February 1979 she cut aid to Afghanistan, withdrew some embassy staff and protested about increasing Soviet influence in Afghanistan.

Inevitably the PDPA Government leaned heavily for help on the USSR, which had sought and obtained good relations with all Afghan governments since 1921. Since the mid-1950s the USSR had been Afghanistan's major supplier of economic aid and military equipment and training, at an estimated cost of $2.5 billion up to 1973 and over $1 billion in 1973-8. After April 1978 she established even closer relations with the PDPA regime. A number of agreements were signed, including a Treaty of Friendship and Good Neighbourliness in December 1978. The number of Soviet civil and military advisers increased from about 3,000 before the revolution to about 4,500 (other estimates ranged between 1,500 and 30,000). Large sums were made available for economic development, new military equipment was supplied (including T-62 tanks, MiG-21 fighters and Mi-24 helicopter gunships), and it was rumoured that Soviet pilots were flying combat missions and military advisers were employed at company level.

From the spring of 1979 the Soviet Union began to demand a greater say in the policies of the Afghan government. Evidently alarmed at the extent of the hostility to the regime and the prospect of being drawn into a protracted civil war, and concerned about the possible international complications of Afghan disputes with Pakistan and Iran, she began to argue for less radical policies, conciliation of the opposition, and the formation of a broader-based government. The abandonment of land reform and the Afghan Revolutionary Council's July 1979 declaration in favour of a more broadly based government may have been connected with this initiative. There was, however, reason to believe that these initiatives were opposed by Amin, and that the USSR was behind Taraki's abortive attempt to oust him in September. Amin's victory was therefore doubly unwelcome to the Soviet Union. Faced with an apparent choice between withdrawing from Afghanistan, with an inevitable loss of prestige, and supporting a man whose policies she believed to be unworkable, the USSR maintained her support but at the same time prepared to overthrow Amin and to instal of a more co-operative leadership in Kabul.

The Soviet Invasion

A steady build-up of the Soviet presence in Afghanistan had been visible since the autumn of 1979. Indeed, the US State Department issued a series of diplomatic warnings and protests, beginning in September, and at least four of these protests were made in December alone. However, they apparently contained no precise threats of action – or, if they did, were insufficient to prevent the Soviet invasion.

One of these protests was on 14 December, when the Soviet Union moved between 400 and 800 combat troops to Kabul, and the State Department noted that there were about 4,000 military 'advisers' in Afghanistan. On 18 December the number had risen to 5,000 (1,000 of them combat forces), and they were fanning out to key positions. On 24 December 1,500 troops, the equivalent of an airborne regiment, were airlifted to Kabul, and at least 30,000 troops were noted to be poised on the border. From Christmas day to the 27 December at least 5,000 additional airborne troops, were flown into Kabul international airport from the USSR with armoured vehicles, tanks and other equipment. In that two-day period as many as 150 flights were made by An-12 and An-22 transport aircraft (which carry 90 and 150 men respectively), and five divisions, or at least 50,000 men, were reported to be assembled on the border.

On the night of the 27 December an explosion at the central telecommunications station in Kabul cut all telephone connections and apparently signalled the start of the Soviet operation. Soviet troops took over the radio and television station, the presidential palace, and the Darulaman palace where Amin had taken up residence, perhaps on Soviet advice, only a few days before. There was some resistance from Afghan troops, but it was quickly put down. Simultaneously, Soviet troops poured across the border at three points, heading for Kabul in the centre of the country and then fanning out to the Pakistan border, and to Herat in the northwest. On 28 December Kabul Radio broadcast a speech by Babrak Karmal, the former Deputy Prime Minister and head of the PDPA's Parcham faction, announcing that Amin had been deposed and that he had taken power. This speech was apparently a pre-recorded message, and Karmal was not seen in Kabul until the night of 1 January, when he addressed the nation on television.

The Soviet Union's initial justification for her invasion was that she had been invited by the existing government to protect it against the counter-revolution which was being supported from outside the country, particularly from China, Pakistan, Iran and the United States. However, the cynicism of these claims was made manifest in the immediate murder of Amin and his replacement by Karmal, a man whom the Soviet leaders felt would be more amenable to their needs and whose greater pragmatism they hoped would be more acceptable to the Afghans.

By 5 January, a week after the coup, there were at least 50,000 heavily armed Soviet troops in the country, maintaining control over the main roads and the main cities. Most of them were reservists recently called up from the Turkmenistan, Uzbekistan and other border republics, and many of them spoke the same languages as the Afghans. For the first weeks of the occupation, Soviet commanders relied on Afghan army troops when force was needed, an indication that an effort was being made to avoid alienating the Afghans and to keep Soviet troops from being entangled in direct engagements with the guerrillas. If that were the motivation, it failed. By early February, the Afghan army had been reduced to less than half of its original strength by defection and desertion. With the exception of the air force, what was left could no longer be regarded as an effective fighting force. Soviet troops, having to take on the burden of consolidating control, found themselves the objects of intense hatred, sniper fire and heavier opposition, and on 4 February American intelligence sources claimed that they were suffering about 500 casualties a week and had lost a total of at least 2,500 since the 24 December. The Soviet Union also now began to replace the earlier, reservist-dependent units from the Islamic part of the USSR with main line forces from other areas.

Throughout February, the Soviet Union continued to move in more troops and sophisticated equipment such as BMP mechanized infantry combat vehicles, T-62 and possibly T-72 tanks, MiG-21 strike aircraft and Mi-24 helicopter gunships. By the end of the month, between 70,000 and 80,000 combat troops were deployed in Afghanistan, organized in 6 divisions – three in the West near the Iranian border, and three facing Pakistan in the north and east, with elements in Kandahar and in Kabul. There was little doubt that this number of troops would be able to secure the main cities, towns and roads. But if the Soviet leaders planned to extend pacification into the foothills in an effort to wipe out the guerrilla forces operating in the mountains, a far larger force would be needed (estimates ranged from 250,000 to 400,000), and even then success would not be assured.

At the begining of 1980, it appeared unlikely that the Soviet forces in Afghanistan would soon be withdrawn or even reduced. What seemed more likely was an ever-increasing involvement by the Soviet Union in maintaining a government of her preference in Kabul and providing it with a minimum of authority.

There were those who saw the Soviet move into Afghanistan as the first step in a thrust towards the Indian Ocean and the Gulf region. But it was difficult to see how the Soviet Union, having invaded Afghanistan and then bogged down in civil war there, had measurably improved her strategic position in the region as a whole. Rather than increasing Soviet influence, the invasion had alienated not only the West but the non-aligned countries of the region as well, and had generated efforts to resist Soviet military pressure in the future. Bases in Afghanistan could bring Soviet forces closer to the Gulf, but – given the USSR's 1,300-mile border with Iran, the range of her transport aircraft and the growth of her navy – distance had long since ceased to present a major obstacle to military action in the Gulf, had the USSR wished to undertake any.

But the strategic implications for the region were nevertheless profound. The Soviet Union's demonstrated readiness to use her forces to create political *faits accomplis* beyond her borders would overshadow relations with other countries as well. Repeated, unsubstantiated accusations against Pakistan, China and Iran of providing the Afghan rebels with weapons could foreshadow a Soviet attempt to use force against these countries. In particular, Iran's uncertain future might provide the Soviet Union's security-obsessed leaders with another case in which Soviet state interests demanded military action against neighbouring territory. Moreover the ethnic and tribal divisions and aspirations in the region might lend themselves to Soviet exploitation in order to undermine existing regimes. Even in the unlikely event of a total withdrawal of Soviet forces from Afghanistan, therefore, there would be no return to the *status quo ante*.

EAST ASIA

East Asia had not been able to escape the growing violence and instability that characterized the world of the 1970s. In 1979, however, its conflicts were unique because they were wholly between Communist nations: Communists were actually at war with other Communists across agreed borders. This fighting was not the result of the familiar East–West confrontation, but grew out of the constant tension between the various parts of Indochina, reinforced by Sino-Soviet antagonism. The danger of the conflict was enhanced by the possibility that non-Communist nations would be drawn into the vortex that it generated. The members of the Association of South-East Asian Nations (ASEAN) were threatened by a possible spill-over into Thailand of the fighting in Kampuchea, and the United States could be affected as her support for China grew and her relations with the USSR deteriorated.

The Soviet Union was quick to exploit the opportunities which the fighting in Indochina offered for expanding her influence on the mainland of Asia. Vietnam's invasion of Kampuchea had left her vulnerable to economic, political and military pressure from China, and Hanoi's turn to Moscow for support to counterbalance this resulted in an increase in the Soviet presence in the area. However, the Vietnamese action, and the Soviet support, deeply concerned the other nations in the region. It generated closer co-operation among the non-Communist states in the area (acting through ASEAN), which, while they would have preferred to remain non-aligned, were now being pushed by events into closer relations with China and the United States. In north-east Asia, too, the growth of Soviet military investment in the area moved Japan to a gradual reassessment of her future security requirements.

WAR IN INDOCHINA

Heavy fighting in the lowlands of South-east Asia tends to be cyclical, closely following the rhythms of the wet and dry seasons. During the monsoon, roughly from May to late October, roads are unusable for heavy equipment, much of the land is flooded and the dense vegetation becomes almost impossible to penetrate. During this period guerrilla forces can operate, and may even be at an advantage, but large-scale actions are effectively ruled out until the dry season returns, from November to April, and massed armies can move again. This pattern was followed in 1979, when two short, sharp interconnected wars were fought during the dry season, and guerrilla warfare in Kampuchea continued during the remainder of the year.

While both the wars could be said to have nominal victors (Vietnam over-running Kampuchea and replacing the Pol Pot regime with its own proxy government, and China 'punishing' Vietnam for her action) neither was conclusive, and the threat of further fighting in Indochina remained high. The losers were easier to see: while armies clashed, once again the people of the area suffered. One clear result of the fighting was its devastating economic effects on both Kampuchea and Vietnam, and the flood of refugees spawned by the troubles ebbed only slowly. Whatever the final result of the political and military struggles, damage to the fabric of society, particularly in Kampuchea, would take a long time to repair.

Vietnam Invades Kampuchea

US Security Adviser Brzezinski characterized the Vietnamese invasion of Kampuchea as a 'proxy war', and there was a measure of truth in this. In the years since the end of the second Indochinese war in 1975, Chinese and Soviet diplomatic, economic and military aid to Kampuchea and Vietnam respectively had done much to turn the two smaller Communist countries into clients of the larger ones. This was particularly true during 1978: as the crisis between Vietnam and Kampuchea grew, so did the amount of support which the Soviet Union and China gave, and so too did the Soviet and Chinese stakes. In this respect, then, the Vietnamese attack on Kampuchea represented an extension of the Sino-Soviet conflict to an armed struggle waged through governments and armies that were not their own.

Yet the war had other roots as well, for the tortured relationship between the two Indochinese nations was nurtured by historical resentments on which more recent antagonisms between the two Communist parties had been superimposed (see *Strategic Survey 1978*, pp. 76–7). Each had its own ambitions, quite aside from those of China and the Soviet Union. The unsavoury Pol Pot regime in Kampuchea had been carrying the fight to Vietnam for two years before the invasion, partly to rectify what it considered Vietnamese encroachments on to Kampuchean territory and partly to prevent what it saw as an effort to consolidate Vietnamese control over the whole of Indochina. Vietnam did indeed hope to extend her influence and control throughout Indochina, but she would probably have preferred to do it more quietly and more gradually. However, the constant Kampuchean harassment of Vietnamese border towns and refusal to engage in meaningful negotiations left Vietnam little choice, in her view, but to move quickly and decisively.

Vietnam prepared carefully for her invasion. In early November 1978 she signed a Treaty of Friendship and Co-operation with the Soviet Union which, among other things, called for 'consultations with a view to taking effective and appropriate measures' if either were attacked or threatened with attack. This was clearly intended to reduce the possibility of Chinese action against Vietnam when she moved against Kampuchea. On 3 December 1978 Hanoi organized a front group called the 'Kampuchean National United Front for National Salvation' and put at its head Heng Samrin, a defector from the Pol Pot regime. Having secured its rear as far as possible and established an alternative government to carry into Kampuchea with it, the Vietnamese army launched its massive attack in the last week of December with about 120,000 men in twelve divisions, accompanied by tanks and armoured cars.

The invasion was a swift success, partly because of its weight and the preparations that had been made, but also because the Pol Pot regime had decided not to stand and fight but to retreat to mountain and jungle outposts from which to conduct a guerrilla campaign against the invaders. In the first week of January 1979 provincial capitals fell one after the other with extraordinary speed. On 7 January the Vietnamese forces, and the few Kampuchean units opposed to Pol Pot that they had brought in their wake, captured the capital, Phnom Penh, without a battle. On 8 January Heng Samrin formed a Kampuchean People's Revolutionary Council, with himself as chairman, and proclaimed the existence of the People's Republic of Kampuchea. By the end of January the Vietnamese had gained control of all the country's cities, and the first major battle of the war was over.

The Soviet Union and her allies moved quickly to endorse this *fait accompli*. Vietnam and Laos had recognized the new government immediately on its formation, and by 11 January Ethiopia, Afghanistan, the Soviet Union and all the Communist countries except Romania and Yugoslavia had followed suit. But no other country recognized it. Instead, China and the ASEAN countries led efforts in the United Nations to condemn the Vietnamese action as blatant aggression. This failed on 15 January, when the Soviet Union vetoed the resolution that had been brought in the Security Council and asserted that the events in Kampuchea represented 'a true people's uprising' on the part of dissident Kampucheans.

After the invasion Pol Pot's forces became the dissident Kampucheans. Forewarned by Vietnam's massive preparations for the invasion, the regime, with Chinese advice and aid, had pre-positioned supplies and arms mainly in the difficult mountainous and jungle areas of the south and west of the country, and it was estimated that as many as 60,000 of Pol Pot's Khmer Rouge forces managed to elude the invaders. Throughout the spring these forces mounted fairly large attacks (at times involving as many as 1,000 troops) on Vietnamese units and even on some of the provincial capitals. The Vietnamese forces, however, gradually gained control over more of the country than just the cities and the major roads, and by late spring and early summer appeared to have bottled up most of the Khmer Rouge in the north-west of the country, hard against the Thai border, with some in scattered areas in other provinces. As a result, in the last half of 1979 the Khmer Rouge were on many occasions forced to cross into Thailand along with refugees from the fighting in order to escape attacks by Vietnamese troops, up to 200,000 of whom were now in Kampuchea. Thailand, which was reported to have covertly helped supplies from China to reach the Khmer Rouge, was reluctant to offend Vietnam directly by harbouring the Pol Pot forces. She therefore turned both guerrillas and refugees back into

Kampuchea, but at points different from those at which they had entered – thus allowing the guerrillas to escape their pursuers, regroup and continue fighting.

China Invades Vietnam
The invasion of Kampuchea and the swift establishment of a Vietnamese-controlled government there presented China with a difficult dilemma. Throughout 1978 she had made considerable efforts to prevent just this outcome. And although she would have preferred to support a more malleable and reasonable government than the brutally repressive Pol Pot regime, she felt that there was no choice if Vietnam – and through Vietnam the Soviet Union – were to be stopped from expanding her influence throughout Indochina. To this end, China had exerted economic pressure on Vietnam in the summer of 1978 by cancelling all her aid commitments and withdrawing all her advisers from the country. At the same time she began to build up her military forces on the Chinese–Vietnamese border, and throughout the autumn of 1978 she fought a number of small skirmishes there, partly in support of the Hoa (Chinese who had lived in Vietnam for generations) whom Vietnam was forcing out of the country and partly to warn Vietnam of the risks she would face if she expanded her border fighting with Kampuchea into a full-scale invasion. But these actions had an effect opposite to that intended. Instead of being intimidated, Vietnam moved closer to the Soviet Union in order to counter the Chinese pressure.

As the Vietnamese preparations for the invasion of Kampuchea mounted, so did Chinese preparations. China moved more troops to the border area throughout the autumn of 1978 and, partly as a result of the Vietnamese–Soviet pact, negotiated the full normalization of relations with the United States. During his visit to the United States in January 1979 Vice Premier Deng Xiaoping spoke out twice to threaten Vietnam with 'punishment' for her invasion of Kampuchea, thus implicitly seeking to tie the United States to the projected Chinese action. Finally, on 17 February, China launched her attack, calling it a 'lesson' to Vietnam that would be limited in space and in time.

By the time she opened her attack on Vietnam, China had massed about 180,000 men on the border. Not more than 100,000 were used within Vietnam, however, and the remainder were kept in reserve. There was no way to know what goals were set for these troops initially, but after two weeks of fighting China claimed that her ultimate goal was the capture of the provincial capital of Lang Son, on the strategic Route 1 which leads from the Chinese border directly to Hanoi. Lang Son was captured on 3 March; China then announced that her aims had been met and that she would withdraw, and by 16 March Chinese troops were back again across their own border.

Vietnam met the Chinese onslaught by means of border security troops and militia in heavily fortified positions throughout the mountainous border area. If one of the Chinese aims was to damage Vietnam's regular forces in the battle, then this was not achieved, because they were mostly kept out of the mountains in a defensive ring in front of Hanoi, and so played no part in the fighting. Although the Vietnamese forward units were unable to prevent the Chinese advance through the narrow defiles in which the battles were fought, they did make it very difficult, and they were estimated to have inflicted at least 20,000 casualties on the Chinese forces, all of which were infantry, fighting without air support. China had deployed a large number of aircraft to border airfields, but she relied on heavy artillery barrages to prepare the attack, perhaps because her obsolete air force would have been no match for the more sophisticated Vietnamese air arm, perhaps because the nature of the terrain would in any event have reduced the effectiveness of air support.

China undoubtedly had many and mixed motives for her action. She might have thought that her onslaught would cause Vietnam to move some troops out of Kampuchea to meet it, and thus would relieve some of the military pressure on the Khmer Rouge. Also, having spent so much political and diplomatic capital in trying to prevent the Vietnamese move, and yet having failed to do so, she probably considered it necessary to take some action so as to prevent a complete loss of face or national honour. On a deeper level, China wanted to indicate that further efforts to consolidate Vietnamese control over the entire Indochina area would meet with serious risks in the future. She also wanted to reassure other nations in the area, particularly Thailand, that her verbal support would be backed up with deeds. Moreover, she probably wanted to indicate to other nations, particularly the United States and the West, that fear of

Soviet reactions should not deter necessary military actions taken in pursuit of their national interests.

Judgements on the success of China's action must be as mixed as the motives that led her to take it. Vietnam did indeed suffer as a result; before they left, Chinese troops laid waste to the six provincial capitals they had briefly occupied and destroyed the economic infra-structure in the area. But Vietnam was not required to reduce her actions in Kampuchea to meet the Chinese threat, and she further consolidated her hold over Indochina, moving more troops into Laos (Laos subsequently requested the remaining Chinese to leave) and firming up her grip on Kampuchea. Moreover, the Chinese action forced Vietnam to rely more heavily on the Soviet Union. ASEAN, too, condemned the Chinese invasion, for it seemed to confirm the fears of some of the south-east Asian nations about Chinese aggression. On the other hand, Thailand was heartened by it, and it is questionable whether without some clear Chinese response to Vietnam and the Soviet Union she would have been as willing to give even such a limited degree of aid to the Khmer Rouge as she reportedly did give.

Conditions in Kampuchea

When the Vietnamese army conquered Kampuchea it found that it had taken over a country which had been devastated by its own rulers. There had been recurrent reports of what the Pol Pot regime had been doing inside Kampuchea since it came to power in 1975, but the reality was even worse than the reports. The regime had systematically destroyed the basis for a modern civilized society: schools, hospitals, water supply systems, factories were wrecked; managers, doctors or anyone who looked like an intellectual had been murdered or had died from being forced to work in the countryside under impossible conditions (it was said to be dangerous to wear glasses, since people who did could be killed as a result); typewriters, gramophones, television sets, hospital equipment and automobiles had all been destroyed because they were signs of decadent living.

One of the results of this wholesale murder and destruction of the managerial and professional classes was that it was now necessary for Vietnamese to run Kampuchea. This increased the difficulty of trying to present the new regime as an indigenous Kampuchean one and exposed Vietnam to attack for having taken over the country. And, even though those who had managed to survive the previous three years detested the Khmer Rouge, their innate abhorrence of the Vietnamese prevented their giving much support to the new regime in these circumstances.

The major problem that the new Vietnamese regime inherited was that of food production. The new government had been urging people to return to their villages and farms and to replant rice paddies. But this was difficult. The upheavals caused firstly by the forced movement of people by the Khmer Rouge and then by the ruin of the early rice planting during the fighting, as a result of both the farmers' inability to work their fields during the conflict and the deliberate destruction of the crops by the retreating Khmer Rouge forces, meant that the people were left with little to replant. They found it necessary to consume their seed rice to avoid starvation. Some rice and other help was given by Vietnam and the Soviet Union, but it was too little to make up for the deficits, and, according to information from relief agencies, over 2.5 million Kampucheans faced the prospect of starvation during the autumn of 1979.

In this regard the new regime showed itself to be as much concerned with ideological and political considerations as the Khmer Rouge had been. Efforts by international relief organizations to bring food and other aid to the Kampuchean people were frustrated by the Vietnamese and their puppet government. They insisted that they must control the distribution of any such relief, claiming that the humanitarian efforts mounted by the West were merely a cover for supplying the Khmer Rouge rebels, and they attempted to prevent the distribution of food to anyone but those whom they designated. Their hope was clearly to end the rebellion by starving out the isolated pockets of resistance. At the end of the year some relief was reaching some of the people, either by being brought in through Thailand or as a result of the willingness of humanitarian donors like Oxfam to deal through the authorities in order to prevent wholesale starvation. But the amount was inadequate, and badly needed aid was still being withheld by governments unwilling to agree to the demands of the Vietnamese and Heng Samrin governments. The prospects were that famine in Kampuchea would grow to major proportions by the spring of 1980, unless there were some changes of attitude or the fighting ceased.

As a result of her absorption of Kampuchea Vietnam became heavily dependent on the Soviet Union, both economically and militarily. Without Soviet diplomatic and military support, Vietnam would be faced with an acute physical security threat from China. And without the Soviet and COMECON economic aid she was receiving (estimated at $2 million per day at the end of the year) neither her own weakened economy nor the devastated Kampuchean economy would be able to survive. On the other hand, and despite the considerable cost incurred, the Soviet Union had gained a firm ally against China, an entrée to the mainland of Asia which had been denied to her since World War II, and the use of military and naval facilities in Vietnam. The presence of her naval forces in the waters off the coast of South-east Asia increased visibly. At the height of the Sino-Vietnamese war, she sent a 14-ship task force, headed by a missile-carrying cruiser, to Vietnamese waters, and several of these ships called into Cam Ranh Bay. In early May 1979 it was reported that a *Foxtrot*-class submarine had arrived in the Bay (the first report of a submarine using this facility), and the Soviet Union continued to use the logistic facilities both there and at Danang for ship visits, even if Vietnam's insistence that they had not become formal Soviet naval bases remained technically correct.

Prospects
At the beginning of 1980, a full year after the Vietnamese had swept through the country to what appeared to have been an easy victory, about 25,000 Khmer Rouge were still fighting a low-level guerrilla war against the puppet regime. Their task was not an easy one, however. Efforts to form a united front against the Vietnamese-dominated government were largely unsuccessful, because of the universal detestation felt for the leaders of the previous government; even when the Khmer Rouge leaders tried to improve their image by shuffling the top positions of command (Pol Pot was replaced by Khieu Sampan at the end of the year), this failed to bring about any reconciliation with the other guerrilla forces, including the Khmer Serei, and with Prince Sihanouk, who from September 1979 onwards attempted to form a new national front with himself at its head. This inability of the various forces opposing Heng Samrin and the Vietnamese to join in a common government, an outcome desired and supported by China and ASEAN, left the latter with no alternative but to go on giving political and diplomatic help to a regime which continued to rule the small areas under its sway through draconian repression. But, so long as the Kampuchean opposition was dominated by the Khmer Rouge, it seemed likely that more and more nations would find it difficult to continue their support for it. In early December 1979 Britain withdrew her recognition of the Khmer Rouge government without recognizing the Heng Samrin government – and the same position was likely to be taken by many other countries as well.

Meanwhile the possibilities for an early compromise over the Indochina dispute were not high. China was clearly unwilling to accept the replacement of her client regime by a Vietnamese puppet government, particularly since it appeared that the ensuing Vietnamese-controlled Indochinese federation would be closely tied to the Soviet Union. While another attempt to 'punish' Vietnam probably would not take the form of a direct attack, China retained the option of increasing her support for the rebels in both Kampuchea and Laos. This would throw a heavy strain on Vietnam which, with almost 200,000 troops in Kampuchea and perhaps 50,000 in Laos, would at the same time have to support a good many more to guard her homeland against another possible Chinese attack from the north. If the Kampuchean forces opposing the Heng Samrin government could be brought to form a coalition of national unity, ideally under Prince Sihanouk, the difficulties Vietnam faced would mount.

In this situation there were the seeds of a more direct confrontation between the super-powers. The Soviet Union, heavily committed to Vietnam's support and deeply hostile to China, might intervene directly if the tensions between China and Vietnam should again lead to open military conflict. As a result of her response to the developments of 1979 the United States found herself closer to China, sharing the Chinese interest in blocking Soviet expansion and actively supporting it by reversing her earlier refusal to supply militarily relevant technology and materiel to Peking. Thus, the spectre of an even larger war growing out of the antagonism that had erupted over Kampuchea at the end of 1978 had, if anything, been strengthened by the developments of the ensuing year.

CO-OPERATION IN SOUTH-EAST ASIA

The Vietnamese invasion of Kampuchea and the attendant installation of a client government in Phnom Penh accelerated the evolution of the Association of South-East Asian Nations (ASEAN) as a political community. ASEAN's immediate disapproval of Vietnam's establishment of the Heng Samrin regime was sustained consistently throughout the year, but its political efforts to force a Vietnamese troop withdrawal were not matched by any novel forms of military co-operation. China's consequent invasion of Vietnam evoked mixed feelings which reflected the underlying diversity of strategic interests between ASEAN states. Nonetheless, the common positions on troop withdrawals which they adopted in respect of both military actions effectively favoured the Chinese cause. Thus, despite the perception of some members that China posed a major long-term external threat to their security, the Association as a corporate political entity was drawn into a degree of support for China through its opposition to the consolidation of Vietnamese domination throughout Indochina.

Background
Formed in August 1967 as a vehicle for intraregional reconciliation in the wake of the confrontation between Indonesia and Malaysia, ASEAN soon revised its order of priorities. At the outset, its five founder members – Thailand, Malaysia, Singapore, Indonesia and the Philippines – had stressed 'economic growth, social progress and cultural development in the region', and made only secondary references to the promotion of 'regional peace and stability ... through abiding respect for justice and the rule of law in the relationship among countries of the region.' This less publicized priority soon became a more important central concern, however, when decisive changes were perceived in the balance of external influences bearing on Southeast Asia.

The turning point in ASEAN's evolution occurred with the convening of its first summit meeting in Bali in February 1976, as a direct outcome of revolutionary Communist success in Indochina in April 1975. By the time the summit was held, it was evident that the Kampuchea of the Khmer Rouge had rejected the role of servile client of Vietnam, and that a monolithic Indochinese Communism had not been established. Nonetheless, ASEAN had become sufficiently alarmed for common political priorities to be incorporated into public pronouncements. The Declaration of ASEAN Concord issued at Bali affirmed a commitment to the proposal, originally advanced in 1971 at a meeting of ASEAN foreign ministers, that South-east Asia should be recognized as a Zone of Peace. Moreover, the five heads of government explicitly stated that political stability and internal security were indivisible within the Association, and that 'the stability of each member state and of the ASEAN region is an essential contribution to international peace and security'. Each member state resolved to eliminate threats to its stability posed by subversion, thus strengthening both national and ASEAN resilience.

At Bali the heads of government sought also to promote a wider structure of ordered relations within South-east Asia by promulgating and signing a Treaty of Amity and Co-operation. With Vietnam in mind, this 'code of interstate conduct' was explicitly left open 'for accession' by other regional states, but it drew a hostile response from Hanoi, which regarded ASEAN as an insidious instrument of American and Japanese interests. And at the Conference of Non-Aligned States held in Colombo in August 1976, Vietnamese and Laotian opposition denied the Zone of Peace proposal a place in the final communiqué. In the middle of 1978, however, the marked deterioration in Sino-Vietnamese relations prompted a reversal of Vietnamese suspicion and mistrust of ASEAN which was most clearly shown in the tour of ASEAN capitals made by the Vietnamese Prime Minister, Pham Van Dong, in September and October 1978. A striking feature of the functioning of the Association at this juncture was the way in which its five members, through secret diplomacy, upheld a common and harmonious position in the face of Pham Van Dong's persistent, but unsuccessful, attempts to conclude bilateral treaties of friendship with each of them.

After Vietnam's Invasion
Pham Van Dong's assurances of non-interference in the internal affairs of regional states were received with some satisfaction. But the subsequent conclusion of a Soviet-Vietnamese Treaty of Friendship and Co-operation in November 1978 revived underlying apprehensions, and these were confirmed by the Vietnamese invasion

of Kampuchea the following month. Indeed, the shock to ASEAN's collective nervous system which the invasion caused was all the greater because of Vietnam's so recently and freely dispensed assurances of non-intervention. These had given the ASEAN governments the impression that in Vietnam's attempt to reach a better political understanding with her non-Communist regional neighbours she had accepted their common priority that the independence of Kampuchea should be respected. In the face of a perceived act of treachery, the ASEAN governments closed ranks and affirmed solidarity with Thailand, which was now confronted by client governments of Vietnam along its entire eastern border. At a meeting in Bankok on 12 January 1979, the foreign ministers of the Association 'deplored the armed intervention' and called for 'the immediate and total withdrawal of the foreign forces from Kampuchean territory'.

In the circumstances, the ASEAN governments could do no more than take a diplomatic initiative, which was weakened by an unwillingness to identify Vietnam expressly in the joint statement. Although ASEAN exhibited a strong sense of common concern over regional security, it possessed neither the structure nor the capability of a viable alliance. There had been bilateral military co-operation along common borders between Thailand and Malaysia and between Malaysia and Indonesia since before the formation of the Association. However, such co-operation in counter-insurgency and the exchange of intelligence, as well as in bilateral (and occasionally trilateral) military exercises, had been undertaken outside the formal auspices of ASEAN with the specific object of giving the lie to charges that such co-operation made ASEAN an embryonic or *de facto* alliance. The Association therefore was not in a position to contemplate concerted military action in order to reverse the apparent political *fait accompli* effected by the force of Vietnamese arms.

This military weakness made the invasion of Kampuchea especially alarming. Vietnam had moved from gradual subversion to overt intervention across a political boundary in order to overthrow and replace an independent, if repugnant, government. This willingness to violate a cardinal rule of the international system was of most concern to Thailand, but all ASEAN governments were conscious of the principle involved and of the danger of appearing to endorse a precedent which might well be applied to their disadvantage in future. They were also, in varying degrees, apprehensive that the political entrenchment of the Heng Samrin regime in Kampuchea would serve to consolidate Vietnam's dominance throughout the whole of Indochina. Such an outcome would revive the political spectre, which had materialized briefly in April 1975, of a decisive and unpalatable change in the regional balance of power.

Even for states such as Indonesia and Malaysia – which were somewhat ambivalent, since Vietnam's political dominance would impede the extension of Chinese influence – the fact that the Vietnamese invasion was facilitated by Soviet political support and military and economic assistance was a major source of concern. For Indonesia and Malaysia, which had reached a compromise over the issue of the Zone of Peace in place of the latter's more precise proposal for the neutralization of South-east Asia, the common political denominator was a desire to exclude the threat of great-power intervention in the region.

Relations with China

In taking a common stand at the January 1979 meeting of ASEAN foreign ministers, the five governments were conscious of the danger of appearing to side with China in her conflict with Vietnam. While there was a convergence of interests between themselves and China, they were concerned that ASEAN would not be able to avoid being drawn into a major-power confrontation. This apprehension, already made clear at the meeting of ASEAN foreign ministers in June 1978, was underlined by China's military intervention into northern Vietnam in February 1979.

China's move to 'punish' Vietnam brought a quick response from the Association. Indonesian Foreign Minister Mochtar Kusumaatmadja, as chairman of ASEAN's Standing Committee, issued a statement calling for 'the withdrawal of all foreign troops from the areas of conflict in Indochina'. Though intended to avoid partiality, this pleased China, who had already made clear that her action was a limited one, while irritating Vietnam. In March the ASEAN governments, acting together, secured non-aligned sponsorship for a draft resolution making the same request before the United Nations Security Council. It failed as a result of a Soviet veto.

The ASEAN members were divided in their private attitudes to the Chinese action, for fears of Vietnamese expansionism were not held with equal intensity by all members. Indonesia, in particular, viewed the risks of such expansionism with less concern than the others, and indeed would have been less concerned still but for the close relationship which had developed between Vietnam and the USSR. As a result of this relationship, however, Indonesia reassessed her own perspective and even contemplated the normalization of relations with China. Singapore was particularly vocal about the role of the Soviet Union in supporting Vietnamese objectives.

The reactions to the Chinese attack clearly demonstrated the ambivalence of feeling within the Association. While there was disappointment that China had not been able to chastise Vietnam to the extent of affecting her political will, there was at the same time common satisfaction that the action was limited. There was satisfaction, too, that the Soviet Union was not drawn directly into the conflict, and ASEAN governments were conscious of the pressures that were likely to encourage some kind of Soviet military response if China sought to administer a second 'punishment'. A common concern over the prospect of a relationship of undue dependence between Vietnam and the Soviet Union, especially if it entailed Soviet enjoyment of operational naval base facilities, was reflected in the ASEAN governments' rejection in September of a request for port visits by Soviet warships. Ideally, the ASEAN states would have preferred Vietnamese disengagement from Kampuchea and a greater assertion of Vietnamese independence from the Soviet Union. However, Soviet support for Vietnam was a function of Sino-Soviet relations, and the management of these lay well beyond ASEAN's competence.

Thailand harboured the greatest apprehension of Vietnam's actions in Indochina and was most pleased at the retribution China handed out to Vietnam, although she sought to avoid appearing to be a party to Chinese attempts at intervention in Kampuchea and Laos. China's adamant refusal to be reconciled to the transfer of power inside Kampuchea made it easier for the Thai government to refuse to foreclose yet on the option of the Pol Pot resistance as a means of denying Vietnamese dominance in Indochina, a position which China encouraged by the sale of oil at 'friendship' prices. Chinese willingness to take military action against Vietnam encouraged the development of an informal alignment with Thailand. This was reflected, for example, in a tour of Thailand in December by the Deputy Chief-of-Staff of the People's Liberation Army, Gen. Wan Shangrong, who affirmed that 'if Thailand and other ASEAN countries were invaded by outside forces, the Chinese government and people would resolutely side with them'. Although its worth was still questioned, such an alignment was encouraged by the current condition of Sino-American relations and the open US opposition to Vietnam's role in Kampuchea.

A New Solidarity

The common diplomatic position adopted by the ASEAN governments concealed certain private misgivings which were set aside because of the overriding priority of asserting public solidarity with Thailand. The invasion of Kampuchea, and the consequent Chinese intervention in Vietnam, posed a problem for ASEAN because the five governments had never shared a common strategic perspective and did not take the same view of the source of the major external threat. For Thailand, the prospect of her historical enemy, Vietnam, dominating Indochina conjured up the fear of being confined to the role of an oriental Finland. Other member states did not have this sense of immediate threat.

Nevertheless, the cohesion of ASEAN as a diplomatic community came before any prospect of cultivating a special relationship with a Vietnam perceived as a bulwark against China. Thus, although Indonesia, and also Malaysia, sought to avoid closing the door on any dialogue with Vietnam, in the hope of reducing her near-exclusive relationship with the Soviet Union, solidarity with Thailand was paramount. Any sign of reluctance or indecisiveness on this score might well have damaged ASEAN cohesion irreparably, and would have encouraged a greater tendency for Thailand to respond to the political advances of China, the only state prepared to take practical measures to deny Vietnamese dominance in Indochina. In consequence, the diplomatic initiatives of ASEAN as a corporate entity were governed by the priorities of the member most exposed to a security threat. These diplomatic initiatives were, to some extent, a substitute for practical action. Indeed, the Association's abortive attempt to secure the passage of the Security Council resolution in March was an effort to overcome a sense of military impotence and to register its claim to have a right to share in managing regional order in South-east Asia.

In June, the foreign ministers of ASEAN convened their annual meeting in Bali. They reaffirmed their joint statement of the previous January which had strongly deplored the armed intervention against the independence, sovereignty and territorial integrity of Kampuchea and also reiterated the demand for the immediate and total withdrawal of foreign forces. In addition, they expressed grave concern over 'the deluge of illegal immigrants/displaced persons from Indochina' and agreed that Vietnam was responsible for the unending exodus of 'illegal immigrants and has a decisive role, too, in resolving the problem at source'. But there was also a measure of disagreement at Bali. For example, Singapore sought a much stronger condemnation of Vietnam's invasion of Kampuchea. For countries like Malaysia and Indonesia, on the other hand, the issue of the refugees, with their predominantly Chinese identity, appeared to represent more of a threat than Vietnam's invasion of Kampuchea. On balance, the outcome of the meeting demonstrated that member governments had a greater ability to arrive at viable political compromises than to embark on significant forms of co-operation. The fissures which the refugee issue opened up in the wall of intra-ASEAN solidarity were temporarily sealed as a result of the UN meeting on refugees and displaced persons in South-east Asia, held in Geneva in July, and the resulting agreement by a number of countries outside the region to take in more of them for settlement and Vietnamese efforts to slow the outflow of refugees. In August, the ASEAN foreign ministers met once again, in Kuala Lumpur, to ensure a harmony of policies before the annual session of the United Nations General Assembly and again used the opportunity to reaffirm their joint statement issued in Bangkok on 12 January. When the General Assembly convened in September, the ASEAN states played an active role in the successful reconfirmation of the ousted Pol Pot government in the Kampuchean seat, and in November the Assembly voted overwhelmingly for their resolution calling for an immediate withdrawal of all foreign forces from Kampuchea.

Thus the ASEAN states during the course of the year maintained an effective measure of political solidarity and a unity of purpose over the issue of Kampuchea, despite the fact that their interests were less than wholly identical. Indeed, this visible expression of political solidarity helped deny the widespread international recognition which Vietnam and the Soviet Union sought for the Heng Samrin government. Yet, although ASEAN proved itself a viable instrument of multilateral diplomacy, it was unable to bring any tangible influence to bear on the actual conflict in Indochina. In this respect, it was not a factor in the balance of forces; nor indeed did it try to become one. ASEAN was also unable to demonstrate the utility of its Zone of Peace proposal for South-east Asia. The conflict over Kampuchea indicated how difficult it was to insulate an intra-regional conflict in South-east Asia from the competitive involvement of extra-regional powers.

Towards Military Co-operation?
In the latter part of 1979, with the onset of the dry season in Indochina, there were reports that ASEAN was contemplating a more positive security role. In November Malaysian Deputy Prime Minister Dr Mahathir Mohammad announced that, although ASEAN was not a military pact, its members had 'an understanding in military aspects'. The Thai Ambassador in Manila was reported to have said soon afterwards that ASEAN would hold a conference of defence ministers to discuss regional security before the end of the year. However, this prospect was almost immediately dismissed by the Secretary-General of Malaysia's foreign ministry, and the Thai Prime Minister, Gen. Kriangsak Chamanand, then indicated that the idea of such a meeting would be explored, but only to exchange ideas and not to discuss military ties, which would violate ASEAN principles.

Despite additional reports that some members had taken steps to set up intervention forces, the formal and practical sides of intra-ASEAN co-operation did not suggest the addition of a military dimension to the functioning of the Association. The obvious focus of any such military co-operation would be Thailand in the event of a Vietnamese invasion. However, while the conflict within Kampuchea could lead to hot pursuit into Thailand, or to the use of portions of Thai territory to encircle and liquidate the Khmer Rouge resistance, it did not foreshadow an actual invasion of Thailand. In addition, Thailand made it clear that she was reluctant to play host to ASEAN armies from different cultures, and in any case almost every ASEAN government would prefer not to get drawn into a military role in support of Thailand. Thus, while reinforcing their separate general capabilities as a result of developments in the region, the members of ASEAN did not go so far as to attempt to set up formal military co-operation within the structure of the Association.

External stimulus served to promote the political and diplomatic solidarity of ASEAN. In seeking to confront external challenge, however, the Association demonstrated a limited capacity for collective action. Indeed, it did not possess the collective capability to influence the future pattern of power in Indochina, which pivots on the outcome of the conflict within Kampuchea. Nonetheless, it took a calculated risk in maintaining a diplomatic position not matched by military capability, facing the prospect of alienating Vietnam without necessarily being able to prevent her achieving her political goals in Kampuchea. But, according to ASEAN's foreign ministers in their joint statement at the end of the year, to do otherwise than recognize Pol Pot 'would be tantamount to approving the act of foreign military intervention and the imposition of a regime which is sustained by foreign military forces'. The dilemma for ASEAN was that the success of this stand on principle could not be accomplished by diplomatic gestures alone. Yet such gestures were all that the Association had at its disposal.

THE DEFENCE DEBATE IN JAPAN

How Japan can best defend herself has been the subject of considerable debate since at least 1950. Over the years, however, the focus of the debate has shifted. From questioning whether Japan's military structure – the Self-Defence Forces – are allowed under the 'Peace Constitution', it has moved to questioning how strong they can be and still remain consonant with the Constitution and what strategies are appropriate to deal with the new problems of national security which have resulted from changes both in Japan and in the international scene. During 1979 these last issues were the ones which formed the core of discussion, for the Japanese general public, though without great enthusiasm, now seemed to accept the existence of and necessity for Self-Defence Forces within the limits set out in the Peace Constitution.

The questions in the forefront of public discussion of national security during 1979 were the Soviet military build-up in the region and the problem of ensuring an uninterrupted supply of essential sources of energy and raw materials. The second of these was of greatest concern and came into even sharper focus during the crisis between the United States and Iran at the end of the year. Japan's equivocal stand at the outset, when the US embassy in Tehran was seized and the hostages taken, and her activities in the international oil market immediately afterwards fell short of the solidarity the United States expected from a major ally. But it accurately reflected Japanese anxiety over the problem of maintaining a steady flow of oil to service the national economy, an anxiety which was strengthened further when it became known that American international oil companies were cutting supplies to Japan to enable them to help meet the shortfall of Iranian oil. However, along with a recognition that energy dependence had become a serious threat to Japan's security, there was full agreement that the threat could not be dealt with by military means, and that Japan would have to continue to rely on her economic power and diplomacy to protect her interests in this field.

The problem that the Soviet Union posed for Japan's security, primarily a military one, was felt particularly keenly at a time when US forces in the region were stretched as a result of the crisis in South-west Asia and when Soviet strategic interests in the region around Japan were visibly more pronounced. Japan's attention centred on the development of Soviet military facilities on the islands of Etorofu, Kurashiri and Shikotan – three of the four Northern Islands which she claims – and on the Soviet naval build-up in the seas surrounding Japan. The main purpose of the Soviet actions on the islands was probably to provide a defensive screen behind which to convert the Sea of Okhotsk and its approaches into a Soviet preserve, from which naval power could be projected into the Pacific, and to protect the new Soviet *Delta*-class missile submarines deployed there. Japanese reaction was particularly acute, since this development directly challenged Japan's territorial claims to the islands. In addition, there remained the possibility that the Soviet Union, in a crisis, could use these positions as a springboard from which to launch a limited assault on the Wakkani Peninsula in northern Hokkaido.

The Japanese response to the USSR's military build-up in the Far East and her increasing naval and air activities was a more realistic appreciation of the need to improve the capabilities of the Self-Defence Forces, particularly in the fields of air defence, anti-submarine warfare and logistics. At the same time Japan realized that basically she must rely on the United States to deter the Soviet Union. Heightened awareness of this on the part of the Japanese public contributed to an atmosphere in which the government was able to take steps to facilitate the presence of US forces in Japan (such as cost-sharing arrangements) and to enhance the quality of the Japan–US security arrangements (for example, through studies of joint military planning and joint military exercises).

In the autumn of 1979 it was announced that in the spring of 1980 units of the Maritime Self-Defence Forces would for the first time participate in joint exercises with the US, Canadian, Australian and New Zealand navies. Taken in the face of questions by the opposition parties about the legality of participating in multinational exercises, the decision was a further indication of Japan's readiness to assume a more active role outside the narrow confines of her territorial waters.

The danger of a Soviet attack on Japan had been considered most likely in the context of a global crisis involving a direct confrontation between the Soviet Union and the United States – a contingency which was thought to be fairly remote. Moreover, despite strong verbal warnings and threats, the Soviet reaction to the signing of the Sino-Japanese Treaty of Peace and Friendship in August 1978, and to Prime Minister Ohira's visit to China in December 1979, had been symbolic rather than substantive. During 1979 the Soviet Union even made a number of diplomatic gestures (including sending a Vice Foreign Minister to Tokyo in May for an exchange of views with the Japanese Foreign Ministry) which were intended to indicate that, despite the signing of the treaty, the USSR continued to look for good relations with Japan.

In Japanese eyes, however, these gestures were sharply contradicted by the increasingly rapid build-up of the Soviet military presence in the Far East. Under these circumstances, the value of the Japanese-US security arrangement for the defence of Japan was heightened, and the credibility of the US commitment became a key issue in the defence debate in Japan. The withdrawal of American troops from Vietnam and then from Thailand, and the Carter Administration's announcement that it intended to withdraw ground troops from Korea, roused Japanese misgivings about the durability of the United States presence in Asia.

These misgivings had been lessened by a series of measures taken by the United States in 1978, and in 1979 the level of anxiety was further reduced. President Carter's freeze on the plans for withdrawing ground forces from Korea and a general stiffening of American attitudes towards the Soviet Union, underlined by increased military expenditures, dampened fears about US reliability. A new worry surfaced, however, when the United States announced her so-called 'swing strategy', under which American naval forces in the Pacific would be transferred to the Atlantic or Indian Oceans in an emergency. Since Japanese defence planners thought that the outbreak of hostilities between the super-powers would probably occur first in either Europe or the Middle East, they were concerned that Japan might be left unduly exposed at a time of severe tension and danger.

The debate within the defence community thus became polarized between those who wanted to see a bigger Japanese defence effort in order to make a greater contribution to the partnership with the United States and strengthen the mutual security system, and those who called for increased armaments on the grounds that in a crisis Japan might have to rely on herself alone. While all agreed that the Japan–US security arrangements for the defence of Japan were indispensable, and that Japan's present defence capability was far below the required level, the differences between the two schools, which centred on the credibility of the US commitment, could have important future political consequences. During the year, however, the first was still the predominant official view, and the relationship with the United States over security was smooth and growing.

In contrast to a harmonious security relationship and a striking absence of serious domestic opposition to it – underscored by decisive shifts in favour of the Mutual Security Treaty by two important centrist opposition parties, Komeito and the Democratic Socialist Party – the American-Japanese economic relationship continued to be a source of friction between the two countries. There was some improvement in terms of the balance of payments, but it was thought that this might only be a temporary phenomenon and that 1980 might see a return of large Japanese surpluses, as exports provided the main growth factor in an economy affected by a domestic recession.

Friction with the United States in 1979 had been most noticeable in the area of global policies, and was brought into sharp relief by the Iranian crisis and the oil question. In early 1980 it moved into the security realm. Particularly after the Soviet invasion of Afghanistan, the United States began to make clear her unhappiness with Japan's unwillingness to raise the level of her defence spending. Defense Secretary Brown, visiting Tokyo on his way home from Peking in January, encouraged the Japanese government to increase its spending, citing the Soviet invasion and the recent build-up of Soviet forces on the Kurile islands. Heavier American pressure could be expected, although this could bring new tensions into the US-Japanese relationship. Another possible source for misunderstanding was the American move to provide militarily associated equipment to China. While Japan was willing to support the economic modernization of China, she was wary about military support (she would not provide it herself) for fear of Soviet reaction.

Japan thus stood on the threshold of the 1980s beset by the increasing uncertainties of the international environment. Having outgrown her dependence on the United States in every respect except that of security, she faced difficult choices in her relations with the Soviet Union; and she was forced to perform a delicate balancing act in order to reconcile her increasingly close association with China with the demands imposed by her interests in South-east Asia and her membership of the club of industrialized nations.

In the area of defence, the prospect of an economic recession in the 1980s and the possible impact of resultant difficulties in national financing effectively made it difficult for Japan to sustain any substantial increase in defence spending. It was only after a heated debate within the government that the proportion of the GNP to be devoted to military expenditure in the fiscal year 1980 was set at 0.9% – the same level as in 1978 and 1979. In money terms, however, this represented a continuous increase, from just under $8 billion in 1978 to $8.9 billion in 1979 and a projected $9.3 billion in 1980.

In the face of both economic and political restraints, defence planning was to concentrate on improvements in air and naval capabilities, underlined by the gradual introduction of the F-15 interceptor, the P3-C anti-submarine aircraft and airborne warning and control systems (AWACS). A modest start was to be made on modernizing defence systems and improving logistical facilities, particularly ammunition storage capacity, which had been allowed to sink to half of that in 1957. The relatively modest increases of Japan's defence forces reflected not only political and financial restraints but also emphasized a continued uncertainty in the country about the role of a military capability in ensuring Japan's security, which seemed to be most threatened by challenges that defied military solutions.

CHINA'S DEFENCE INDUSTRIES

Equipment deficiencies in their armed forces were brought forcibly home to the Chinese military planners as a result of the short war against Vietnam. A review conducted by the Military Affairs Committee in the summer of 1979 was reported to have pointed critically at poor communications equipment, lack of night sights and remote sighting equipment, lack of armoured personnel carriers and other problems. None of these could be new to China's leaders, for the obsolescence of equipment had been a long-standing problem in their effort to bring their army up to modern standards.

The Chinese-produced tanks are copies of Soviet models from the 1950s, without the speed or the infra-red range finders, modern electronics or heavier armour of present-day models. Chinese-built aircraft are copies of Soviet designs – MiG-17s, MiG-19s and a few Mig-21s – and even these are no longer produced in the numbers reached in 1972. China's artillery is also obsolescent and without modern sighting devices; she has no anti-tank guided missiles; and her anti-aircraft defences depend on out-of-date weaponry. The country is clearly unable to design and build rapidly all the sophisticated weapons needed for a modern, well-equipped army, and it has been searching in the West for military aid in large quantities. Even this road to better military equipment will be barred for a long time to come, however, because of the backward state of the military machine-building industry, the backbone of Chinese weapons development.

The Need to Modernize
Over the past fifteen years military research and development in China has been seriously hampered by ineffective management, a shortage of skilled man-power and equipment, and the effects of the Cultural Revolution. A key weakness at all levels has been the shortage of well-trained scientists, engineers, and technicians. The core of China's professional researchers is composed of a small cadre of foreign-trained scientists and engineers, and these are followed, in descending order of ability, by people trained in China before 1966 and those educated since 1970. Because many military research personnel were chosen for their political reliability more than their technical qualifications, they are often less competent than their counterparts in non-military institutes and production facilities. Additionally, the rigid compartmentalization throughout the military industrial sector, prevents researchers and technicians having easy access to information from inside their organizations or from outside.

The anti-science policies of the Cultural Revolution era and the 'Gang of Four' period severely disrupted progress in military research and development. Long-term research programmes were curtailed, military industrial and technological institutes closed, laboratories ransacked and destroyed, and faculty members and scientists everywhere harassed and disgraced. There were some exceptions, however, where organizations were able to shield personnel from political activity and prevent total disruption of research and development programmes. This was particularly true of professionals in the missile and nuclear fields, who were able to keep programmes moving, if at a reduced pace. Despite China's new policy towards science and technology, however, the legacy of the anti-science period persists in the attitudes of many military researchers. The continuing fear of another political turnabout prevents many military scientists and engineers giving full commitment to their work, and many professors and scientists in the 60–65 age group, who had been subjected to debilitating criticism during the Cultural Revolution, probably have little enthusiasm to resume work.

Until recently, China largely ignored the application of effective management to military research and development. Basic research, aimed at the creation of new knowledge, has been forbidden for more than a decade. Applied research, which is expected to have practical results, was disrupted by the Cultural Revolution and did not resume until 1976. Development, which is aimed at putting research findings into practice, has been only partially applied: advanced development has been largely ignored, and routine development work has been aimed at relatively minor modification of products brought into being by previous research and development. Nearly all Chinese-produced weapons are thus based on outmoded Soviet models, and even then China has encountered a great deal of technical difficulty in duplicating them.

Weaknesses in Chinese military industrial production are reflected throughout the entire technological spectrum, from basic research to the maintenance of finished products. The most critical shortcomings in both military and non-military machine building industries – in design technology and manufacturing know-how – are compounded by a host of other manufacturing constraints, including poor production and quality-control methods, limited standardization procedures, inadequate machine tools, limited instrumentation and equipment, and shortages of special metals and materials.

The lack of a modern design capability is a basic weakness. Chinese design technology in the strategic weapons area – nuclear warheads and ballistic missiles – though slightly more advanced than in the conventional weapons field, is still at the technical levels achieved by the Soviet Union in the early 1960s. China appears to lack the scientists, or the competence, to improve the designs of such antiquated weapon systems as the MiG-15 and MiG-19 fighters, and where design modifications have been made the dependability of the modified equipment is probably less than that of the original. Limitations in design capabilities are compounded by a host of manufacturing deficiencies, including the lack of modern production techniques and quality-control methods, which are common throughout China's military machine-building industry, including the much-touted electronics sector. According to comments made in November 1977 by Wang Cheng, former head of the Fourth Ministry of Machine Building, the electronics industry continues to be backward and is unable to meet the needs of national defence and economic construction. From this it can be concluded that China needs to give greater attention to long-range strategic planning, to the management of research and development activities, and to methods of increasing the return on investment. Factory management, manufacturing techniques, production scheduling, inspection methods, instrumentation, quality control, and improved electronic production methods are all greatly in need of improvement.

Changes in the Bureaucracy

To help in overcoming many of the problems facing the military industrial sector, China has reorganized the bureaucracy that controls military production. Changes in organizational leadership emphasize her determination to establish strong civilian control over the military-industrial complex. Ministerial heads of all the machine-building industries have been replaced since late 1977, and five of the new appointees are civilian replacements for men formerly associated primarily with the People's Liberation Army (PLA). With these changes, all eight of the Ministers of Machine Building are now civilians (see table).

The revised organizational structure consolidates China's military-industrial and scientific functions into a more manageable framework. Administrative control bodies abolished during the mid-1960s have been re-established, under the State Council, with broad authority over the operation and planning of Chinese industrial and scientific activities.

One military industrial element, the National Defence Industry Office (NDIO), seems to have emerged as the principal co-ordinating unit between the State Council and the military machine-building industries. The NDIO operates in concert with the State Planning Commission on matters of production and allocation of funds – a function previously handled by the Ministry of National Defence.

The State Science and Technology Commission (SSTC) has also re-emerged, with seemingly broad powers over the planning, funding, and supervision of all scientific and technical work in China. It has thus taken over from the military some of the functions which had been assumed by the National Defence Science and Technology Committee (NDSTC). The NDSTC probably continues to be responsible for defence-related scientific and technical projects, but direct control over the military research academies and institutes appears to have reverted to individual ministry subordination. In late 1977, for example, the Fourth Ministry of Machine Building (responsible for electronics) was claimed to have 51 research institutes directly affiliated with it.

These reorganizations indicate that the leadership found it necessary to strengthen control over the defence industry to help in minimizing potential military objections to new policies. The defence establishment has long been accustomed to special treatment in the allocation of scarce resources, by virtue of its priority claim on scientists and technicians, precision machinery and instruments, and high-quality imported materials. The present structure provides the Chinese government with a better mechanism for sharing these scarce resources with producers of civilian industrial equipment. In the past, such sharing of resources appears to have been thwarted by a bureaucracy dominated by the PLA, as happened when Lin Biao was in power.

China's aim is to eliminate duplication between civilian and military efforts and, within the defence industry, to concentrate resources on the most important projects. The reorganization enables her to bring military production into line with economic priorities and to permit more efficient use of existing plants and equipment. These developments underscore the current tightness of funds for new investment and the need to maximize output from the country's existing industrial facilities.

Ministries of Machine Building

	Minister	Appointed
1st MMB (Civilian machinery)	Chou Tsuchien	Oct. 1977
2nd MMB (Nuclear)	Liu Wei	March 1978
3rd MMB (Aircraft)	Lu Dong	March 1978
4th MMB (Electronics)	Qian Min	Aug. 1978
5th MMB (Munitions)	Zhang Zhen	March 1978
6th MMB (Shipbuilding)	Chai Shufan	March 1978
7th MMB (Missiles)	Zheng Tianxiang	Feb. 1978
8th MMB (Space)	Joiau Ruoyu	Sept. 1978

Looking to the West

China's bureaucratic reorganization of the military industrial complex has gone hand in hand with a comprehensive search for Western technological assistance. In late 1976 she began a massive effort to survey a broad spectrum of foreign military technologies and manufacturing processes, and from 1976 to mid-1979 several thousand military, technical, and industrial representatives were dispatched from, or travelled to, China to discuss possible Chinese acquisition of Western military equipment and manufacturing know-how. These exchanges increased markedly in late 1977, following Vice Premier Deng Xiaoping's return to power, and reached peak proportions in late 1978. Since early 1979, however, there has been a noticeable decline in the numbers of military equipment delegations travelling to and from China, accompanied by an apparent slow-down in negotiations for a number of major foreign military equipment packages. This appears to have resulted from the economic reassessment and consequent readjustment of China's overall modernization plans carried out in late 1978.

The technical missions travelling to and from China strongly indicate that she is interested in limiting her dependence on any one country for technology and equipment. However, these contacts with virtually all the major developed states also suggest that China is in the process of formulating long-term programmes to investigate the defence philosophies of other countries, for, in addition to industrial and technical contacts, she has received a number of military officer delegations from Japan, Eastern and Western Europe, Africa and the Philippines and sent similar missions of her own to these countries. The visits seem to be part of an overall programme to promote anti-Soviet policies, solicit advice on the kinds of military weapons and technology China needs and foster discussion of military philosophy and doctrine.

Her inquiries for Western technology over the past three years indicate that China's ultimate goal is to establish an industrial base that will support the large-scale development and manufacture of conventional and strategic weapons systems. During the initial stages of planning, Chinese attention focused largely on the acquisition of a variety of foreign weaponry and subsystem technologies, but the Chinese leadership apparently realized that buying technology and licences to manufacture such equipment was meaningless unless an adequate industrial base was first established.

Basic Technology Needs

The ability of the Chinese industrial infrastructure to support programmes for the development and manufacture of modern weapons are uneven. While the country produces most of the materials and basic types of machinery required to support the current weapons production effort, it needs to import a variety of modern industrial technologies to raise the level of its military manufacturing processes.

Special Metals

One serious deficiency in China's military machine-building industry is her inadequate capacity to produce alloy and special steels and certain non-ferrous metals. China has sufficient metallurgical competence to produce small quantities of superalloys, electrical steels and stainless steels, but substantial increases in high-grade steel production will require considerable investment in new capacity. A key weakness that particularly hampers modern aircraft and ballistic missile development is the inability to produce and fabricate quality non-ferrous metals, such as aluminium, magnesium, titanium, cobalt and nickel. The technology currently being used to process these metals is undoubtedly based on 1950s Soviet equipment and methods.

China appears intent on overcoming her basic metallurgical deficiencies by acquiring complete processing facilities from Japan and other foreign suppliers, and negotiations for the purchase of facilities to process aluminium, copper, nickel, titanium, tungsten and zinc are under way. In order to double steel production to a target of 60 million tons by 1985, China had earlier planned to build three large new iron and steel complexes and to modernize seven others, but these plans have since been revised.

Chemicals

Considerable attention is being given to the technological development of the Chinese chemical industry through the acquisition of foreign equipment and manufacturing processes. In fact the chemical industry has largely dominated China's plant import programme since 1972. Petrochemical plants, including synthetic fibres, rubber and plastic processing facilities, are among the manufacturing technologies imported from the West, and these and other types of polymer technology have wide application in developing and producing advanced weaponry.

Machine Tools

China has developed a substantial machine tool industry, consisting of several thousand plants that range in size from backyard shops to factories employing thousands of workers. It can supply the country's low- and medium-grade machine tool needs and offers some good-quality, durable, general-purpose machine tools for export. But China is far less capable of making the precision tools needed to produce weapons and is still in the early stages of development in numerically-controlled machine tools and computer-aided manufacture. While some military industrial facilities have attempted to meet their specialized equipment needs through on-site development, the machinery produced is usually below standard or fails to operate. China is expected to satisfy her precision machinery and equipment needs by direct purchase from Japanese and Western suppliers.

Electronics

Starting from a primitive base in 1949, China has developed a strong and rapidly expanding electronics industry. The industry has held a priority claim on her resources because of its importance to both military development and industrial production: half to three-quarters of its output is procured by the military, with most of the remainder destined for civilian industry. In terms of volume of production, it compares favourably with those of some of the developed countries of Western Europe. However, the level of Chinese technology is still substantially behind world levels, and despite rapid gains in the industry over the years China has had to import strategically important advanced electronics products from non-Communist countries to help keep military and industrial programmes moving. Practically every major sector of the electronics industry lags in design technology, and lack of quality control and sub-standard production of manufactured items are also major problems.

China's interest in acquiring foreign know-how to bolster her electronic industry covers the entire technological spectrum. Turnkey facilities currently under discussion include technologies to produce polycrystalline silicon, integrated circuits, minicomputers, micro-processors, large-scale computers and facilities for producing computer memories, peripherals and computer interface equipment. Negotiations are also in progress for modern telecommunications technology, including high-speed data transmission, optical fibre, microwave, underground cable and satellite communication system technologies. In addition, China has stepped up her search for foreign laser and optical equipment technology and is actively negotiating with suppliers in Japan, the United States and Western Europe.

Intermediate Technologies

Resting on top of the basic technologies base is a broad range of sophisticated activity which must be mastered if a country is to produce advanced weapons systems. Many of these intermediate technologies have been high on the Chinese agenda during the three years since the overthrow of the 'Gang of Four'. China has been willing to consider contractual arrangements with foreign manufacturers of civil aircraft and space systems to help her gain access to and exploit the close association of military and civilian technology that prevails in the developed world. China's interest in foreign aviation technology covers the entire gamut of modern aircraft manufacture. Among the technology transfer mechanisms being considered are turnkey facilities and joint ventures to manufacture entire civilian aircraft. These negotiations will involve licensing arrangements to produce aircraft wings, brakes, bearings, jet engines, turbine blades, and the casting technology needed to produce jet engine housings. Negotiations are also in progress to purchase modern aircraft and test facilities including wind tunnels, engine test cells, and ancillary instrumentation.

By indicating her desire to purchase several foreign communication satellite systems and earth-resource satellite receiving stations, China has gained valuable access to the aerospace industries of Japan, the United States and Western Europe. Hundreds of Chinese scientists and technicians have been dispatched abroad to gain first-hand knowledge of the technology and equipment needed to launch and maintain modern satellite systems, and can thus acquire familiarization with modern propulsion, guidance control and tracking subsystems.

Integration of Civilian and Military Output

A programme to expand the Chinese military industrial base apparently began in the mid-

1960s and continued into the early 1970s. Under the general slogan of 'war preparation' China mounted a wide-ranging campaign to build hundreds – and possibly thousands – of small-, medium-, and large-scale industrial projects throughout her remote interior regions. This effort was apparently of such magnitude as to cause dislocations in the economy. An article prepared in the National Defence Industries Office in early 1977 claimed that the Lin Biao clique 'one-sidedly expanded the plan of construction for national defence industry – as a result, the development of the national economy was impeded'.

The military industrial construction effort apparently created considerable excess capacity to produce what are essentially obsolete weapons. To help put this industrial capacity to better use, China has adopted a new policy which involves converting a sizeable proportion of military manufacturing capacity to non-military production. Under this new 'integration policy', an increasing number of military factories are sending specialists to civilian organs in local areas to familiarize themselves with the market for non-military items. The programme has led to new lines of production in military plants, ranging from cameras to mining equipment; the Xiangtan Tank Plant, for example, has started to produce sewing machines, electric fans, bulldozers and tower cranes, while an ordnance factory in Wuxi has reportedly begun to make equipment for use in ear surgery. China has also claimed that about 80% of the defence industry enterprises in Liaoning Province has begun to use part of its equipment and technical forces to produce daily necessities for local consumption and for export.

In the course of the economic reassessment carried out in late 1978 and early 1979, criticism surfaced over lack of judgment and co-ordination in importing technology and equipment. This, together with the bureaucratic reorganization, the cutback in travelling military delegations and construction activity, and the new emphasis on civilian production at military factories, clearly indicates that China has decided on a slower military modernization programme. The burst of activity in 1976–8 has given way to a more sober assessment of what the country can actually afford and assimilate in its attempt to acquire Western military technology. Nonetheless, there has been no change in the long-term goal of eventually obtaining the basic and intermediate technologies needed to become a major military power.

Comments made in the Chinese press have also suggested that the military modernization effort has been slowed, and the consensus has been that military modernization *per se* should not begin on a large scale at least until the Sixth Five-Year Plan gets under way in 1981. Whether this arrangement will hold remains to be seen. The Sino-Vietnamese war in spring 1979 made the PLA's shortcomings painfully clear. Military planners are also aware that the Soviet threat is a reality, and that prolonged postponement of modernization is a high-risk gamble. But they know, too, that economic plans are not set in concrete; the reassessment of economic modernization goals in early 1979 is a clear reminder that a start on comprehensive military modernization in 1981 is not necessarily assured. These factors guarantee that decisions over the allocation of scarce investment resources will remain contentious and subject to change.

THE MIDDLE EAST

The process of peaceful accommodation with Israel, begun by President Sadat of Egypt with his visit to Jerusalem in November 1977 and followed up by the Camp David Summit and Accords in September 1978, culminated in the signing of the Egypt–Israel Peace Treaty in Washington in March 1979. The subsequent gradual implementation of the Treaty's provisions, especially over Sinai, marked a fundamental shift in the political and strategic balance of the Arab–Israeli conflict. Egypt, reacting to pressure from Arab governments opposed to this accommodation, continued to disengage from those areas of Arab politics affected by the conflict with Israel, and to accelerate the reorientation of her policy towards the West which she had begun as early as 1972. This caused a realignment of Arab states in an attempt to force Egypt back into confrontation with Israel.

Nevertheless, throughout 1979 Egypt remained impervious to these developments in her determination to forge a new policy independent of the other Arab states. Although the Arab League split when most of its members severed their relations with Egypt and withdrew from the League's Cairo headquarters (a rival headquarters was established in Tunis), the Baghdad–Damascus attempt to undermine Egyptian policies did not succeed, even with Saudi support. And developments in Iran, and later in Afghanistan, tended to move the centre of conflict in the region away from its Arab core (which included the conflict with Israel) to the eastern peripheries of the Gulf and south-west Asia.

With the opening of the border between Egypt and Israel in the middle of 1979, followed by an exchange of Ambassadors on 25 February 1980, as had been agreed in the peace treaty signed eleven months earlier, a new start was made in the Middle East. After thirty years of unremitting hostility, Israel was fully recognized as a sovereign nation by her largest and most powerful Arab neighbour. But the thorny problem of the Palestinians, which had figured prominently in the lengthy and sometimes acrimonious negotiations between Israel, Egypt and the United States, continued to trouble the region as a whole. There was no indication that any convergence of views on this key question had been reached in the many meetings since President Sadat's visit to Jerusalem in 1977. This failure threatened to reverse the progress made so far, for unless some solution to the Palestinian question could be achieved the region would remain permanently unstable, and the possibility of further fighting would increase.

ISRAEL AND THE PALESTINIAN ISSUE

Egypt and the United States saw the agreement reached at Camp David on autonomy for the Palestinians as providing the nucleus of a Palestinian homeland; Israel was adamant on a narrower interpretation. Of the territories occupied by Israel in the 1967 war, those which she referred to as Judea and Samaria she considered as being an integral part of historic Israel, and the Begin government insisted that the Jewish people have an inalienable right to this land. Thus, while Egypt and the United States insisted that autonomy would be a transitional phase, during which the Palestinians would increasingly acquire the attributes of statehood, Israel demanded that she must permanently retain sovereignty and remain the sole source of state authority, with the Palestinians only handling their own educational and municipal affairs. The limited Israeli interpretation also excluded East Jerusalem from the area to which autonomy would be granted – a restriction that Egypt, seeing herself as negotiating on behalf of the Arab world, could not possibly accept, especially in the face of a resurgence of Islamic militance in the Middle East.

Recognizing that this gulf could not be easily bridged, Egypt and Israel sought to postpone these sensitive issues to a later stage, preferring to complete their bilateral arrangements first. Israel was convinced that Egypt was in fact seeking a separate peace. She therefore expected that the staged Israeli withdrawal from the Sinai would be so enticing a territorial incentive that Egypt would not want to link progress on the Palestinian issue (which looked unpromising) with the Israeli evacuation of Egyptian territory

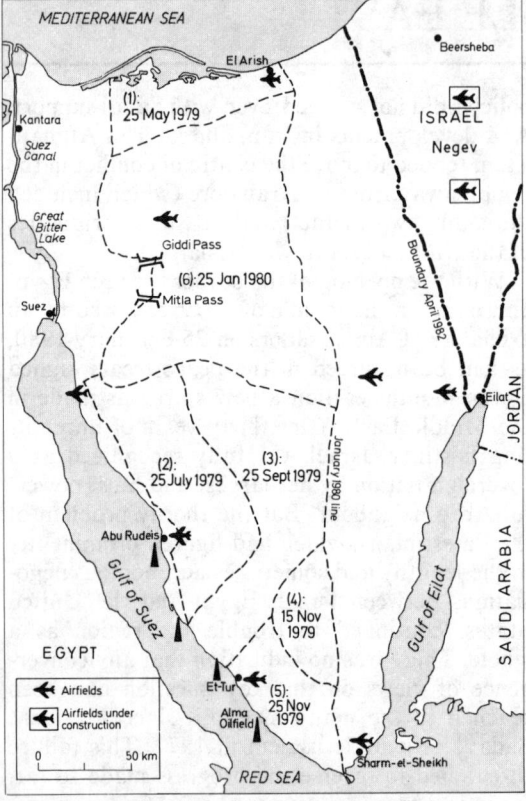

Israeli withdrawals in the Sinai, 1979

Egyptian control a region of strategic importance in which Israel, since she occupied it in 1967, had constructed sophisticated early-warning, surveillance and command-and-control systems and airfields crucial to her defence. In addition, this area held the oil fields which not only had supplied all Israel's energy requirements since 1967, but had also considerably aided her ailing economy. According to the agreement, Egypt would sell 2 million tons of oil to Israel in 1980, at OPEC price levels, with sales in subsequent years being at spot-market prices. Israel thus felt that she had made considerable sacrifices and taken considerable risks in carrying out her part of the Camp David agreements.

President Sadat viewed the matter very differently. For him, the peace treaty he had put his name to had laid the foundations for progress on all other matters outstanding between Israel and the Arabs. He felt that Israel's agreement to withdraw to her pre-1967 southern borders and dismantle all her settlements beyond that line in exchange for full Egyptian recognition should provide a model for the others with whom Israel was in conflict, including the Palestinians. To ensure that Israel would not hinder Egypt's prospects of regaining the Sinai, and to improve his image as a moderate, rational leader (in contrast to his Israeli counterpart), Sadat deliberately concentrated for the time being on issues relating to the two states. But it seemed only a matter of time before he concentrated his efforts on the Palestinian question.

The various meetings held by Egypt, Israel and the United States at ministerial level, and the working groups which assembled on several occasions, made progress only on technical issues relating to the autonomy plan, mainly to maintain the momentum. But without substantial progress Sadat could not hope to win the support of the moderate leaders in the Arab world nor of the Palestinians. However, developments within the Arab world assisted him. The weakening of the Syrian–Iraqi link, the internal political instability which occurred in Syria and, to a certain extent, in Saudi Arabia, and the dwindling impact of the Rejectionist Front all helped him maintain his position internationally and domestically.

Israel: A Weakened Government

While Sadat managed to consolidate his position, the Israeli Prime Minister was losing much

(which was moving ahead). Mr Begin's government was further encouraged by Egypt's continued participation in the prolonged autonomy talks, despite their small promise of progress. Moreover, Egypt's low-key reaction to Israeli military action in the Lebanon against the PLO and Syria (in which, in two encounters, Israel shot down a total of ten Syrian MiG-21 fighters with no losses of her own), and President Sadat's restrained response throughout the year to the establishment of further Israeli settlements in the West Bank, were taken as proof that Egypt was indeed seeking a separate peace.

From the Israeli point of view, the price she was paying for this was considerable. By the end of January 1980 she had completed her six-stage withdrawal to the interim line which stretched from El-Arish on the Mediterranean to Ras Muhammad on the Red Sea, and the third of the Sinai which she retained was to be returned to Egyptian control in April 1982 (see map). Israeli forces were redeployed to new bases in the Negev, well within Israel's 1948 borders, financed and built by the United States at a cost of $2 billion. This Israeli withdrawal returned to of his domestic and international prestige. The fragmentation of the government coalition over internal religious, personal and political issues, and especially its failure to control the constantly rising rate of inflation (estimated at 150% by the end of 1979), made many Israelis disillusioned with the quality of his leadership, on which they had pinned great hopes. Criticism of the government's inability to govern came from all quarters, including Begin's own *Herut* party.

One result was the formation in October of a new political party, *ha-Tehiya* (the revival), which presented a challenge to Begin from the right. Its founding members included some hardliners who had been loyal to Begin ever since being under his command in the underground before the birth of the state of Israel. Its other main component was drawn from members of the ultra-nationalist religious *Gush Emunim* (the Block of the Faithful), who not only rejected the Camp David Accords but were disillusioned with the National Religious Party (NRP), which they blamed for being too soft on the issues of autonomy and of establishing further Israeli settlements in the West Bank.

Begin moved to accommodate this shift to the right by appointing his Minister of Interior, NRP member Yosef Burg, instead of Foreign Minister Moshe Dayan, to lead the Israeli delegation in the talks with Egypt and the US. This action indicated that autonomy was a domestic issue and also had the effect of appeasing the NRP and weakening the position of the Foreign Minister. On two occasions later in the year Dayan visibly distanced himself from the official majority view of the government. During August and September he met Palestinian leaders from the occupied territories, who were known to be strongly identified with the PLO, just as the government was bitterly protesting at meetings that Andrew Young, the US Representative to the United Nations, was having with PLO officials. Then in October, despite previously criticizing the US refusal to implement Carter's pledge to arrange the permanent stationing of the multi-national UN Emergency Force (UNEF) in the Limited Force Zones in the Sinai, Dayan agreed to the proposal that the US Field Mission in the Sinai should carry out this surveillance. The cabinet, which had been previously stirred up on this issue by Dayan himself, was therefore now forced to endorse his new position.

The opposition Labour Party tried wholeheartedly to exploit the rifts in the government

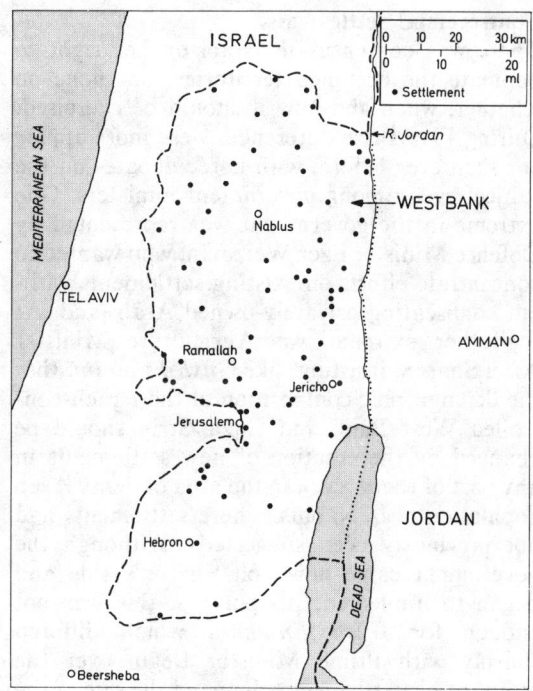

Israeli settlements in the West Bank

majority, but it was itself divided over policies and the question of its own leadership and proved incapable of presenting serious alternatives to the government's policies. The most prominent opposition to these policies came from the expanding Peace Now Movement (PNM), an amalgam of people united in their opposition to the government's approach to the Palestine issue and its policies on settlements but in little else. Although the PNM's popularity was growing, its lack of a positive programme reduced its ability to translate this into real political power.

Despite the government's dwindling popularity and its internal quarrels and splits, its slim majority in the Knesset and the opposition's disunity enabled it to survive. The resignation on 21 October of Foreign Minister Dayan, who had exerted a moderating influence on some of the government's policies, particularly on the Palestinian question, strengthened the hard-liners within the government. They were also aided by the replacement of Simha Ehrlich as Minister of Finance by the Liberal leader Yigal Hurwitz. Hurwitz, who had previously resigned from the cabinet in protest at the Camp David Accords, soon instituted stringent policies aimed at reducing inflation, but at the same time allocated increased sums for enlarging existing settlements and establishing new ones (see map).

Controversial Settlements.

There was consensus in Israel on her right to populate the occupied territories, but none on whether, when and how it should be exercised. During 1979 these differences were more apparent than ever before; with fierce debates on the subject even among government ministers. One extreme in the government was represented by Defence Minister Ezer Weizman, who wanted to concentrate efforts on existing settlements without confiscating privately-owned Arab land. At the other extreme was Agriculture Minister Ariel Sharon, insisting, like *Gush Emunim*, that the demographic composition of the Israeli-controlled West Bank and Gaza Strip should be changed by the creation of new settlements in any part of them (even in the area of dense Arab population near Nablus, where settlements had not previously been suggested). Although the government came down on Sharon's side and began to implement his policies, this was not enough for *Gush Emunim*, which differed sharply with Prime Minister Begin over the tempo of his settlement policy and the size of the required resources. They wanted to do more, faster, and with greater government backing.

The issue was fully joined over Elon Moreh, a *Gush Emunim* settlement established on 10 June near Nablus, on land expropriated from private Arab ownership on the grounds that Israeli security required a settlement at this site. The Arab owners brought a court case challenging this and arguing that Israel had no right to seize their land. On 22 October the Israeli Supreme Court ruled that the settlement was illegal, despite the government's claim of a security justification for its existence, and ordered that it be dismantled and the land returned to its legal Palestinian owners. Haim Bar-Lev, a respected former Chief-of-Staff and now Secretary of the opposition Labour Party, and other former high-ranking officers argued before the Court that Israel's security needs could be better realized by other means than the establishment of a settlement at Elon Moreh. That they were joined in this opinion by the Defence Minister convinced many Israelis, and not only the members of the High Court, that the high-handed methods used to establish Elon Moreh stemmed from political-ideological considerations rather than security reasons.

For the first time since 1967 a serious public debate took place over the real security value of the settlements. Apart from those in the Jordan Valley, still widely viewed as a legitimate and integral part of any Israeli defence system, it became increasingly obvious that a civilian settlement in a remote area, amidst a hostile Arab population and away from the principal traffic arteries, could be more of a security threat than an asset. Rather than stopping an invading army, it could force the Israeli army to rush to its protection, thereby fragmenting the Israeli forces and hindering their freedom of action, as had indeed happened in the Golan Heights during the 1973 war.

Reactions on the West Bank

The Palestinians in the occupied territories, previously reluctant to turn to the Israeli High Court for redress of their wrongs – lest this be construed as acquiescence, if not acceptance, of the sovereignty of Israeli law in the occupied territories – were as surprised as the government by the outcome of the Elon Moreh case. The positive verdict buttressed their feeling that change was now possible.

The publicity given their cause since Camp David had further strengthened their bargaining position. The dialogue between the PLO and Jordan, reopened in late 1978, and Jordan's attacks on the Egyptian-Israeli peace treaty, enabled the West Bank Palestinians to close ranks, conceal their traditional divisions and co-ordinate action both among themselves and with the PLO. They declared the PLO to be their sole and legitimate representatives, which made it a symbol. The Palestinians could not openly support any political arrangement which appeared purposely to exclude the PLO and present the local mayors as an alternative leadership, and this strengthened the PLO's position in the occupied territories. At the same time, however, the Palestinian mayors, as the representatives of West Bank communes, bolstered their own political positions, and their rising popularity caused the PLO to view their activities with ambivalence. The PLO needed the mayors, in order to co-ordinate political action in the occupied territories and to help strengthen its position among the Palestinians over whom it had no direct control, yet the power thus devolved to them might make them less amenable to PLO instructions.

Israel at first looked upon this development with some favour, just as she welcomed the signs that Jordan was trying to assert herself in the East Bank, feeling that both these trends would inhibit the PLO. It soon became clear, however, that the mayors' activities were in fact co-ordinated with, and guided by, the PLO in Beirut. Israel decided she could no longer accept this, and in mid-October outlawed the Preparatory Committee of the Palestine National Front, which had organized at least some of the demonstrations and public meetings which had been held on behalf of the PLO.

The growing solidarity among the Palestinians reached its peak in November, when the Israeli authorities decided to expel the mayor of Nablus, Basam Shakah, a staunch supporter of the PLO. The affair was handled clumsily by Israel (charges that he had assisted PLO operations appeared to be trumped up), and overnight Shakah became a popular hero. Demonstrations of support for him soon turned into protests against autonomy and in favour of the PLO, and all the other mayors in the occupied territories resigned. Under heavy international pressure, most seriously from Egypt and the US, Israel was forced to release Shakah from custody, and in early December she withdrew her order to exile him. The Palestinians greeted this as a considerable political victory and saw in it evidence of Israel's growing weakness. Thus, through yet another ill-conceived move, the Begin government had contributed to the unity, however temporary, of the Palestinian population as well as helping the cause of the PLO.

A Shift in US Policy

The Carter Administration, from its early days, had been moving gradually towards a new definition of the relationship with Israel, under which the United States would continue to supply support for Israel's security but would not automatically support her policies. The Begin government's domestic and foreign policies did much to justify this distinction, and Israel's growing negative image in the United States helped the Carter Administration to redefine its Middle East policy without seeming to be yielding to pressure from the oil-producing Arab states, with whom the US was trying to gain more influence.

The new American emphasis became even more visible during the year. The American pledge to Israel not to negotiate with or recognize the PLO so long as it did not accept UN Resolution 242 and recognize Israel's right to exist (first made by Secretary of State Kissinger in 1976, as part of the agreement on the disengagement of forces on the Sinai) did not prevent the United States from making unofficial contacts with PLO leaders. And American financial support for Israel was less generous in 1979 than previously. Israel, citing world-wide inflation, the burden of having to import the oil she had previously extracted from Sinai and her increased security costs, had requested economic aid of nearly double the 1979 figure of $1,285 billion. But the United States only agreed to increase the 1979 figure by $200 million, despite repeated Israeli appeals, citing the huge sums which Israel was spending to establish settlements which the US administration continued to regard as illegal.

This more reserved US policy did not produce any major changes in Israel's behaviour, however. The Israeli government assumed that, in a Presidential election year, Carter would be forced to modify his policy in order to gain support from Jewish voters. Moreover, the Begin government seemed to interpret as acquiescence the President's relatively restrained reaction (protests but no real pressure) to its uncompromising intention of expanding settlements in the West Bank. This, and a perception of American weakness in response to events in Iran, tended to harden the views of the Israeli government and discourage those who argued for a more flexible Israeli position.

At the year-end it seemed increasingly probable that Israel's rigidity over the Palestinian question would sooner or later lead to open disagreement between the two states. US strategic and economic interests in the Gulf – not least concern for the stability of regimes in the region – argued for more pressure on Israel, rather than less. Overtures to the Arab world and especially the new US–Egyptian link (manifested in early February 1980, when American military aircraft took part in combined exercises in Egypt without prior notification of Israel) clearly implied that Israel was no longer the only strategic asset the US had in the area. The Soviet invasion of Afghanistan reinforced this. Contrary to the Begin government's hopes that this would compel the US to recognize the strategic significance of Israel as her only true friend in the Middle East, the United States turned to Arab states for military partners in the area.

Prospects for Compromise

At the end of the year, the issues had at least emerged even more clearly. Israel's position had further deteriorated. Not only had there been a marked shift in American policy away from very close support for Israel towards a more distant position, but Israel's expectations that Egypt would acquiesce in a purely bilateral peace-treaty without pressing the case for the Palestinian autonomy scheme seemed increasingly unjustified. With the recovery of two-thirds of the Sinai, Egypt would now be more likely to insist on a more ambitious approach to the Palestinian problem than Israel had so far been willing to concede. Rather than defusing the Palestinian question, the Camp David agreement and subsequent developments underlined this as the central issue in any Middle East settlement. The United States and the West, on the other hand, found themselves again faced with a familiar, but sharpened, dilemma. To move Israel towards greater flexibility over the Palestinian issue would be essential for peace in the Middle East, and more than helpful in the strained situation in the Gulf; yet to apply too much pressure to her could well be counter-productive, leading neither to Israeli concessions nor to more pro-Western Arab policies.

EGYPT AND THE ARAB STATES

Whatever the present currents in the region, Egypt was certain to retain a central role in the Arab world. She remained a spiritual and cultural centre of Arab Islam by virtue of the al-Azhar University and its affiliated institutions; there was a vast Egyptian presence throughout the Arab world, made up of an estimated 1 million important administrative, professional and technical cadres; and Egypt continued to train officers from other Arab armed forces and educated nearly 50,000 students from other Arab countries. For these reasons she could not easily be cut off or isolated from the rest of the Arab world, whatever the political differences between regimes.

While there were isolationist trends in Egypt, termed 'Egyptianism' or 'Pharaonism', this could not mask the fact that Egypt was very much an Arab country, and her real cultural, economic, political and strategic interests lay in the Arab world. Nevertheless, in contrast to other Arab countries, Egypt had historically performed an important role of political-cultural synthesis between Africa and the Arab world, Europe and the Arab world, the Mediterranean and the Desert, Islam and Christianity. It was the confidence that derived from this historical experience which led President Sadat in 1977 to his initiative of establishing relations with an alien entity, Israel.

The staged implementation of the Camp David peace treaty provisions had created new conditions, but these were not yet irreversible and would not become so until the process continued beyond the initial stages. Only when Egypt could point to significant gains, not only for herself but also for the Arab world as a whole, would other states in the area be forced to follow her lead. Sadat had no doubt that his country had a leading role to play in bringing peace to the region, but he had also insisted on maintaining a balance in his policies between Egypt's national interests and her wider interests as a member of an Arab cultural entity and political community.

Domestic Pressures in Egypt
While President Sadat's policies were not seriously threatened during the year, and even seemed to be confirmed by events abroad, the domestic situation remained worrying. Egypt's major problem for the foreseeable future would be that of feeding her rising population. It has been estimated that by the end of the century she will have a population of 60-70 million, an increase of 50% or more in twenty years. Of the present population (estimated to be 40 million at the end of 1977), 40% was under fifteen years old, and in 1979 only some 25% (9.5 million) made up the working population. Despite the industrialization programmes of the last twenty-five years and the expansion of industry, 44.7% of this working population was on the land, 35.9% in services and only 19.4% in industry.

A new economic policy, commonly referred to as the Open Door Policy, had been inaugurated in 1974 to tackle the country's parlous economic condition. Its main features were: a shift to a free market economy in the hope of attracting foreign capital investment, determination to strike a better balance between industrial and agricultural development, revitalization of the public sector by promoting keener competition from an enlarged private sector, and a conscious effort to provide the structures to cope with the economic and social problems looming increasingly large on the horizon. By 1979 it was still too early to say whether this policy would create the new economic structures required, but it had established a parallel domestic market for foreign exchange, reduced exchange restrictions, reformed banking laws, and to some extent decentralized economic decision-making. Perhaps more important, it had increased the private sector's participation in the economy. Nonetheless, major obstacles remained.

Although Egypt had abundant cheap labour, most of it was ill-fed and either uneducated or poorly educated and trained. There was therefore a manpower problem. Municipal and other public services, so crucial to the success of the new policy, were in disarray or had collapsed and could only be restored with massive outside assistance, since technicians, craftsmen and artisans, even managers of small-scale businesses, were in desperately short supply. Even more serious was the deplorable condition of the state administration, with its overmanned and wasteful bureaucracy.

It was the social consequences of these economic problems which created an underlying threat to Egypt's foreign policy. It still remained to be seen if Egypt's opening to the West would produce the tangible economic advantages that she expected, but meanwhile rising inflation (currently estimated at 40%) had eroded the living standards of the small 'middle class' which emerged after 1952: the professional classes, the salaried bureaucracy and the officer corps. Whereas the harsh economic conditions of the last thirty years were justified by the requirements of a wartime economy, the growing chasm between the few rich and the rapidly increasing poor could create conditions parallel to those of the period 1950-52. That many of the new rich acquired their wealth through access to influence and power only helped to fuel the resentment of the rest of society, but there was little to indicate that Egypt's leaders were becoming more sensitive to these sharp disparities.

Internal Dissent
Although the response of most Egyptians to President Sadat's 'peace policy' was one of welcome relief, opposition to the policy continued. This was voiced in particular by formerly dormant popular religio-political movements. Notable among these was the resurrected Muslim Brotherhood, which became especially active among students and in the press and provided a platform of steady opposition to the regime and its policy of peace with Israel.

A more immediate concern for the regime was potential disaffection among officers who, affected by inflation, observed civilians enriching themselves in quick-return enterprises under the new economic policy and also viewed with great suspicion the better pay and conditions and the sophisticated weaponry of the police forces. There was already a heavy defence burden on the budget which would remain for some years to come – rising from the current $2.17 billion to perhaps more than double that in the next five years – since the conflict with Libya, and the remaining uncertainties in the Middle East, made an early reduction in defence expenditure unlikely. The 1979 budget showed a deficit of a little over $1.7 billion.

Even with peace, therefore, the short-term prospects both for the economy and the social fabric of the country remained grim. Austerity measures might help the former but would strain the latter. The bread riots in 1977 showed that such measures would prove highly unpopular, especially if they eliminated state subsidies for essential food commodities, and if not accompanied by an extensive programme of reform they would be meaningless. And while oil revenues and the anticipated rise in Suez Canal revenues, once the current development programme was completed, would help Egypt's foreign-exchange position, this would be of no immediate benefit to the millions of poor.

The success of the regime's 'peace policy' and its ability to withstand or counter Arab opposition therefore continued to rest on its ability to cope effectively with the changing domestic scene. In 1979 Egypt's pressing economic problems and their social consequences led to a deterioration of the domestic political situation. As a result, the so-called liberalization policies of 1975–8 (in any case more cosmetic than substantial) were discarded, if not in fact reversed. There was a tightening of internal security and a move towards a greater autocracy in decision-making and policy formulation. But in the light of dynamic domestic developments it was clear that these measures would not in the long run be sufficient.

In the short run, however, fairly massive American financial aid ($1.2 billion in 1979) and military assistance (a $3.5 billion long-term arms sales agreement) obviated for the moment Egypt's earlier dependence on help from the rich

Arab states. While she remained isolated in much of the Arab world, she had gained some time in which to seek, through negotiations with Israel and the United States, for a solution to the root problem of the Middle East: an acceptable answer to the Palestinian question.

Arab Reactions

Other Arab states began the year with a concerted effort to punish and isolate Egypt for her policy towards Israel, but this became increasingly ineffective as the year went on. The cohesion of the anti-Egypt coalition was undermined by the usual rivalries and clashes of interests between Arab states, and in addition by considerations of state security in the light of the turmoil in Iran and the Soviet attack on Afghanistan.

In November 1978, after the full import of the Camp David accords was realized by Arab states opposed to Egypt's peace policy, they met in Baghdad under the sponsorship of three of the leading Rejection Front states: Syria, Iraq and Libya. For each of these three, however, Israel and the Palestinians were not the only issues involved. Libya's relations with Egypt had been deteriorating for several years; Syria, without her Egyptian military ally, felt betrayed and exposed in the conflict against Israel; and Iraq saw in the new arrangement a chance for greater influence in the region. The PLO, too, was anxious to pre-empt any developments on the Israeli-occupied West Bank which would favour any group of resident Palestinians at its expense or extend Egyptian influence over that territory. In fact, the absence of a positive policy in the anti-peace Arab camp made it difficult not to conclude that the fierce opposition to Egypt's policies was connected not only with Israel and the fate of the Palestinians but also with conflicting aspirations to the leadership of the Arab region.

Saudi Arabia, too, felt unable to support Sadat's moves. Although at first reluctant, she joined the Baghdad group of Arab states and by its second meeting in March 1979 had become a leading force behind the effort to unite the Arab world against Egypt. Saudi Arabia had played an increasinlgy important role in inter-Arab politics since as far back as 1967 and, after 1973, was particularly loth to see this diminished; however, it was likely she also felt that joining the Baghdad group would give her an opportunity to influence it in the direction of moderation (indeed, at the November 1978 meeting she was the primary sponsor of the moderate resolutions which stopped short of completely isolating Egypt).

Jordan had already improved relations with Damascus and was taking care not to alienate the West Bank Arabs. She, too, joined the new coalition, not least perhaps because Iraq and Syria had begun to consider a union between their countries, and membership of the group might serve to placate her two powerful neighbours to the north and east.

Soon after the March 1979 meeting, however, the efforts to achieve a Syrian–Iraqi union (see *Strategic Survey 1978*, pp. 59–60) began to weaken. A serious crisis was caused by internal developments in Iraq, the most important of which was the retirement of President Bakr in July, ostensibly for reasons of ill health, and the speedy succession of his deputy and kinsman, Saddam Hussein. It soon transpired, however, that Saddam had engineered his own succession without proper consultation with the regime's *Ba'ath* elite, and especially within the army officer corps. Protests by some officers led to the summary execution of several of them in August, to a wider purge in both the *Ba'ath* party and the military, and to Iraqi accusations of Syrian complicity in an attempted coup.

Fundamental to the breakdown of efforts towards Syrian-Iraqi unity, however, was the old rivalry and distrust between the two countries, which proved too strong to overcome. Ever since independence in 1946, every Syrian regime had been interested in carving out a major role for Syria in the Fertile Crescent area, which includes Jordan and Iraq. Consequently, rivalry between Syria and Iraq for the domination of this region has been a political fact of life which continually jeopardized any schemes of closer co-operation or unity between the two countries, even though both were governed by *Ba'ath* party regimes. The two regimes automatically suspected each other of trying to acquire regional leadership by subverting one another's security. Syria, moreover, unlike Iraq, had faced Israel over the Golan since 1967, and since 1976 had carried the heavy military and financial burden of occupying the Lebanon as the main contributor to the Arab peace-keeping force.

Syrian Domestic Problems

President Hafez al-Asad, in power in Damascus for ten years, was the leading member of the minority Alawite sect, which during the last ten to fifteen years had come to control the two main centres of power in Syria, the military and the ruling *Ba'ath* party. Despite a large measure of cultural uniformity, Syria continued to be characterized by strong religious and ethnic diversity. Almost 82% of the population were Arabic-speaking, but there were significant non-Arab minorities, of which Kurds were the most numerous (8%), followed by Armenians (4%), Turcomans (3%) and Circassians. In religious terms, nearly 68% of the population were Sunni (orthodox) Muslims, who regarded the major religious minorities – Alawites (11%), Druzes (3%) and Ismailis (1.5%) – as heterodox, heretical sects of Islam. Just under 5% were Greek Orthodox, constituting the most important element in a Christian community of 14%.

This sectarian and ethnic diversity had always tended to produce a fragmented political system in Syria. Political interference by European powers in the past strengthened both the function of religious minorities as political units and their communal consciousness. Under the French Mandate (1920-46) sectarian loyalties were actively encouraged in order to counter the rise of Arab nationalism, particularly in the Latakia and Jabal Druze regions, where most of the Alawites and Druzes respectively were concentrated. As part of this policy, France favoured the recruitment of special military detachments from religious and ethnic minorities (Alawites, Druzes, Kurds, Circassians) to form the *Troupes Spéciales du Levant* which she used to suppress local insurrections and rebellions. This situation was deeply resented by the Sunni establishment in Damascus, Aleppo and the other main towns of Syria, which constituted the 'ruling class' of notables and merchants who came to dominate the offices of state and politics after independence in 1946.

Minorities such as the Alawites had for a long time been underprivileged agrarian communities, whose members' only hope of upward mobility was to take up a military career. Over the years, they attained a representation in the armed forces proportionately greater than their numerical strength in the population. When the *Ba'ath* party was formed in the early 1940s, its ideology (secular with an element of socialism) attracted many minorities, including the Alawites, and within thirty years minorities came to dominate both the *Ba'ath* party (in power since 1963) and its military organization which after 1966 came to dominate the civilian wing.

This background explained the manifestations of opposition and discontent in Syria in 1979, and the challenge they presented to the Asad regime. The trouble began with the massacre of sixty cadets in the Aleppo Artillery School in June; the government accused the Muslim Brotherhood (a Sunni religio-political movement, an offshoot of the Muslim Brotherhood in Egypt) of responsibility for the killings. In August two leading Alawite sheikhs were assassinated by terrorists in the Latakia region, and the Muslim Brotherhood leader, Abdal-Sattar Zaim, was assassinated in September, possibly in retaliation. By this time sectarian and intercommunal violence in Latakia was growing serious, and between June and October nearly one hundred assassinations were reported in the Alawite community.

Opposition to Asad's regime was more widespread than these outbreaks of sectarian violence suggested, however. Conservative Sunnis had resented the regime's assistance to the Lebanese Christians during the 1975–6 civil war between Christians, Muslims and Palestinians in Lebanon. The monopoly of state power by Alawites and their allies from the other minorities was also difficult for the Sunni majority to accept, and the older political formations of the Damascene establishment continued to oppose the *Ba'ath* party. There was suspicion of the role of the President's brother, Rifaat al-Asad, whose 'companies of defence' (*saraya as-difa*), some thirty thousand strong, were seen by many as the Alawite regime's praetorian guard. A widespread sense of grievance against what some saw as the corruption which had tainted the regime was compounded by inflation and economic inequality. There were also rivalries among Alawite officers and political aspirants themselves.

These domestic difficulties, the cooling if not already hostile relations with Iraq, and the negotiations between Egypt and Israel, led President Asad to seek ways to check any further deterioration of his position. He tried to broaden the base of his support by replacing some fellow-Alawites who had acquired positions of power and influence, especially in the security services of the state, but since his position depended on Alawite support, there were limits to this approach. Moreover, the *Ba'ath* party, never a grass-roots party, remained dominated by the military, which in turn continued to be dominated by Alawite and other minority officers. To the extent that Asad was forced to turn his attention to these problems, he was diverted from his efforts as part of the anti-Egyptian front.

Jordan and the PLO
Late in the year, in view of the worsening political situation in Syria, deteriorating Syrian-Iraqi relations and the continued negotiations between Egypt and Israel, Jordan reassessed her position regarding the West Bank and the Palestinians, and reconsidered her ties with Syria and Iraq. Despite repeated American pressure, however, she saw no urgency to join the negotiations with Israel. Having declared herself publicly in favour of Palestinian autonomy on the West Bank, Jordan still hoped that in the end she might play a determining role in the West Bank's future. Thus, during 1979 she took a number of steps to shore up her position on the West Bank to counter PLO influence there.

After an initial, brief effort to gain support from the Ayatollah Khomeini and the Iranian revolution, the PLO concentrated on a diplomatic offensive aimed at securing recognition from Western (especially EEC) countries and, if successful, using this to obtain recognition from the United States as well. The Iranian digression bore little fruit. Events in Iran heightened the suspicion and apprehension of the PLO's financial backers, such as Saudi Arabia, Kuwait, the Gulf States and even Iraq, and there was thus little to be gained from an alliance with the revolution in Iran. Subtle and complex historical antipathies between the Shi'a majority in Iran and the Sunni majority in the rest of the Arab world also precluded a close relationship between the PLO and the new regime in Qom/Teheran.

Under Yasser Arafat's control, PLO policy therefore continued to stress diplomatic efforts, as opposed to the military, subversive and terrorist activities favoured by some of his opponents. However, his efforts at the Havana Conference of Non-Aligned Nations in September to condemn and discredit Egypt for her peace negotiations with Israel were frustrated. And, while there was a guarded improvement in relations with King Hussein of Jordan, all the PLO's activity during the year had no appreciable effect on Egyptian policy.

Libya
Libya, too, was forced to reduce her anti-Egyptian activity, at least temporarily. Firstly, latent domestic strains were evident in religious opposition to the Gaddafi regime which was ruthlessly suppressed, with several of its leaders being executed. And secondly, Gaddafi, who had long been attempting to subvert the Sadat regime (allegedly subsidizing Muslim radical groups and even leftist groups in Egypt) found that fears of Egyptian retaliation placed heavy constraints on his actions, now that Egypt no longer had to concentrate her forces in the Sinai.

The Rejection Front was further weakened by a rift that developed between Yasser Arafat and the Libyan leader, who had become disenchanted with the passivity of the PLO's military role and demanded that it should engage in widespread terrorist action against Egypt and Israel. Instead of providing financial help to Arafat's *Fatah* (the mainstream group within the PLO), Libya now restricted her support to the rejectionist and more radical Palestinian groups, in order to weaken *Fatah* and to prevent Arafat making diplomatic overtures to the US and Egypt. The resulting deterioration of relations led to the closing of the PLO offices in Tripoli, and the arrest of Palestinian student members of the *Fatah* by Libyan police.

The Changing Scene
In early 1980 four problems dominated the perception of regional politics by Arab regimes in the Middle East. One was the possible outcome of the Egyptian-Israeli peace process. Another was the long-term impact of events in Iran and populist religious sedition in other states. A third was the apprehension all the Arab regimes felt about the Soviet incursion into Afghanistan. A fourth (or a corollary of the third) was the fear that the United States could not, or would not, protect them from this marching Soviet threat. The emphasis in Arab capitals was upon guarding against domestic sedition and against subversion, if not occupation, from outside.

For some of these states such concerns would be hard to allay, given their worsening economic situations, military weakness and domestic uncertainties. In these circumstances, protection by a foreign power might soon become their first priority, and new relationships between clients and super-power patrons could be in the offing. Oman was one example, seeking more direct Western (and particularly American) military support. A minority sectarian government in Syria could find itself isolated and seek to forge an even closer relationship with its Soviet patron.

Saudi Arabia could be plagued by further disturbances at home, and if the two Yemens were to unite (probably under the domination of Marxist South Yemen), would stand in more urgent need of her American patron's protection.

Power in the states of the region had long rested in the hands of older traditional ruling elites, sectarian and other 'class' minorities: monarchs and tribal sheikhs, a ruling family in South Arabia, the Sunni minority in Iraq, the Alawite minority in Syria, the Christians in Lebanon and soldiers in many countries. The profound demographic changes in the last decade had meanwhile produced a mass of discarded humanity which provided radical, populist religious movements with a vast resource of potential political malcontents for whom Islam was the sole ethic and basis of political identity and social cohesiveness. And events in Iran had shown that such masses could be led, not only against their own political establishments, but also against those they believed to have obstructed or undermined their cultural autonomy – invariably some foreign power.

These developments pointed to a period of renewed super-power rivalry in the Middle East, conducted less by proxy and more by direct involvement. Regional politics thus threatened to become proportionately more difficult, and more dangerous.

AFRICA

SOUTHERN AFRICA

During the first half of 1979 the chances for peaceful, internationally recognized solutions to the Rhodesian and Namibian conflicts appeared to be rapidly slipping away. In Rhodesia the internal election, held in April and the intensification of the war by both sides had hardened their positions and further eroded the trust and willingness to compromise which must be key ingredients of any lasting peace settlement. In addition, a ground swell of Western sympathy for Bishop Muzorewa's new administration threatened to drive a wedge between the West and major black African states. In the Namibian conflict, South Africa's bitter denunciation of alleged Western and UN perfidy led to a suspension of negotiations and a sharp escalation in South Africa's counter-insurgency war and her moves to prepare Namibia for an internal settlement.

But the last few months of the year saw renewed prospects for the peaceful resolution of both conflicts. This was particularly true of the dramatic developments arising from the London talks on Rhodesia. War-weariness on both sides, neither of which could foresee a clear military victory, together with growing internal problems in Rhodesia and some of the 'Front Line' states, were strong inducements for the two sides finally to enter serious negotiations for a settlement. An astute chairman, the British Foreign Secretary, Lord Carrington, took advantage of each side's weaknesses – and of the Front Line states' fears that a deadlock would lead the British government of Margaret Thatcher to recognize Bishop Muzorewa's administration and lift sanctions – to press hard and successfully for major concessions and rapid progress towards a cease-fire. Astonishingly, the cease-fire held, free and fair elections took place, and the war torn country moved towards a peaceful transition to black majority rule.

Recent movement in the Namibian negotiations has been less substantial and far less dramatic. A breakthrough in the long-stalled talks came with a suggestion from the Front Line states for a demilitarized zone on each side of the Namibian border. This proposal, formalized in a UN working paper in September, had received initially favourable responses from all the interested parties by the year-end. However, further steps toward a negotiated international settlement in Namibia would probably be delayed while both sides watched the outcome of the fragile transition period and elections in Rhodesia.

Many uncertainties and potential pitfalls remained in both the Rhodesian and Namibian peace negotiations. Prolonged violence and warfare create their own momentum, and the antagonisms and mutual mistrust accompanying civil war die hard – particularly when resort to arms remains an attractive and available option. In Rhodesia the main danger now seemed to be the possibility that regional and tribal political differences might lead to renewed violence, which in turn might well prompt outside countries to intervene militarily. In Namibia the key question was how the South African leadership would resolve the conflict between the potential benefits of an internationally recognized settlement and its strong determination to control future developments in the territory.

Rhodesia

Prospects for peace and stability in southern Africa improved dramatically in the closing weeks of 1979, when the signing of a peace treaty brought a formal end to seven years of guerrilla war in Rhodesia. Against heavy odds, and with the dreary precedent of more than a dozen failed Rhodesian peace initiatives over the years, the British government brought the combatants together at Lancaster House in early September. The step-by-step negotiations were tough, sometimes acrimonious and often close to collapse, but after 15 weeks Britain and the Rhodesian combatants had hammered out arrangements for a new constitution, a transition to independence and a cease-fire, all covered by a comprehensive peace treaty signed on 21 December.

A switch from warfare to relatively peaceful election campaigning began almost immediately. After the sweeping electoral victory in March 1980 of his ZANU(PF) party, which won 57 seats in the 100-member parliament, Robert Mugabe moved quickly to broaden his support, alleviate white fears and set a tone of moderation for his government. Important issues remained unresolved, however, and the new government would be exceedingly fragile. Nor was there any guarantee that political factions which had fared poorly in the election would continue to accept the results; the temptation to use force to enhance political fortunes or settle old scores remained strong. But even such worrying contingencies could not diminish the very considerable achievement of the Lancaster House Conference in bringing Rhodesia so far towards peace. Astute diplomacy by the chairman, aided by the increasing pressures on the various parties to reach a settlement, brought success where earlier efforts had failed.

Early in 1979 there had been no signs that serious negotiations, let alone an internationally recognized settlement would take place. The war was being intensified by both sides, and casualties were rising rapidly. The guerrillas were far from achieving a military victory, or even challenging the superior Rhodesian government forces in skirmishes, but their isolated attacks had become more frequent and more daring. The internal settlement was faltering badly, and white emigration continued at the very high level of almost 1,000 per month. As a means of winning support – both within and outside Rhodesia – and bringing an end to sanctions, the government of Ian Smith was pinning high hopes on the forthcoming internal elections, as a result of which the country's first black-dominated parliament would come into being.

In spite of guerrilla harrassment, these elections took place with relatively little disruption. Bishop Muzorewa's United African National Congress won 67% of the votes cast, and his new government, with eleven black cabinet ministers, eagerly sought international recognition. Since some 65% of the eligible voters had voted in the election, and foreign observers had seen no signs of fraud or intimidation at the polling booths, the government claimed that the major criterion for Western recognition had been met – the majority of voters had expressed their preferences in a free and fair election. However, critics saw serious flaws in the election process. For one thing, parties opposed to the internal settlement had been banned from political activity since September 1978. Moreover, the government, the army and white employers had launched a massive campaign to get Africans to the polls; since staying away was the only available way of voting 'no' to the internal settlement and its constitution, this campaign undoubtedly produced an artificially high 'yes' vote. More fundamentally, there were those who questioned how far it was really possible to hold completely free and fair elections in the midst of a civil war which had caused more than 200,000 people to flee the country and led to millions in the countryside being uprooted from their normal lives and terrorized by roving bands of guerrillas, armed thugs and government troops conducting punitive raids.

Changing Attitudes
Britain's newly-elected Conservative government showed early signs of inclining towards recognition of Bishop Muzorewa's administration. Largely because of black African sensitivities, Mrs Thatcher hoped to postpone a decision until after the Commonwealth Prime Ministers' conference in August or, preferably, until November, when the renewal of sanctions was due to be voted on in the British parliament. Meanwhile the policy was suspected to be one of 'creeping *de facto* recognition', under which official recognition and the removal of sanctions would be delayed, while efforts would be made to end the war and Britain would build up permanent consultative arrangements with the Salisbury government.

In May Mrs Thatcher set the tone for future British policy. In an interview with *Time* she buried the already moribund Anglo-US plan, saying 'we must go from where we are now: there is an internal settlement'.

In the United States, too, there was growing restiveness over the Carter policy of neutrality towards the Rhodesian combatants. On 14 May the Senate voted by 75–19 to call on the President to end sanctions within ten days of the Muzorewa cabinet being sworn in, and within a month it voted 89–7 to ask the President to lift sanctions by 30 June. This show of support for the new Rhodesian government was, in large part, a reaction against the Carter Administration's policy, which was widely perceived as being sympathetic to the guerrillas.

The internal settlement, and particularly the April elections, were thus seen in the West as having brought about a new situation. There was a democratic constitution; there had been elections in which the majority of voters had taken part; and a government with black cabinet ministers was functioning. To many in the West such a government – despite its imperfections and the fact that effective political power remained in white hands – seemed to offer better chances for peace and progress towards genuine majority rule than the guerrillas attempting to win power through the barrel of the gun.

During the summer the pressures on all those involved, directly or indirectly, in the Rhodesian conflict continued to increase, revealing the vulnerabilities of each of them. President Kaunda failed to win the Salisbury government's agreement to supply the several million tons of grain needed to relieve Zambia's serious and growing food shortages: a situation exacerbated by prolonged bottlenecks on Zambian railways and in the Tanzanian port of Dar-es-Salaam, the major conduit for Zambian trade. Prime Minister Muzorewa suffered major defections from his party and also came under British and American pressure to reduce the role of whites in his government and liberalize the constitution. Even his military commander, General Walls, was convinced that he could not win the war and was urging new elections and a new constitution as the only way to gain international acceptance. The guerrillas and their supporters the 'Front Line' states (Zambia, Tanzania, Angola, Mozambique, and Botswana) feared that Western recognition of Muzorewa and an end to sanctions were imminent. Even the Organization for African Unity (OAU) seemed to be weakening in its support of the guerrilla war: in July it called for all-party talks on Rhodesia, and failed to give the guerrillas the ringing endorsement they had expected. Britain, too, was subject to growing pressure. A number of African states tried to persuade her of the serious consequences that would flow from recognition of the Salisbury regime, and in late July Nigeria took over British Petroleum's 20% interest in BP-Shell Nigeria – a move which the Nigerian foreign minister acknowledged to be aimed at influencing Britain's policy on Rhodesia.

At the Commonwealth Conference in Lusaka in early August Mrs Thatcher disclosed an important shift in Britain's Rhodesia policy. She called for an all-parties conference in September (at which delegates must have full negotiating powers) to agree on constitutional changes; and to secure general acceptance by 15 November of a referendum or new election under Commonwealth or UN supervision. Whether this shift towards more neutral ground was caused by the threat of Commonwealth economic actions against Britain or by assessment of the risks involved in unilateral recognition of the Muzorewa government, it came as a shock to the right wing of the British Conservative Party and to the Salisbury leadership. The new policy differed from that of Britain's previous government only in that failure of an all-parties conference would almost certainly lead to a settlement with Salisbury alone. This difference, however, was to play an important role in the Lancaster House Conference, making the political alliance of the two guerrilla movements, the Patriotic Front (PF), and its backers acutely aware of the likely consequences of a deadlock or PF walk-out.

The Botha administration in South Africa, which had been the Muzorewa government's major outside backer, was also distressed at the shift in British policy. South Africa had provided extensive financial and logistical support for the internal election in April, and had procured major consignments of weapons for Rhodesia's counter-insurgency effort. On 30 November Mr Botha acknowledged that South African troops – said by other sources to number one or two battalions – had for some time been defending vital transport links *inside* Rhodesia, and on several occasions during the summer and autumn there were warnings that South Africa would intervene militarily if there were chaos in Rhodesia or if the Muzorewa government were overthrown by force.

The Lancaster House Conference opened on 10 September. Although the combatants probably expected talks to fail, each side was determined that the blame for that failure would rest on the other; hence neither the Muzorewa team nor the PF delegation of Mr Nkomo and Mr Mugabe was prepared to walk out. Indeed, the PF leaders were under strong pressure from Presidents Nyerere of Tanzania and Kaunda of Zambia to remain at the conference table, since the war-weary Front Line states were heavily committed to a successful conclusion of the London negotiations (which had also received formal endorsement from the OAU).

The pattern which Lord Carrington initially imposed on the talks was applied throughout their fifteen difficult weeks. Britain would submit a proposal and ask for a prompt response from the two delegations. After their objections had been heard, the counter-proposals offered and discussed, Britain would prepare a compromise proposal and pressure both delegations into quick acceptance with few, if any, further changes. When the PF were too long in responding, British officials threatened to go ahead with the 'second-class solution' (i.e., a settlement with Salisbury alone); and when the Salisbury delegation seemed truculent, it was reminded that British sanctions would not automatically lapse in November but would remain in force until the implementing legislation had been removed by executive order. The chairman's tactics proved to be effective, in part because the opposing delegations could justify to their followers substantial compromises on the ground that this was the best deal they were able to squeeze out of Lord Carrington.

The Constitution Issue
At the start of the talks Lord Carrington pushed first for agreement on a new constitution, since that appeared to be the least contentious issue. Bishop Muzorewa tried to limit the discussion to changes in the existing constitution. He was outmanoeuvred, however, by the PF, which succeeded in getting general agreement that the new constitution would be only the first item on an agenda covering transitional arrangements, security forces, a cease-fire and new elections, and that agreement on any single item would not be valid until the entire agenda package had been agreed. On 12 September Britain submitted her constitutional proposal. This removed the mechanism in the existing constitution which enabled whites to block constitutional change by providing that, although twenty parliamentary seats were reserved for whites, it would take 30 votes to block legislation or to amend the constitution. The proposed constitution also provided for a head of state, with power to appoint a prime minister and to make senior appointments in the public service and armed forces, and included a justiciable bill of rights. Other major provisions were intended to protect the standards of the civil service and the pension rights of public employees.

After receiving criticisms and initial (and widely divergent) counter-proposals from both parties, Britain tabled a 'final' draft constitution on 3 October. Meanwhile Muzorewa had successfully beaten back an effort by former prime minister Ian Smith, a member of his delegation, to persuade the delegation to reject the constitution unless the entrenched white blocking mechanism was restored. On 5 October, therefore, Muzorewa accepted the British proposal. But the PF rejected it, thus throwing the conference into its first serious deadlock. The PF objected to guaranteed pensions for whites, but the real sticking-point was the required compensation to white farmers for land which the new government might take from them.

The stalemate lasted another two weeks, towards the end of which Lord Carrington announced that the conference would go on without the PF, which could resume its place only if it accepted the constitution. The Front Line presidents, fearing that the PF would be permanently excluded from the conference, encouraged President Nyerere to go to London to try to break the deadlock. On 18 October it was announced that he had found an acceptable compromise: in order to avoid the new Zimbabwe government-to-be having to pay large sums (estimated at $2 billion) to compensate white farmers for expropriated land, Britain agreed to propose a multi-national fund, to which the US, the European Community, the World Bank and others would be asked to contribute. This solution, flimsy and imprecise though it seems, was sufficient to win PF acceptance of the constitution. Five weeks had now passed since the initial British proposal had been tabled, and the three major contentious items on the agenda were yet to come.

The Transition.
On 19 October Britain submitted a relatively simple plan for a two-month transition period before new elections. Executive power would be vested in a British governor, who would have full control over the armed forces and police; the existing police force would be responsible for law and order; and no attempt would be made to integrate PF forces with those of the government.

Muzorewa showed strong reluctance to relinquish power – and thereby lose the important advantage of holding office right up to the new elections – but, after holding out for a week, accepted the proposal. The PF vetoed it. The guerrillas wanted to share power with the governor during the transition, and they also argued that two months was far too short a time for them to get their people back inside the country and prepare for the elections. They also strongly opposed the notion of the Rhodesian police having the sole responsibility for law and order during this period.

The ensuing three-week deadlock was broken only after urgent intercession by President Kaunda. While he failed to move Lord Carrington away from his basic proposal, Britain did accept Kaunda's suggestion that she should arrange to feed and house the guerrilla forces during the transition, and this proved decisive in winning over the PF. She also agreed that the PF forces would have equal status with those of the government.

The final terms of the transition, accepted by the PF on 15 November, provided for:
- the Muzorewa government to step down, and a British governor to take authority during a two-month transition;
- this transition to begin only after an effective cease-fire had been established;
- order to be maintained by the Rhodesian police, under the supervision of a special group of British police;
- the cease-fire to be supervised by a commission of military men from all the parties involved;
- the elections to be supervised by a council, similarly drawn from all parties, under a British chairman;
- Patriotic Front forces to be fed and housed during the transition;
- Britain, assisted by other countries, to help resettle Rhodesian refugees returning from adjacent states.

Four weeks had gone by since the initial British proposal, during which there had been a rapid influx of guerrillas into Rhodesia, particularly along the Mozambique border, where an estimated 12,000 guerrillas of Mr Mugabe's Zimbabwe African National Union (ZANU) had crossed over.

The Cease-fire

As Britain and the two Rhodesian sides began discussing the problems associated with a cease-fire, Rhodesian forces launched a devastating attack inside Zambia, where a number of major bridges were destroyed in an effort to stem the infiltration into Rhodesia of guerrillas from Mr Nkomo's Zimbabwe African People's Union (ZAPU). Zambia responded with full mobilization and accusations of British complicity.

These developments prompted Lord Carrington to table a cease-fire plan on 22 November and call for responses in four days. This scheme called for a brief (7–10 day) cease-fire, a monitoring force of several hundred Commonwealth troops, and 14 assembly points for the guerrillas inside Rhodesia. Muzorewa accepted on the 26 November, but the PF had serious reservations. It favoured a monitoring force of thousands, with a greater proportion of troops from non-white Commonwealth states, and a longer cease-fire period. It also demanded the right to assemble throughout Rhodesia, and not at the designated assembly points, and it was particularly concerned about the continued presence of South African troops inside Rhodesia.

Britain went a considerable way to meet these objections. She agreed to a monitoring force of at least 1,200 – including contingents from Britain, Australia, New Zealand, Fiji, Kenya and an unnamed Asian country – and to its remaining until a new government had been elected and independence granted. Britain was also ready to order the Salisbury forces to disengage and return to their bases during the cease-fire, but was not prepared to allow the guerrillas to gather all over the country at places of their own choosing.

There the talks stuck, despite growing Front Line pressure on the PF leadership and British threats to move towards elections without the Front. The PF was nudged into a preliminary agreement on 6 December, but still withheld its final signature. On 12 December Britain increased the pressure on the PF by sending her Governor-designate, Lord Soames, to Salisbury and announcing an end to sanctions. On 17 December Nkomo and Mugabe signed the cease-fire, after Britain had made some final concessions: increasing guerrilla assembly points to an initial 16, the last to be located in the heartland of Rhodesia, and announcing that any guerrillas not reaching an assembly point within the two-week cease-fire deadline would not automatically be considered unlawful.

The Uneasy Peace

Four days later, on 21 December, all parties signed the final accord in London. On the same day the UN Security Council lifted sanctions, and Lord Soames removed Rhodesia's embargo on grain shipments to hard-pressed Zambia. The cease-fire took effect on 28 December, and a two-month election campaign began on 4 January 1980, with elections taking place on 27–29 February for the 80 black-elected MPs, and on 14 February for the 20 to be chosen by whites.

By early January the cease-fire took hold, despite a number of subsequent incidents. Almost 20,000 guerrillas had reported to the various assembly areas, where some of them quickly set up defence perimeters under the eyes of the monitoring force. The former guerrilla leaders were already launching their electoral campaigns. Mugabe announced that ZANU would campaign separately from the ZAPU wing of the PF. In a dramatic reversal, Rhodesia seemed to have moved from war to peace.

The elections were suprisingly peaceable: no shooting at the polling places, no stolen ballot boxes, no riots. And the process was judged to have been reasonably free and fair by virtually every outside observer. Even more surprising was the clear result. Contrary to the almost universal prediction that no party would win a majority of the 80 seats elected by black voters, let alone an overall parliamentary majority, Robert Mugabe's ZANU (PF) won 57 seats, which gave him a comfortable margin in the 100-seat assembly. This spared Lord Soames having to choose a Prime Minister, from among several roughly equal claimants, to head a coalition of black parties. It may also have prevented recourse to arms by a leader who felt slighted in the jockeying for coalition leadership.

Mugabe's parliamentary majority could perhaps bring Rhodesia, henceforth to be called Zimbabwe, a more stable government than it would have had with an uneasy and shifting coalition of small parties. But this would be so only if Mugabe were able to win and retain the support of Nkomo's and Smith's parties, either of which could bring civil war to the country if it perceived its interests to be conclusively threatened or damaged. His initial moves were conciliatory and initially reassuring to his former opponents. He laid down broad guidelines for a policy of national unity, stressing moderation and gradual reform, though making clear that fundamental change in the society was the ultimate goal. A coup still could not be ruled out, of course – particularly during the first year after the election, when delicate adjustments and fragile accommodations would have to be made. Various armed groups – whites, ZAPU guerrillas still in Zambia, and former Rhodesian irregulars – could probably be organized quickly. But the whites and Mr Nkomo were likely to wait and see what the new leadership did, and what opportunities it offered, before considering any drastic moves. In any event they would be unlikely to launch a coup without a guarantee of South African support.

For her part, South Africa had threatened to intervene militarily only if there were 'chaos' inside Zimbabwe leading to an unchecked flow of black refugees into South Africa, or if the Zimbabwe government allowed guerrillas to use its country as a base from which to attack South Africa.

Within Zimbabwe the apparent acceptance of the negotiating process begun at Lancaster House, and the broad willingness of all the parties involved to accept its results, had given that process a momentum which would be difficult to stop or reverse. While the period immediately ahead would be a perilous one for the new government, its chances of survival looked good, at least in the short term.

Over the longer run the Mugabe administration faced another set of problems. Black expectations – for land, jobs, housing, education – were high. With black farming in disarray and black unemployment at 50%, urgent measures would be needed. Some 60,000 or more jobs would need to be created each year just to keep pace with new entrants to the labour market. Yet if Mugabe should feel forced to adopt radical reforms – for example, in such areas as job preferences, income redistribution, or property expropriation – he would discourage much-needed foreign investment as well as alienating Zimbabwe's whites, causing many to emigrate and perhaps prompting some to consider a coup.

Another future problem arose from the merger of the Rhodesian security forces with the ex-guerrillas of ZANU and ZAPU. This would almost certainly create a force too large for Zimbabwe's security needs, however loosely defined. Yet the government might find it politically difficult to make deep cuts in the armed forces – particularly if civilian jobs continued to be scarce.

If all went reasonably well, the Zimbabwe settlement would make southern Africa a less unstable region. Relations between the West and black Africa (particularly Angola, Mozambique, and the new Zimbabwe leadership) would be strengthened by the success of their efforts for a settlement. Peace in Zimbabwe would mean fewer opportunities for the USSR to stir up anti-Western sentiment or to embarrass the West in southern Africa. Moreover, in time Zimbabwe, with her impressive economic potential, could easily become a new power centre which could help poorer states in the area to reduce their heavy dependance on South Africa. In South Africa itself the ZANU victory – which came as a shock to the Botha government — would encourage black resistance, and Mr Botha would have to abandon the notion of a constellation of conservative southern African states with South

Africa at its centre. It seemed doubtful that negotiations over Namibia would be vitally affected, although a moderate and non-interventionist Zimbabwe might possibly somewhat lessen South African antipathy to the idea of SWAPO rule in Namibia. The Front Line states, with the successful outcome of Rhodesian negotiations behind them, would probably be more inclined to join the West in seeking a peaceful transition in Namibia, and ultimately perhaps in South Africa.

If the peace held and the people of independent Zimbabwe laid aside their weapons and took up the task of reconstruction, the future held considerable promise. The country's soil and climate made it a potential exporter of agricultural produce, and this, together with its extensive industry and infrastructure and its relatively high proportion of educated and skilled blacks, held out favourable long-term economic prospects. The biggest and most important question of course, would be what effect the war had had on the people of Rhodesia, and on their capacity for forgiveness and co-operation in the task of building Zimbabwe.

Namibia

South Africa and five Western powers (the US, Britain, France, West Germany and Canada) had been negotiating intermittently on the future of Namibia (South West Africa) since April 1977. During this period South Africa had conducted a two-pronged policy of negotiating for an internationally-sponsored settlement while at the same time keeping the option of an internal settlement very much alive.

This policy reflected South Africa's two conflicting sets of interests in the territory. Faced with growing Namibian insurgency and the increasing threat of international sanctions if she continued to defy the UN's demand for free elections and total independence for Namibia, she had a strong incentive to reach an internationally approved settlement. Yet she also had vital political, strategic and economic interests in the territory which she felt bound to protect. In strategic terms she saw Namibia as an important buffer against outside attack against the Republic itself, and therefore had a prime interest in ensuring that the government of an independent Namibia would be friendly. She was also most concerned over internal political stability in the territory, since racial or tribal unrest might well spill over into South Africa. In addition, Namibia's large deposits of uranium, diamonds, phosphates and other minerals made a substantial contribution to South Africa's economy.

The Pretoria leadership clearly did not believe that these interests would be protected in an independent Namibia dominated by the South West African People's Organization (SWAPO), which had been waging a low-key but growing guerrilla war against South Africa for thirteen years. Yet it feared that SWAPO, as the only national liberation movement in the territory, might win any popular election held in the near future – particularly if it were to be conducted under the auspices of the UN, which already recognized SWAPO as the legitimate representative of the Namibian people. South Africa had therefore shown little faith that the outcome of Western-sponsored talks would be congenial to her interests.

In 1978, however, talks had moved further than at any time in the past, and at last a settlement seemed to be in sight (see *Strategic Survey 1978*, pp. 85–9). A UN settlement plan had been accepted by South Africa, subject to certain 'clarifications', in April, and by SWAPO – also subject to specific conditions – in July. But movement came to a halt in the late summer of 1978, when South Africa balked at, and finally rejected, the details of the plan's provisions concerning the UN's role in Namibia. In December she went ahead with internal elections to a constituent assembly in the territory, though she took care to declare that she would continue to seek an internationally recognized settlement. Negotiations between Pretoria and the UN resumed in late December and continued into early 1979.

Going It Alone

But prospects for a negotiated settlement suffered a major setback in February 1979, when South African Prime Minister Botha issued a stinging and detailed condemnation of UN Secretary-General Waldheim and the 'Western five', alleging duplicity in the negotiations. Time and again, he charged, South Africa had agreed to certain conditions, only to find later that they had been changed without consultation. The latest alleged breach of faith concerned the important issue of SWAPO bases during the transition period which was to precede UN-supervised elections. The plan to which South Africa had agreed, he claimed, clearly stipulated that UN forces would monitor SWAPO bases in the sanctuary states (i.e., Angola and Zambia). But South Africa had subsequently become aware of 'scheming behind the scenes'. The Western five had allegedly handed Waldheim a document, without South Africa's knowledge, aimed at 'clarifying' certain parts of the settlement. This, Botha claimed, showed that the five were now supporting the 'astonishing concept' that SWAPO personnel inside Namibia at the time of the cease-fire should be established in bases there. Further, the document purportedly stated that the military component of the United Nations Transition Assistance Group (UNTAG) would not be required to monitor the restriction of SWAPO to bases outside Namibia. Moreover, Botha accused Waldheim of assuring the Front Line states that SWAPO bases in their territories would not be monitored.

Therefore, when Waldheim's final report was circulated on 26 February, South Africa saw it as a 'drastic departure from the settlement plan', objecting in particular to Paragraph 11, which she saw as giving SWAPO the right to obtain bases in Namibia which they had never previously had, and to Paragraph 12, which she felt gave no assurance of effective monitoring of SWAPO bases in neighbouring states. South Africa therefore rejected the UN plan as presented, and these two paragraphs subsequently remained the major obstacles to a settlement.

This angry rejection of Dr Waldheim's report of 26 February put the talks on ice for five months. Meanwhile, South Africa declared her intention of going ahead with an independent initiative to achieve peace and order in the southern part of Africa. In a major speech on 7 March her foreign minister said that South Africa would work at solving her own regional problems with local leaders, black, white and coloured, and would establish a 'sub-continental solidarity' which could become the basis for regional co-operation in all major spheres of activity. He also said the government would consider forming a constellation of seven to ten African states south of the Cunene/Zambezi line, and in a subsequent speech suggested the possibility of establishing 'international secretariats' to regulate the affairs of the southern African states.

The fact that the foreign minister's speech came so soon after Prime Minister Botha's denunciation of the West over Namibia, and the unreality of some of the notions it contained (independent African states joining a constellation dominated by South Africa), suggested that it was more an angry gesture of defiance than a carefully considered policy change. Nonetheless, there were indications that behind the rhetoric lay a decision to tighten the *laager*. But the *laager* was to be enlarged to include Rhodesia and Namibia. Prime Minister Botha confirmed that his government considered Rhodesia to be part of South Africa's regional defence responsibilities. Heavy South African support of the Rhodesian internal elections in April 1979, and the later re-entry of South African troops into Rhodesia, were concrete manifestations of this new policy.

In Namibia, South Africa's go-it-alone policy was reflected in several initiatives, and most obviously in the intensification of counter-insurgency activities. In early March a joint air and land operation destroyed more than a dozen SWAPO camps 20–30 kilometres inside Angola and Zambia, though it caused few SWAPO casualties. And two months later some 8,000 reservists were called up for another operation, designed to wipe out roving SWAPO units, totalling a few hundred men, which had successfully infiltrated northern areas of the territory. The number of South African troops in Namibia rose to an estimated 30,000 in 1979, from 20,000 a year earlier, and Defence Department land purchases in the Caprivi area suggested that South Africa did not plan an early withdrawal from the territory.

A second independent initiative was devoted to building and strengthening Namibia's internal political structure and restoring unity to the divided white community. In May 1979 the Constituent Assembly, elected in December 1978, successfully petitioned Pretoria to declare it a National Assembly with broad powers of taxation and budgetary control. It was allowed to constitute itself for only one year at a time, however, and executive authority would continue to rest with the Administrator-General appointed by Pretoria. This was a major move to strengthen both self-government and the multiracial centre parties, but it increased dissension in Namibia's white community too, and particularly angered the Afrikaner right-wing party, AKTUR. This party had long dominated the old – and now suddenly emasculated – South West African Legislative Assembly. Smarting over its loss of influence and concerned that the multiracial National Assembly would start to remove legal segregation in the territory, AKTUR petitioned the courts to nullify the act creating the National Assembly. Prime Minister Botha blocked this move, but the turmoil in the white community, involving growing incidents of right-wing violence, convinced him that caution was needed in moving to end racial discrimination in the troubled territory.

South Africa also cracked down hard on the (legal) internal SWAPO political party. Leaders were jailed, government officials in both Pretoria and Windhoek threatened to ban the party, and its executive committee dissolved itself in the face of continuing government harrassment. The government's apparent objective was so to weaken the party that it could be allowed to enter any future election without any risk of its winning.

Having strengthened the multi-racial centre parties and crippled the left-wing SWAPO party, the Botha administration now turned its attention to the restive AKTUR. On 1 August, in a surprise move, it recalled Administrator-General Steyn (who had alienated the Right by issuing executive orders nullifying discriminatory laws) and replacing him with Prof. Gerrit Viljoen, a university rector and chairman of the *Broederbond*. While his appointment was seen as a sop to the Right, Viljoen would be expected to use his influence in this quarter to keep right-wing whites from disrupting future negotiations with the UN. Meanwhile he revived the notion of a three-tier government (national, regional, and municipal) for the future Namibia: a scheme that would give the whites control over their own communities and the power to avoid local desegregation.

At the year-end it was not clear how far desegregation had proceeded (although it had been announced earlier that segregation of public transport and other amenities was to be terminated during 1979). Also unclear was the relationship between Viljoen and the main party of the centre, the Democratic Turnhalle Alliance (DTA). The DTA had proposed a strong central government for Namibia, in contrast to the loose, three-tier confederation favoured by the Administrator-General. The question was, which of these views would prevail?

The Talks Resume

In mid-August South Africa and the Western five resumed the talks on Namibia. Thanks to suggestions made earlier in the summer by the leaders of the 'Front Line' states, who were anxious to end the deadlock, some promising new elements were offered as a basis for renewed discussions. The late President Neto of Angola proposed a demilitarized zone (DMZ) extending on both sides of the Angola-Namibia border, and official Angolan supervision of SWAPO bases on Angolan territory. He also expressed a willingness to have some sort of UN presence, though not monitors, inside Angola. And at the Commonwealth Conference in Lusaka in August the Front Line states reportedly persuaded SWAPO to drop its claim for bases inside Namibia at the time of a cease-fire, provided South Africa gave up her demand that the United Nations should monitor SWAPO bases in Angola and Zambia. The South African government called the DMZ proposal a 'positive step', though not an adequate substitute for UN monitoring at every existing SWAPO base.

On 21 September Secretary-General Waldheim's office drew up and circulated a working paper, *Monitoring and the Establishment of a Demilitarized Zone*, which put forward a number of proposals. It envisaged SWAPO forces in Angola and Zambia returning to their bases when a cease-fire took effect – there to be restricted under Angolan or Zambian supervision – though any members wishing to return, unarmed, to Namibia would be able to do so. A DMZ extending 50km on either side of the border between Namibia and Angola would be established fourteen days after the cease-fire took effect, and any SWAPO bases within it would be closed and their occupants moved to bases outside it; certain 'selected locations' (i.e., South African permanent military bases) would be allowed to remain with the DMZ, but South African personnel there would be confined to base. UNTAG would operate freely within the DMZ with the co-operation of the local police forces, would monitor them until a week after elections had been held in Namibia, and would take prompt enforcement action if the DMZ were to be violated.

This working paper formed the basis for further discussions during mid-November in Geneva. The Front Line states, SWAPO and the South African government all 'accepted the concept' of the DMZ but, each having some reservations, none went so far as to approve it in principle. SWAPO's leader, Sam Nujoma, refused to agree to disarm his forces inside Namibia, or to ask them to leave the territory at the start of a cease-fire. South Africa, formally replying on 5

EUROPE – THE OPPOSING ALLIANCES

The North Atlantic Treaty Organization (NATO) celebrated its thirtieth anniversary during 1979 with mixed feelings of self-congratulation and concern. There was good reason for the self-congratulation. Despite all the problems that it had faced over those thirty years, the Alliance had served its purpose well by providing security for Western Europe and helping to keep the peace. Yet there were equally good reasons for concern. The overwhelming military superiority which NATO had been able to count on in its earliest years, particularly in nuclear weaponry, had long since disappeared, and the balance between the two alliances in Europe was threatened by the constant improvement in Warsaw Pact weaponry. Althought NATO was able to reach agreement on one aspect of the weapons spectrum – modernizing nuclear forces – and to reaffirm its commitment to increased spending in support of the Long Term Defence Programme, these agreements concealed divergences of view among its members which would doubtless come to the surface again in the future.

On the other side of divided Europe, the Warsaw Pact was shortly also to celebrate an anniversary, its twenty-fifth, in 1980. It, too, would undoubtedly find much reason for self-congratulation but would also have much to question. The economic strain of continuing to modernize and strengthen its forces was at least as real for the Warsaw Pact as it was for NATO. While the political diversity and independence of action represented in NATO was hardly matched on the other side, the discipline and control over the Pact that the Soviet Union would wish to exercise was far from complete. Soviet leaders would surely have doubts as to the ability and willingness of various East European nations to pursue Soviet aims, should armed conflict break out in Europe. Also, though disputes were not conducted in the open, as in the West, there had clearly been disagreements within the Pact over existing mechanisms for co-operation and co-ordination. These disagreements, though muffled by cooling East–West relations after the invasion of Afghanistan, would not disappear.

MODERNIZING THEATRE NUCLEAR FORCES IN NATO

Questions about the adequacy of NATO's military posture in the face of continuing improvements in all areas of Warsaw Pact forces and an increasingly unstable international environment continued to dominate Alliance politics. The culmination of the SALT II negotiations, the subsequent ratification hearings in the US Senate, and the debate over the proposal to modernize NATO's Long Range Theatre Nuclear Forces (LRTNF) focused attention on the continuing credibility of NATO's strategy of flexible response, and particularly of the US strategic guarantee to Europe. Doubts over NATO's current doctrine and capabilities were given added impetus in September by Henry Kissinger's remarks at a Brussels seminar celebrating the Alliance's thirtieth anniversary. In a critical exposé of what he considered the inadequacies of current US strategic doctrine, Dr Kissinger called for the development of a more realistic and credible deterrent strategy.

His comments were largely directed towards supporting the proposal to introduce into Europe American long-range cruise missiles and ballistic missiles – the most dominant issue under consideration in the Alliance. The thorough preparation and intense consultation that preceded the LRTNF modernization decision reflected favourably both on Alliance solidarity and on American diplomacy, but the final decision concealed serious reservations on the part of several smaller countries, caused by the widespread uneasiness in significant sections of their public and parliamentary opinion about the introduction of further nuclear weapons into Europe. In fact the LRTNF debate revived a number of long-standing questions about the role of nuclear weapons in Alliance strategy, the problems of reconciling the often conflicting demands of NATO's defence and detente policies and, particularly, the role of arms control in ensuring Alliance security interests.

While these issues found particular focus in the LRTNF debate, they were equally relevant to conventional defence – especially NATO's commitment to 3% real increases in national defence spending and to the Long Term Defence Programme (LTDP). In 1977 NATO ministers had agreed to the 3% goal, but the record of compliance had been mixed. Some countries – notably the US, Britain, France and the Netherlands – had met it but others fell short. Though the 3% figure was arbitrary and of limited value as an indicator of real defence capabilities, it did have political and symbolic significance. Failure to reach it represented a potential source of tension – particularly in the United States, where Congress was attentive to indications that Europe did not bear its share of the common burden of defence.

NATO's determination to reverse the adverse trends in the military balance between itself and the Warsaw Pact was signalled by the endorsement of the LTDP in 1978, a significant milestone for the Alliance. The LTDP incorporated 123 measures in nine functional areas of conventional defence. In a number of key areas, such as readiness and reinforcement, considerable progress had already been made, due in part to the short-term measures adopted by NATO Defence Ministers in 1977. In the field of readiness, great emphasis was being put on expanding and modernizing anti-armour capabilities, and the West German forces particularly were developing significant capabilities in this area. Attention was also being given to the question of increasing the number of anti-tank war reserve stocks, but, as in other areas of reserve stocks, the difficulty in establishing NATO-wide standards for rates of consumption remained an obstacle. With regard to reinforcement, efforts were made to accelerate the movement of men and material to the forward areas in the critical early phase of a crisis or hostilities. The US was preparing to preposition equipment in the Central Region of Europe for three additional heavy reinforcing divisions to be sent from the US during this phase. The Allies were also studying the use of civilian assets, particularly aircraft, for military purposes, as well as the substantial improvement of host-nation support for incoming reinforcements.

Despite these advances, much of the commitment to the LTDP amounted to promises of intent rather than programmes of action, and its real effectiveness would only be seen when members were called on to implement the measures they had endorsed. In many cases agreement in principle had still to be turned into hard-and-fast requirements, an agreed blueprint produced, realistic costings worked out, and mechanisms devised for integrating the measures into national defence planning systems.

Events in Afghanistan and the general instability in the Gulf area underlined another of NATO's problems, reinforcing the views of those who believe that the main challenge of Soviet military power lay less in Europe than in the uncertain regions of the Third World, particularly the Gulf. However, while Alliance members unanimously condemned Soviet actions in Afghanistan and declared their support for, and readiness to co-operate with, the United States in her problems in Iran, no consensus emerged on formulating an Alliance policy for regional disputes beyond NATO's boundaries. This reluctance by many European members to be too closely identified with the United States in her role as a global super-power, and their desire to avoid a return to confrontation politics, was likely to produce new tensions within the Alliance during the coming year.

Nuclear Modernization

The major event of 1979 was the agreement by NATO Ministers on 12 December to modernize the Alliance's Long Range Theatre Nuclear Forces by deploying in Europe 108 US *Pershing* II medium-range missile launchers and 464 US ground-launched cruise missiles (GLCM), all with single warheads. This was accompanied by an offer to the Soviet Union to establish permanent limitations on theatre nuclear forces through arms-control negotiations. The proposal thus involved both modernization and arms control.

There were two sources of Alliance concern over theatre nuclear forces. The first was the perception that the condition of strategic parity codified by SALT, in conjunction with the continuing Soviet TNF modernization, would emphasize European vulnerabilities at the theatre nuclear level. This concern was expressed most forcefully by Chancellor Schmidt in the 1977 Alastair Buchan Memorial Lecture (reprinted in *Survival*, Jan/Feb 1978, pp. 2–10), where he noted that SALT, by neutralizing the strategic capabilities of the two super-powers, magnified the significance of East-West disparities in tactical nuclear and conventional weapons. The second source was an apprehension that the United States was considering negotiating substantial constraints on cruise missiles in the SALT II negotiations. It was feared that these constraints would effectively prevent cruise missiles being used in the European theatre.

As a result of these concerns, the United States agreed that the theatre nuclear force balance needed special examination, and a High Level Group (HLG) was established under the authority of the Nuclear Planning Group. Its purpose was to examine the role of TNF in NATO strategy, the implications of recent Soviet TNF deployments, the need for TNF modernization, and the technical and political implications of alternative NATO TNF postures.

A number of guidelines were established that provided a basis for the HLG's deliberations. It was determined that the TNF decision should represent only an evolutionary change in NATO's defence posture, and should not entail any increase in the role of nuclear weapons in Allied defence, nor any change in the overall number of nuclear weapons in the European theatre, It was not considered necessary to have a capability to match the Soviet SS-20 mobile medium-range missile but merely to have an offsetting capability to provide a credible response. And lastly it was agreed that, in order to achieve greater credibility in terms of public perception, the system should have as much visibility as possible. The HLG, which began work in the late autumn of 1977, examined the various technological options available and eventually produced the proposal that the US should deploy a total of 572 warheads in five European countries: 108 *Pershing* II launchers (with 108 missiles) and 24 GLCM launchers (with 4 missiles each) in West Germany, 40 GLCM launchers in Britain, 28 GLCM launchers in Italy, and 12 GLCM launchers each in Belgium and the Netherlands.

During the HLG's deliberations, a number of separate but related rationales emerged to justify TNF modernization and generate support for NATO's decision. Militarily it was argued that TNF modernization was needed: to compensate for the consequences of strategic parity of the theatre nuclear balance; to close the gap caused by the substantial modernization of Soviet TNF, particularly deployment of the SS-20 missile and the *Backfire* medium-range bomber; and to replace existing obsolescent and increasingly vulnerable Alliance systems. At the political level, TNF modernization was considered necessary: to reinforce the Alliance strategy of deterrence through flexible response; to demonstrate NATO's ability and willingness to act effectively and cohesively in the face of Soviet force expansion; and to underline the American nuclear commitment to the security of Europe, particularly after the concerns raised by the Carter Administration's handling of the enhanced-radiation warhead (ERW or 'neutron bomb') issue a year earlier (see *Strategic Survey 1978,* pp. 106–7).

Concern over the theatre nuclear balance, while shared in varying degrees by other NATO members, was primarily a German preoccupation. However, although Germany adopted a positive, and at times forceful, attitude towards modernization, she made her participation in it dependent on a number of conditions which reflected her sensitivity about her position both in the Alliance and *vis-à-vis* her Eastern neighbours and were aimed at minimizing any adverse political repercussions. These included the requirement that the Alliance decision be unanimous and that the deployment plan should include at least one continental non-nuclear state besides herself (the so-called 'non-singularity' principle). German officials also stressed that the Federal Republic had no intention of playing any leadership role in questions of nuclear strategy, and that systems based on German soil would remain exclusively under American control.

These criteria focused attention on the attitude of the Netherlands and Belgium to being host countries for TNF, for public anti-nuclear feeling had been widely demonstrated in both these countries during the ERW episode. Public uneasiness about the role of nuclear weapons in NATO was also present in the Scandinavian countries, and in part of the Social Democratic party in Germany. In view of all this, it was acknowledged very early that the Alliance should not embark upon a major nuclear-weapons programme without taking into account arms-control considerations. Public and parliamentary support for TNF modernization would be more likely if a willingness to establish permanent limitations on theatre nuclear systems through arms-control negotiations were demonstrated. Accordingly, a NATO Special Group was established in April 1979 to work in parallel with the HLG and to examine the arms-control implications of the TNF modernization. It concluded that NATO should proceed to a production and deployment decision in December, but should at the same time offer to enter into negotiations with the USSR on theatre nuclear systems. Since the deployment of the NATO TNF systems could not, for technical reasons, occur before 1983, it was implicit that the full implementation of the decision would depend on the success of negotiations, and thus on Soviet willingness to engage in serious mutual restraint. But there was a consensus that the modernization decision should precede these talks, in order to give NATO some bargaining power at the negotiating table.

Doubts and Opposition
While on 12 December it was announced that Ministers had agreed to modernize NATO's LRTNF and that 'all the nations currently participating in the integrated defence structure will participate in the programme', the communiqué did not specify 'the selected countries' in which the missiles were to be stationed. The apparent unanimity of the communiqué concealed the difficulties that several countries had had in endorsing the NATO proposal, and the reservations about participation that the Netherlands and Belgium had been obliged to submit. Of the prospective host countries, Britain fully supported the proposal; as did Italy, despite the opposition of the Italian Communist Party, and Germany, once Chancellor Schmidt had secured the full backing of his party by emphasizing that arms control constituted an essential element of the NATO approach. The Norwegian and Danish governments also supported the decision, although just before the December meeting they had both indicated concern that arms-control considerations were not receiving sufficient attention.

The main centre of opposition to the proposal was Holland, where, as had happened over the ERW issue, widespread public aversion to nuclear weapons had a direct impact on government policy. The opposition Labour Party (the largest single party) was virtually unanimously opposed to the modernization proposal, and a substantial portion of the Christian Democratic Appeal (the major part of the governing coalition) wanted NATO to take no more than a production decision in December, and postpone a deployment decision until arms-control negotiations had been given a chance to produce results. When NATO would not accept this suggestion, the Dutch government agreed with the modernization decision, but submitted a reservation stating that the Netherlands would decide on her full participation in two years' time. In Belgium a similarly weak coalition government inserted a reservation that it would review its position after six months.

While opposition to the NATO proposals was largely founded on a generalized dislike of nuclear weapons, many opponents were also sceptical of the specific military rationale advanced to support the proposal. They rejected the idea that nuclear parity between the superpowers necessarily eroded the US strategic guarantee for Europe, nor did they accept that deployment of the SS-20 gave the Soviet Union any realistic military advantages and options over NATO. While it was accepted that unrestrained Soviet force expansion could not go unchallenged by the West, efforts to restrain that expansion through negotiation should be attempted first, without NATO decisions that could prejudice talks. The opposition had a strong conviction that future stability for the European theatre could be better assured through negotiation than through further escalation in the capability of nuclear weapons, particularly in the form of cruise missiles. It was argued that, given the evident Soviet concern and apprehension over the new American systems, their mere existence would have provided a sufficient base for negotiations, and the modernization decision should therefore have been postponed until arms-control negotiations had been given a chance. As it was, they argued, the decision to introduce cruise missiles to Europe would only prevent any possibility of talks; and it would confer no more than a short-term advantage to the West, since it would cause further unrestrained Soviet force expansion to redress the balance.

The USSR's reaction to the NATO proposal was predictably hostile. She had long insisted that US nuclear systems based in Europe and capable of striking the Soviet Union constituted a fourth arm of the American strategic forces. Soviet apprehension of, and opposition to, the NATO plans to deploy new LRTNF mounted throughout the year, finding their most significant expression in President Brezhnev's speech in East Berlin on 6 October. In a speech directed exclusively to European audiences, and specifically to West Germany, the Soviet leader warned that the introduction of the new NATO systems would lead to a fundamental change in the strategic situation in Europe. The Soviet Union, he said, did not threaten Western Europe, and countries which refused the stationing of the new weapons on their soil would not be targeted by Soviet nuclear forces. He declared that the Soviet Union would be ready to reduce her own nuclear weapons based in Europe, provided NATO did not go ahead with its decision. And, to indicate Soviet willingness to meet Western concerns, he announced an unprecedented unilateral withdrawal of up to 20,000 Soviet soldiers and 1,000 tanks from East German territory.

But the speech came too late and offered too little to prevent NATO's December decision. Its combination of promises and threats, if anything, closed Western ranks. The speech suggested that the Soviet Union would seek to mobilize Western public opinion, even after NATO's decision had been taken, in order to prevent or delay its implementation. But it also indicated, together with statements by the Soviet Defence Minister Ustinov and Foreign Minister Gromyko that the Western move would be met not only with a diplomatic response but also with a military one.

While the Soviet Union was unlikely to rule out negotiations altogether, it was clear that she was not in a hurry to agree on limitations as long as the NATO programme could be undermined by other means. Gromyko had warned earlier that NATO's decision would remove the basis for any negotiation, and this was subsequently confirmed by the official response to an American enquiry in late December: the USSR, it said, would be willing to negotiate only if NATO would publicly renounce its programme. While this did not seem to be the last word on the issue, it did indicate a general hardening of the Soviet position in the light of the uncertainties over ratification of SALT II by the US Senate, the deterioration of US-Soviet relations, and the genuine concern over the military implications of the new programme for Soviet defence.

The Outlook

The future of the NATO programme of both modernizing and negotiating thus remained uncertain at the end of 1979. The modernization programme moved ahead, and the Soviet action in Afghanistan was likely, at least short term, to strengthen the political base for the decision. But in the absence of SALT ratification there was little prospect that the Alliance could move towards the kind of negotiations it clearly preferred: bilateral Soviet-American talks, linked to SALT, which would first establish a common ceiling on longer-range theatre nuclear weapons and then lead to symmetrical reductions. All the signs pointed not to serious negotiation but rather to potential political controversy and a new surge in the East-West arms race. By publicly linking its own programme so closely to the Soviet deployments of the SS-20 missile, NATO had given the USSR a potential lever for the future.

The LRTNF issue was thus not closed by NATO's decision. The December 1979 decision had shown the ability of the Alliance to reach a common position, even if with some difficulty. At the same time, however, it indicated that hard-won decisions could only partially allay political concerns. The European worry over the SS-20 had in reality been a concern over the reliability of the American nuclear commitment to Europe. This concern was almost as old as the Alliance itself, and there was little reason to assume that the December decision had eradicated it.

DEVELOPMENTS IN WARSAW PACT FORCES

The Warsaw Pact, the Soviet Union's multilateral political and military alliance in Eastern Europe, would celebrate the twenty-fifth anniversay of its founding on 14 May 1980. Traditionally the Pact had been seen as Moscow's extended arm in Eastern Europe – both as a forward base for the deployment of Soviet ground forces in Europe and as a uniquely valuable channel through which to entangle the East European states in a web of Soviet discipline and control. As a forward staging area, the Pact had been a clear success. Since the invasion of Czechoslovakia in 1968, the USSR had maintained in Eastern Europe a force of 31 Category I divisions (between three-quarters and full manpower strength with complete equipment): 20 of them formed the elite Group of Soviet Forces in (East) Germany, and there were a further 5 divisions in Czechoslovakia, 4 in Hungary, and 2 in Poland. But Soviet use of the Pact to establish discipline and control had been less successful. Military integration had been limited; the quality of non-Soviet forces, their equipment and the economic effort devoted to them varied markedly between the different countries, and the Soviet armed forces continued to remain in a category of their own. These differences reflected the continuing limits to both military and political uniformity within the Soviet alliance system.

Changing Roles

Initially Soviet policy allocated a deliberately passive role to the East European military forces. This changed in the late 1950s, as a result of

Nikita Khrushchev's emphasis on strategic nuclear forces at the expense of Soviet ground forces. The logical concomitant of this was an enhanced role for indigenous East European armed forces, and the early 1960s saw the first round of decisive improvements in East European military capabilities, as modern Soviet equipment – including T-54 and T-55 tanks, MiG-21 and Su-7 aircraft – were introduced.

Under the then Commander-in-Chief of the Warsaw Pact, Marshal Grechko, multilateral manoeuvres evolved from largely propagandistic exercises in 'fraternal' co-operation into regular, serious and often large-scale combat-training exercises. By the mid-1960s moves were well in hand to standardize military equipment. Nascent arms industries, for example in Poland and East Germany, were wound up, leaving the Soviet Union as exclusive supplier of most weaponry. By this stage, too, some East European units were being trained in the use of nuclear delivery vehicles, although the warheads remained (and still remain) under exclusive Soviet control. By 1965 Poland, East Germany and Czechoslovakia – the strategically important northern tier of states – had emerged as the 'first strategic echelon' in Soviet military strategy in Europe. Thus, both in terms of doctrine and in practice the Soviet Union now seemed inclined to view the East European armed forces as having an active contribution to make to her own ground and air defences.

In aggregate terms, East European countries contribute about 55% of the Warsaw Pact divisions and tactical aircraft in the European theatre, though the Soviet forces stationed in the region contain a considerably heavier concentration of fire-power than the non-Soviet divisions. Nonetheless, the East European countries, with standing armies now totalling well over a million men and para-military and reserve forces estimated at close to 4.5 million, are in a position to add substantially to any Soviet military threat against Western Europe (see table).

The precise nature of the non-Soviet contribution has varied considerably between the different countries, however. The disparity can best be highlighted in terms of financial commitment. The gap between Romania, spending a consistent 1.7% of GNP on defence, and East Germany, spending an above average 5.8%, was a noteworthy example. Measured on a per capita basis the contrast was starker: Romania spent $58 per head of population on defence in 1978, against $253 for East Germany. But these figures concealed important differences in emphasis. East Germany, unlike the other European Allies, seemed to be prepared to commit a substantial proportion of her resources to military R&D. Also, high annual rates of growth in the non-personnel costs of East Germany and Bulgaria (and to a lesser extent Poland, Hungary and Romania) indicated that these countries had made intensive efforts over the past decade to mechanize and modernize their armed forces.

Equipment

Arms procurement had always posed something of a problem for the East European countries, since it was closely tied to several other issues: weapons standardization, Soviet arms sales policy, and the relative elasticity of national defence budgets. Being armed almost exclusively with Soviet or Soviet-designed weapons, Warsaw Pact forces enjoyed many of the economics that standardization brings. Yet this also had the effect of

Non-Soviet Warsaw Pact Forces 1979

	Manpower (000)				Tanks	Combat Aircraft	Est. reserves	Para-military forces	Defence spending (1978)	
	Army	Air	Navy	Total					$ per head	% of GNP
Bulgaria	115.0	25.0	10.0	150.0	1,800	166	240	189.0	66	2.5*
Czecho-slovakia	140.0	54.0	—	194.0	3,400	462	350	132.5	153	3.8
E. Germany	107.0	36.0	16.0	159.0	2,500	335	305	571.5	253	5.8
Hungary	80.0	24.0	—	104.0	1,250	150	143	75.0	76	2.4
Poland	210.0	85.0	22.5	317.5	3,400	679	605	445.0	95	3.0
Romania	140.0	30.0	10.5	180.5	1,500	328	502	737.0	58	1.7
Total	792.0	254.0	59.0	1,105.0	24,350	2,120	2,145	2,150.0		

* 1977 figure

SOURCE: *The Military Balance 1979-1980* (London: IISS, 1979).

tying them to Soviet delivery schedules. For example, after June 1967 the resupply of Egypt and other Arab states took priority over the delivery of equipment to Eastern Europe. And particularly since 1973, when the Soviet Union switched her arms deliveries to the Middle East from an aid to a trade basis, new and sophisticated equipment had turned up in that part of the world – for example, T-72 tanks in Syria and Iraq, and lately even MiG-25 aircraft in Algeria – well before its first appearance in Eastern Europe. Recent Soviet activity in non-European areas could only add to these problems. Moreover, as sophisticated technology pushed up the procurement price of modern weapons, differences in the ability of Warsaw Pact countries to meet these costs had become accentuated. Not surprisingly, East Germany was the first (and so far only) East European country to have received the new Soviet T-72 tank, together with the most up-to-date armoured combat vehicles and some of the newer Soviet rocket launchers and helicopters – reportedly at prices well above the international level for heavy weapons. All were displayed at the parade in East Berlin marking the thirtieth anniversary of the East German state in October 1979.

The Economic Burden
While the East German forces stood out from the other non-Soviet armies of the Warsaw Pact, both in their sophisticated weaponry and the relative size of the budgetary commitment they represented, the substantial weight of the Pact's defence burden still fell squarely on the Soviet Union. This explained repeated Soviet pressure for a redistribution of that burden and a re-scaling of financial contributions. Officially this began with the Soviet call at the November 1978 meeting of the Pact's supreme political organ, the Political Consultative Committee (PCC), for a 5% across-the-board increase in military expenditures by the smaller Pact states. During 1979 all the East European states, with one exception, announced expenditure increases of roughly that order (Romania, in contrast, immediately announced a small reduction in her defence budget).

The economic costs of such increases would be considerable. All the East European economies had been hit hard in the last five years both by the inadequate quantity of oil supplied by the USSR, which had forced them to compete for some of their oil needs in the world market, and by a massive increase in the price of Soviet-supplied crude which was still the main energy source for Eastern Europe (see *Strategic Survey 1978*, pp. 111–12). This had resulted in hefty domestic price increases for basic foodstuffs, commodities and services, inevitably causing a sharp rise in inflation. Increased defence expenditure, by taking a larger share of the national budget, could only exacerbate economic and political tensions throughout the region. In rejecting Soviet pressure to increase defence spending in November 1978 Romanian President Ceausescu publicly articulated a problem much discussed in the other Warsaw Pact capitals: that the security gained through increased defence spending might be eroded by popular resentment over its economic consequences.

Improvements in military capabilities, both quantitative and qualitative, were thus often hard to sustain. Manpower was a case in point. Skilled labour was in short supply throughout Eastern Europe, and in some countries the problem was critical – notably, but not exclusively, in East Germany, with her declining population of working age. It might well prove impossible over the next decade to reconcile existing force levels with the demands of the rest of the economy. Consequently, although the Soviet Union had put increasing emphasis in public statements on the East European contribution to overall Pact defences, for sound 'strategic' reasons the new wave of modernization of the East European Pact forces might be slow to materialize.

Military Integration
In March 1969 an unusually brief (two-hour) session of the PCC in Budapest ratified a series of changes to the military infrastructure of the Warsaw Pact. Coming so soon after the invasion of Czechoslovakia, these reforms were at first assumed to have extended to the military sphere the political doctrine of limited sovereignty in Eastern Europe, with the East European armed forces finally subordinated to Soviet control.

Certainly the decisions clearly pointed to the extension of the formal military structure of the alliance. A Committee of Defence Ministers was established, regularizing previous practice of *ad hoc* ministerial meetings. The Joint Command was reconstituted, with East European Deputy Defence Ministers taking over from their superiors the role of Deputy Warsaw Pact Commanders, so removing the Ministers of Defence from a position of direct subordination to the

Soviet Commander-in-Chief. A Military Council was established – thought to be a consultative body of senior Soviet and East European military officers, though little emerged of its activities beyond terse communiqués, suggesting that it evaluated questions related to the 'current activities of the Joint Armed Forces'. A Permanent Joint Staff was set up in Moscow with East European Deputy Chiefs of Staff; a new committee was established to co-ordinate weapons development; and a new statute was adopted for the Joint Armed Forces (an organization which had long existed on paper but had previously played no identifiable role).

Contrary to initial impressions, however, the new military structure seemed to have reinforced the principle of national control over the East European armed forces in peacetime. Although overall command had been retained by Soviet officers, the East European military and political establishments had apparently achieved greater participation in the channels of command and a formal, institutionalized commitment by the Soviet Union to increased consultation.

The key to the military significance of the 1969 reforms must lie primarily with the Joint Armed Forces (JAF). Immediately after the reforms, both Soviet and East European sources went to considerable lengths to reiterate firmly that the East European armed forces were to remain under national control. There were, however, suggestions that, while particular East European units might have been earmarked for potential assignment to the JAF, they so far remained physically integrated in their own national defence establishments. The two exceptions were East Germany, whose entire armed forces were directly subordinated to the JAF and came under effective Soviet command, and Romania, who had consistently rejected on principle any suggestion that national contingents might be assigned to 'joint' Warsaw Pact command, even on paper.

It might be expected that in practice other states, such as Poland and Hungary, would balk at transferring national contingents to direct Warsaw Pact (i.e. Soviet) command. Soviet emphasis on the principle of national control, therefore, may well have amounted to little more than making a virtue out of necessity. That the USSR at least was still unhappy with existing arrangements was suggested by reports that at the November 1978 PCC meeting the Commander-in-Chief of Pact forces, Marshal Kulikov, called for the setting up of special military units from the Warsaw Pact states to be subordinated to a newly created supreme organ with greater 'supranational' powers than the present Joint Command. Romania was thought to have enjoyed at least tacit support from some of her allies in rejecting this particular proposal.

The actual development of military co-operation, however, showed that, while the USSR demanded that other members integrate themselves more closely into the Pact, she was not prepared to do so herself. For example, the entire air-defence system of the Pact was under the control of the commander of the Soviet Air Defence Force *(PVO-Strany)*. In addition, most if not all offensive air missions were flown by Soviet pilots, and training for the East European air forces was quite strictly curtailed. Judging by the example afforded by the Soviet-led invasion of Czechoslovakia, the Warsaw Pact was in any case not designed to be a wartime command organization. Despite the organizational reforms of the post-invasion period, the retention of Soviet officers in all key command posts suggested that, in the event of a conflict in Europe, military command would automatically be retransferred to the Soviet High Command. Moreover, East European forces were more likely to be deployed in some form of 'corset' formation, involving combined Soviet and East European contingents, rather than being deployed as combat units in their own right. All the same, the recent upgrading of the fire-power of Soviet forces in Eastern Europe and the practice of retaining independent supply lines stretching back to the USSR for each of the four Soviet groups of forces in Europe, suggested that whatever the Pact's institutional arrangements, the Soviet Union would continue to ensure the operational independence of her own forces. Moreover, the 28–30 Soviet divisions based in the western military districts of the USSR and within striking distance of the European heartland helped to ensure a Soviet capability to achieve military objectives in Europe, theoretically without the need for active East European support. The Soviet Union's insistence on military integration within the Pact, while at the same time she continued to minimize her own military dependence on Eastern Europe, seemed to be aimed more at controlling Eastern Europe's military potential than using it.

Further military integration, whatever its ultimate purpose in Soviet eyes, would of necessity require greater consultation in military and political affairs in the interests of operational efficiency, and it was in this area that the reorganized structure of the Pact could, and already had, come into its own. But here again the USSR had sought to maintain some flexibility. Should the intransigence of any of the smaller Pact members bring the multilateral machinery to a halt, the Soviet Union, which had deliberately maintained close bilateral ties with all her East European allies, could bypass it.

Indeed, this might already have happened in connection with external military undertakings. Ever since the 1969 Ussuri River clashes, the Soviet Union had repeatedly tried and repeatedly failed to gain the collective approval of her allies for extending the scope of the Warsaw Pact by committing it (even if only symbolically) to the defence of the non-European borders of socialism – and specifically to the very long and sensitive Sino-Soviet border. More recently, too, she had encouraged the Pact as a whole to develop closer ties with Vietnam. So far all its East European members without exception have reiterated that, in accordance with its statutes, the Pact's military role is strictly European. On an individual basis, however, some East European states – particularly East Germany and, to a lesser extent, Bulgaria – assumed a close military involvement in Africa, Asia and the Middle East, giving mainly technical help where Soviet foreign-policy interests were at stake.

Links between East European military personnel and their Soviet counterparts had always been close. A high percentage of senior East European officers received some part of their training at military academies in the Soviet Union (again the exception was Romania, which had allowed this practice to lapse). Yet the lack of genuine integration on an equal basis caused problems. Even before the invasion of Czechoslovakia in 1968, both Romanian and Czech sources criticized the exclusive appointment of Soviet officers to key command posts in the Pact and called for increased use of the available consultative machinery, particularly with respect to the potential use or deployment of nuclear weapons. More recently some Polish sources indirectly criticized Soviet strategy by discussing the need to develop national military doctrines to supplement the 'unified' Warsaw Pact doctrine. Romania's sentiments on this issue emerged clearly with the adoption of a Law on National Defence, making it a crime to facilitate in any way the entry of foreign troops on to Romanian soil. To underline the point, Romania refused to commit her own troops to Warsaw Pact manoeuvres either, undertaking only to participate in staff exercises, and then only very irregularly.

Such issues were unlikely to fade away and, although the fundamental loyalty of the East European regimes and their armed forces need not be called into question, a debate clearly continued behind the scenes, with neither the Soviet Union nor some of the East European states particularly satisfied with existing mechanisms for co-operation and co-ordination.

Unsolved Problems
Developments at the very end of 1979 could well exacerbate the existing tensions. The Soviet Union clearly wanted the Socialist camp to close ranks in the wake of her invasion of Afghanistan, and the East European countries could soon find even their present modest room for manoeuvre under heavy attack and reduced. It will not be easy for the Soviet Union to achieve this, however. There were already signs of growing Soviet impatience with Romania during the past year, yet Romania nonetheless absented herself from the UN vote condemning the Soviet action in Afghanistan, rather than vote with the rest of the Warsaw Pact.

The 12 December decision by NATO to modernize Western theatre nuclear forces raised once again the issue of costs and the proper contribution to be expected from each member of the Warsaw Pact for their military response. The USSR resumed her pressure on her partners for an increased defence effort. East Germany was the first to respond with an 8.7% increase in defence spending, but many other Pact members continued to demonstrate a lack of enthusiasm for the idea.

Growing Soviet attention to security developments in Asia could again bring up, in the changed conditions and atmosphere of the 1980s, an issue which East European regimes had succeeded in avoiding for the past twenty-five years: the direct involvement of the Warsaw Pact in extra-European contingencies. It is impossible to say to what degree the East European members of the Pact could refuse such a demand by the Soviet Union, but it is safe to say that they would, in their various ways, make every effort to avoid the issue. The 1980s are thus likely to see the underlying complexity of Warsaw Pact politics increasing rather than decreasing.

CENTRAL AMERICA

In 1979, two decades after Fidel Castro took power in Cuba, turmoil in Central America and the Caribbean again preoccupied policy-makers in the United States. The focal point of that concern was Nicaragua, where in July two years of revolution culminated in the overthrow of President Anastasio Somoza Debayle, the dictator whose family had ruled the country for over forty years. His fall did not, as so often in many of the poor countries of Central America, merely open the way to power for a new dictator of basically similar outlook; rather it appeared to portend a broader move towards left-wing governments throughout the region.

REVOLUTION IN NICARAGUA

In Nicaragua as elsewhere in the region, the United States seemed to be reaping the bitter harvest of past policies – in this case, forty years of support for an authoritarian dynasty. And yet newer US policies – in particular the Carter Administration's emphasis on human rights – had themselves played a role in undermining the regime. During Somoza's final years US policy had been hesitant and dilatory: first assuming that Somoza could weather the storm, then trying to pressure him to step down voluntarily (though without repeating the overt US interventions of earlier periods), and finally realizing, too late, that he would in fact be toppled. Regardless of the fact that her support for Somoza had become more and more strained over the years, his fall was therefore bound to be seen as a blow to the United States. Moreover, the revolution which removed him occurred in her own backyard, where her influence was presumed to be strong, even if it was not exercised with the same directness as in the past. That, more than any crucial interests, seemed to give Nicaragua strategic significance for the United States.

The US had intervened in Nicaragua to restore internal order as early as 1909. In 1912 she sent in a marine detachment to protect American property during a period of civil unrest, and (except for a short period in 1925–6) American troops remained in the country until 1933. In 1931, her troops went in to put down a revolt by Augusto Cesar Sandino, a guerrilla leader whose name was to be adopted by the Frente Sandinista de Liberación Nacional (FSLN) in the 1960s. In 1933 the US withdrew, but, to ensure continuing stability, created a 'non-partisan constabulary' called the National Guard, led by a pro-American officer, General Anastasio Somoza Garcia. In February 1934 Sandino, persuaded to disarm his troops, was assassinated on Somoza's orders. In 1936 Somoza overthrew the civilian president and the following year arranged his own election. He ruled until his assassination in 1956, being followed by his eldest son Luis, who ruled until 1963. After four years of a puppet presidency his second son, Anastasio, took power in 1967.

Washington acquiesced in the Somoza dynasty's economic and political hegemony throughout its life. The Somozas proved their loyalty to successive administrations and cultivated friends in the Pentagon and on Capital Hill (in 1979 some members of Congress even tried to torpedo the legislation implementing the Panama Canal Treaty in an attempt to force the Carter Administration to support Somoza). For the United States, they served as a bulwark against Communism throughout Central America. In 1954 they supported a US-backed coup to oust a left-leaning Guatemalan government; in 1961 Nicaraguan territory was used to launch the abortive Bay of Pigs invasion of Cuba; and in 1965 Nicaragua endorsed the US intervention in the Dominican Republic by sending a contingent of her own troops to Santo Domingo.

The Opposition to Somoza

Ironically, the stimulus for the beginning of organized opposition to Somoza was not political, but economic. Somoza departed from the relative moderation that had been characteristic of his family's dictatorship. Despite a total fortune estimated at $500 million, he pushed his way into new sectors of the Nicaraguan economy, and by the early 1970s owned 30% of the country's agricultural land and a wide range of industrial and commercial enterprises. In the wake of a disastrous earthquake in 1972, he and his friends used a substantial portion of international relief and reconstruction funds to further their domination of the economy. That alienated both the middle and lower classes, and touched off a wave of strikes, demonstrations and land seizures during 1972–3.

The moderate opposition coalesced around Pedro Joaquín Chamorro, a prominent anti-Somoza editor and social democrat, who in December 1974 organized a number of political parties and labour confederations into a coherent democratic opposition movement. In the same month the FSLN first came to public prominence by seizing a number of wealthy Nicaraguans in their homes and exchanging these hostages for some imprisoned comrades, a sizeable ransom and a flight to Cuba. Somoza responded by suspending freedom of the press and instituting a reign of terror against rural populations in areas where the Sandinista guerrillas were active – tactics which appalled Nicaragua's moderates and alienated such traditional pillars of Somoza's support as the Catholic church and the business community.

Founded in 1962, the FSLN was one of the many guerrilla organizations spawned in Latin America by the example of the Cuban revolution. During its first decade it was little known in Nicaragua and no match for the US-armed National Guard, but the 1974 operation made popular heroes of the Sandinistas. It was Somoza's tactics, more than anything else, that gradually made the FSLN the focal point of the radical opposition: his cruel repressions alienated the moderates and led them to despair of the effectiveness of non-revolutionary opposition and to overcome their fear of the more radical FSLN.

At the same time there was a shift in FSLN strategy. Internal divisions among the Sandinistas had produced three distinct factions by the mid-1970s. One favoured long-term political re-education of the urban masses and another looked towards prolonged guerrilla struggle in the countryside. A third, however, was prepared for immediate military action to capitalize on popular anti-Somoza feeling and trigger widespread insurrection. Moreover, this *Tercerista* (or 'Third Force') faction was disposed to co-operate with other anti-Somoza elements. This pragmatic attitude, with its lesser emphasis on radical 'purity', made it possible for more establishment opposition groups to support the guerrillas and thus led to the *Terceristas* gaining ascendancy within the FSLN.

In 1977 the human-rights policy of the newly-elected Carter Administration put additional pressure on the Somoza regime and emboldened moderate critics of the government who had been disheartened by the prospect of unwavering American support for the dictator. Under the pressure of reductions in American military assistance, Somoza curtailed National Guard brutality in rural areas and reinstated freedom of the press. In October 1977, however, the FSLN, which Somoza thought he had crushed in 1975, launched attacks on National Guard garrisons in five cities. These were easily repulsed, but they nonetheless served to shatter the myth of Somoza's supremacy and put new heart into the opposition. At the same time, prominent Nicaraguan religious and professional leaders – later called 'The Group of Twelve' – publicly denounced Somoza, called on him to resign, and praised the Sandinistas, saying that they would have to play a role in any long-term solution to the country's problems.

The Crisis
On 10 January 1978 Pedro Joaquín Chamorro was assassinated, touching off two weeks of riots in Managua. Nicaragua's business leaders then called a general strike, which lasted two weeks, in support of a demand for Somoza's resignation. After one week the FSLN endorsed the strike, but at this point the political initiative was with the moderates. During the next six months, the country was affected by intermittent and unco-ordinated violence and strikes organized by a variety of different anti-Somoza groups. During this crucial period the political initiative passed from the moderates to the FSLN. The Sandinistas gathered together funds and arms and extended their influence among the poor, while the moderates – apparently waiting for the United States to push Somoza out of power – talked, delayed and toyed with compromises.

At this critical juncture the US seemed hesitant, unable to choose between her commitment to human rights, her desire for political continuity in Central America and her fear of 'another Cuba'. After Chamorro's assassination she cut military aid to Nicaragua, yet also called on Nicaraguans to avoid violence and wait for democracy until Somoza's term of office ended in 1981. In July President Carter wrote to Somoza congratulating him on his promises to improve his record on human rights. Such apparent indecision convinced the moderate opposition that working with the United States would not unseat Somoza, and they moved, albeit reluctantly in many cases, to co-operate with the radicals. The result was the creation of the Broad Opposition Front (FAO), the first formal link between the moderates and the Sandinistas.

In August 1978, the *Terceristas* seized the National Palace during a session of Congress and took 1,500 hostages. This attack captured the popular imagination and made the FSLN the focal point of the anti-Somoza struggle. As the attackers drove to the airport to fly to Panama with the 59 political prisoners for whom they had exchanged their hostages, thousands of Nicaraguans cheered them in the streets. Soon after that, a new general strike and a wave of guerrilla attacks sparked off major insurrections in several cities. The National Guard, using indiscriminate and excessive force, took three weeks to regain control, killing 3,000 and destroying parts of the cities in air attacks.

The spectacle of his army waging war on its own people finally convinced the United States that Somoza would not be able to restore stability, and from September onwards American policy switched to an effort to build an alternative government not dominated by the Sandinistas. Under the auspices of the Organization of American States (OAS), the United States sought to bring about mediation and the creation of an 'interim government' of the Broad Opposition Front and Somoza's National Liberal Party. But this strategy, which might have succeeded a year earlier, came too late. At this stage the pressure on the FAO to drop its demand for Somoza's immediate resignation and negotiate with him only destroyed the unity and credibility of the moderates. It soon became clear in any case that Somoza was merely playing for time. In January 1979 he rejected the final mediation proposal for an internationally supervised plebiscite, whereupon the US halved (but did not remove) her diplomatic representation in Managua, and cut off military aid.

After some months of recuperation the FSLN launched the 'final offensive' against Somoza's regime in June 1979. Stronger now in both men and weapons, it soon gained control of most of the major cities, nearly all the countryside and half of Managua, despite fierce counter-attacks and rocket and bombing raids by the National Guard.

In late June the FSLN and the National Patriotic Front (a militant coalition of some moderate opposition groups which still had some credibility after the collapse of the FAO the previous autumn) set up a Provisional Government for National Reconstruction. On 22 June the United States finally went on record as favouring Somoza's immediate resignation, but, studiously ignoring the Provisional Government, called for a 'broad-based' representative government' and an OAS peace-keeping force to police a ceasefire. This scheme foundered, and, with the FSLN gaining ground throughout Nicaragua, the US was forced to take account of it. She then tried to put pressure on the Sandinistas to include more moderates in the Provisional Government, but in the end the most the FSLN would do was guarantee the lives of Somoza's associates and the National Guard. On 17 July Somoza fled into exile in the United States, and the Nicaraguan revolution, which had cost more than 50,000 lives, was over.

Aftermath
The five-member junta heading the Provisional Government was a conscious effort to build a broad basis of support. It included Chamorro's widow, a member of the 'Group of Twelve', an industrialist, and two radicals, Daniel Ortega and Moises Hassan. Similarly, the 18-member Cabinet ranged from FSLN militants like Tomás Borge (a Marxist with Cuban ties), to conservative and religious figures.

The government and its policies reflected a tenuous balance of power between the radicals and the moderates. It expressed determination to carry out a social revolution and radically restructure the economy and society, but to do this if possible within the framework of a pluralist democracy. And it had largely respected human rights, avoiding taking retribution on its defeated opponents and banning the death penalty. The government's first task was to begin reconstructing the devastated economy, for the war had left one-fifth of the population homeless and a third of the work-force unemployed. It nationalized the banks and began to redistribute properties confiscated from Somoza and his friends (which amounted to over half the arable land in the country). At the same time, it insisted that efficient private enterprises in all sectors could continue to function, and foreign investment would be allowed.

In foreign affairs, the Junta tried to steer a course that was true to its leftist ideology and yet would avoid sharp moves to the left that might alienate Washington or provoke Nicaragua's right-wing neighbours to the north. One of the Junta's first acts, however, was to establish diplomatic relations with Cuba, and the presence of Cubans was welcomed in agriculture, light industry, political and military training, and medicine.

For her part, the United States seemed to have learned a lesson from the aftermath of the Cuban revolution two decades before. She avoided the sort of punitive response that could have driven Nicaragua towards a more radical course and an even closer relationship with Cuba (as it had pushed Cuba into the arms of the Soviet Union). President Carter personally met two members of the Junta at the White House in September, and the Administration promised to help in the reconstruction effort by providing loans and grants.

Reverberations in the Region
Though there were great differences among the states of Central America and the Caribbean, events in Nicaragua were bound to have a bearing on developments in other countries of the region, since they did have problems in common. Most were very poor: per capita incomes ranged from over $1,000 a year in Costa Rica and Jamaica, through $850 in Nicaragua and $500 in El Salvador and Honduras, to under $300 in Haiti. All were dependent on exports of a few primary commodities, and were thus very vulnerable to swings in world markets. They had growing populations and suffered from high unemployment. And they had outdated political structures – relics of colonial rule in the case of the Caribbean, and anachronistic dictatorships in the case of Central America.

In March 1979, even before revolution finally brought the Sandinistas to power in Nicaragua, the eccentric and brutal rule of Sir Eric Gairy in the eastern Caribbean state of Grenada ended in a coup. The new leader, Maurice Bishop, who seemed to be a man in the radical mould of Jamaican Prime Minister Michael Manley, quickly recognized Cuba and requested military aid from her. The effect of this coup on the tiny, mostly conservative, former British colonies of the Eastern Caribbean was comparable to the shock waves spreading through Central America from Nicaragua. This nervousness was reinforced at the end of the year by concern over the possibility that St Lucia might follow Grenada's example.

In Central America, Somoza's fall increased the exposure of neighbouring right-wing governments in the region, and in October, after considerable violence and popular opposition, the Salvadorean dictator Carlos Humberto Romero was overthrown in a military coup. This time the United States did not obstruct his overthrow.

The military junta which succeeded Romero attempted to broaden its support by including respected civilians on the political left and by announcing a programme of reforms, but the left withdrew from the government over the pace of these reforms. As 1980 began El Salvador seemed to be sliding towards civil war, with another junta, this one dominated by Christian Democrats, unable to control the spiral of violence from both left and right.

The Role of Cuba
There was a temptation in the West, especially the United States, to see behind turmoil in the region the influence of Cuba, and hence indirectly that of the Soviet Union. Cuba's role was important and increasing, but difficult to define with any precision.

Some aspects of the Cuban-Soviet military relationship itself must be more and more worrying to the US, quite apart from implications for regional politics. While the September dispute over a Soviet combat brigade in Cuba made high politics of a minor issue (see pp. 30–31), it underlined the large jump in Soviet military capability in Cuba after 1975. Since that year Cuba had received a squadron of advanced Mig-23 fighter bombers, a squadron of medium-range military transports, and one attack submarine (another was expected), among other weaponry. She was now effectively a huge Soviet intelligence-gathering facility and a base for surveillance, anti-submarine warfare and, conceivably, air attack on the United States in a major war.

There had, however, been clear signs of acute economic difficulties in Cuba and hints of strain in Cuban-Soviet relations. The first real signs of internal dissidence had also appeared (anti-Castro slogans and pamphlets), causing Castro to reorganize his government in January 1980. He also openly acknowledged the economic problems – rooted in continuing low world sugar prices and runaway inflation. These difficulties pushed Cuba closer to the Soviet Union, albeit at some cost to her non-aligned credentials. Though Castro initially remained silent about the Soviet invasion of Afghanistan, Cuba did vote with

Moscow against the UN General Assembly resolution which condemned it, and the embarrassment of the episode caused her to drop her bid for membership of the UN Security Council.

Cuba had for many years played a cautious hand within the region, not wanting to repeat the actions of the 1960s, when her efforts to export her revolution had so frightened even the region's moderate leftist regimes. Castro had often remarked that the best thing he could do for Nicaragua's Sandinistas was to do nothing, and in fact Cuban help tended to follow revolutionary events rather than precede them. To be sure, some of the Sandinistas had received training in Cuba, and some Cuban-supplied arms reached both them and rebels in El Salvador, Guatemala and other countries. All the same, Cuba's most important contribution was probably the verbal encouragement she gave to rebels beforehand and the economic and technical assistance she could supply after they had come to power.

In 1979 Cuba had more than 250 civilian advisors and technicians in Nicaragua, some 70 in Guyana, and (reflecting her increasing attention to the English-speaking islands of the Caribbean) some 350–450 in Jamaica and a smaller number in Grenada, with perhaps some military trainers as well. The form of Cuban influence was well demonstrated in the case of Jamaica. Faced with severe economic problems and a balance-of-payments crisis, Michael Manley's government was both dependent on support from the IMF and closely linked with Cuba, which provided training for its security forces and perhaps limited co-operation in intelligence. For Manley, the Cuban link offered concrete help (mostly economic), some ideological support for his own revolutionary programmes, and also a means of exerting leverage on Western governments and financial institutions.

Outlook for Moderation
In the light of this Cuban role, newly-emergent left-wing regimes were likely for some time to remain confident that they could enjoy the benefits of association with Castro's Cuba without becoming political dependencies. Yet that did not gainsay the difficulties posed for American policy. The dilemmas of 1978 and 1979 in Nicaragua were likely to be repeated in 1980 and beyond in El Salvador and Guatemala. The latter had had military governments and escalating violence between Left and Right since 1954. In January 1980 the Spanish embassy was occupied by peasants protesting against the government, and 39 people died when the police stormed the building. Having seen events in Nicaragua and El Salvador, the Guatemalan military appeared determined to crush resistance at all costs.

There was a risk that the political middleground would evaporate, confronting Washington with a choice between closer identification with repressive regimes, which would be a reversal of a decade of halting attempts to improve the US image in the hemisphere, or watching regimes turn leftward, if not 'Communist'. The spectre of 'another Cuba' in Central America and the Caribbean was a powerful image in American politics, and after Afghanistan it would be all the harder for Washington to resist harsh responses to radical movements. And in the long term such responses might well do more harm than good to moderate forces in the region.

ARMS CONTROL

In 1979 the status of arms control reflected the vagaries of East-West relations. SALT II was signed in June, after nearly seven years of negotiation, but at the year-end its ratification by the US Senate appeared unattainable, having fallen victim to growing American concern over Soviet actions, a concern which reached a peak with the Soviet intervention in Afghanistan. There was little movement in the talks on Mutual and Balanced Force Reductions (MBFR) in Central Europe. There was also no progress in any of the other arms-control forums: the talks on an anti-satellite weapons treaty, on a comprehensive test ban treaty and on conventional arms transfer control all ground to a halt. In effect, the campaign that President Carter had launched in 1977 for a reduction in the conventional and nuclear armaments of both sides and for the control of the transfer of arms collapsed during 1979. Moreover, doubts continued to grow about where arms control should go next in an ever more complicated technical environment, even if it was assumed that the political basis for progress could be recreated.

STRATEGIC ARMS LIMITATION TALKS

As 1980 began, any chance of SALT II being ratified by the American Senate, at least in the near future, had disappeared. In December, 19 senators, including several whose opinions and votes were considered crucial, called on President Carter to defer a vote on SALT until after the American elections in November 1980. As the crisis over the American hostages in Iran dragged on, SALT slid down the agenda of American politics. The Soviet-backed coup and massive intervention in Afghanistan at the year-end seemed the final blow. In January 1980 the President asked the Senate to defer consideration of SALT II, though he indicated that his Administration remained committed to its eventual ratification. Yet delay would mean that ratification would be postponed until after the November elections, and in practice that would mean until 1981. By then the SALT II protocol, adopted as a means of postponing some very difficult issues which would continue to be negotiated in the interim, would have less than a year to run until its expiry on 31 December 1981.

Doubt about the ratification of SALT II was further fuelled by uncertainty about what would follow in strategic arms control, even if it were ratified. In the debate over strategic arms limitation in 1979 it was striking how far technical analysis had come to diverge from the politics of arms control. Among defence and arms-control analysts, even those who supported SALT II, there was deep frustration with the results of SALT thus far, and deep pessimism about how SALT III could be made to do better in a still more complicated technical environment. At the same time, Europeans, in particular, seemed to see progress in strategic arms control as crucial to sustaining some shred of East–West detente; some movement in theatre nuclear arms control would be politically important if NATO were to implement its decision on the modernization of theatre nuclear forces. And in the United States one of the few elements of consensus between the political Left and Right that developed in the SALT II debate was that SALT III had to be better, that it had to produce deep reductions in the nuclear arsenals of the two sides.

The SALT Debate

SALT II fell into its parlous state in the American Senate less because of strong opposition to its terms than for lack of strong support. The issues in the treaty, and the arguments for and against it, were well known by the time it was signed in Vienna on 18 June (for discussion of the treaty and issues connected with it, see *Strategic Survey, 1978,* pp. 116-20; for the text of the agreements, *Survival,* Sept/Oct 1979, pp. 217–30). In fact, it was striking that SALT opponents, effective and well organized before the treaty was signed, lost momentum once Senate hearings had begun and were unable to mount fresh arguments against it. For instance, opponents had argued that SALT II was dangerously unequal in permitting the Soviet Union to retain her 308 'heavy' missiles, while prohibiting the United States from deploying any. Yet that argument lost its force as witness after witness, including the Chairman of the American Joint Chiefs of Staff, testified that the US would not, and should not, build such large missiles, even if she were permitted to do so. In the end, the Senate Foreign Relations Committee voted by 8 votes to 7 against an amendment that would have asserted the right of the United States to match the Soviet strength in heavy missiles.

The same pattern was repeated several times during 1979: when the Senate focused more narrowly on the treaty itself, objections to it waned. One of the central arguments put forward by treaty opponents had been the problem of verification. They argued that the specific provisions that the Administration had agreed with the Soviet Union were inadequate and that the subsequent loss of certain monitoring stations, particularly in Iran, had compounded the difficulties. The Senate Intelligence Committee, which spent four months studying the question and listening to highly classified intelligence briefings, unanimously reported that the treaty strengthened the American ability to monitor Soviet strategic weapons, and that without it the Soviet Union would be able to conceal weapons, deceive the United States and thus make monitoring of these forces far more difficult. With this report in hand, the Senate Foreign Relations Committee turned down, by 9 votes to 6, amendments to the verification provisions that would have required renegotiating the treaty to achieve Soviet agreement.

The Foreign Affairs Committee also set aside efforts to define certain Soviet weapons systems as strategic weapons subject to the treaty. An amendment offered by Senator Stone to require that Soviet diesel submarines capable of carrying nuclear weapons be counted as part of the Soviet aggregate was voted down by a margin of 10 to 5. A more serious issue, however, was the question of the Soviet *Backfire* bomber, which opponents of the treaty insisted could be used in a strategic role. While the Committee turned down, by a vote of 9 to 6, efforts to include *Backfire* in the count of weapons permitted under the treaty, it did adopt a 'reservation' to the treaty which would require the Soviet Union to agree that her assurances that she would neither increase *Backfire*'s range or payload nor speed up its production rate to more than 30 a month (offered in an informal letter from Brezhnev to Carter) were legally binding.

On three other issues of major concern, the Senate Foreign Relations Committee adopted 'clarifications' or 'understandings' that expressed the necessity to meet opponents' objections, but would not require any renegotiation of the treaty. Although the Administration had maintained in its testimony supporting the treaty that there was nothing in it that would prevent the United States from moving ahead with development and deployment of the MX mobile missile, the Committee insisted on a reservation declaring that the United States considered its proposed MX system to be fully permitted by the treaty. A second sticking point had been the protocol to the treaty, which was to expire on 31 December 1981. Opponents claimed that, when that time came, the dynamics of arms control would lead to the extension of the limitations on cruise missile deployment contained in the protocol. To circumvent this, the Committee passed reservations stating that neither the treaty nor the protocol could be extended beyond their expiration dates of the end of 1985 and 1981 respectively. The third issue was the so-called 'noncircumvention' clause, under which, opponents of the treaty claimed, it would prove illegal to share weapons technology with the United States' allies, particularly NATO. The Committee met this objection by an 'understanding' that nothing in the treaty could prevent the US from military co-operation with her NATO allies.

Thus on 9 November, after four months of hearings and a series of votes on individual amendments, the Foreign Relations Committee voted by 9 to 6 to recommend Senate approval of the SALT II treaty with the Soviet Union. All the so-called 'killer' amendments, which would have required renegotiation of the Treaty and thus its likely demise, had been beaten back, though some only by the narrowest of margins. It was therefore clear that, even in the best of circumstances, the treaty would have difficulty passing through the whole Senate unscathed, since each of the 'killer' amendments would be advanced and argued again, and the Senate as a whole was more conservative on these questions than the Committee. Although the Administration needed 67 votes, or two thirds of those present and voting, to assure the passing of the treaty, the most optimistic head-count showed only 60 senators in favour. More pessimistic (some would say realistic) counts indicated that only 50 senators were prepared to vote for the treaty as it came from the Committee.

In the event, as extraneous events intervened and the focus of the debate became more general, the prospect of ratification receded and the Administration decided to postpone the attempt to get the package passed. In fact, the SALT II treaty itself, with its multiplicity of detail, had become less and less central to the debate as time went by. In the end the prospects for ratification had lessened more because, from the perspective of the American Senate, there was no pressing reason to ratify it and enough uncertainty in the international environment to argue for deferring action, than because of passionate and insuperable opposition to it.

Non-SALT Issues

During the course of the year, what had begun as a debate on the SALT II treaty became the great defence-spending debate. SALT II became the hostage of efforts to realize a dramatic increase in defence spending. Former Secretary Kissinger, Senator Nunn and others argued that the United States should increase her defence spending by 4–5% or more, rather than the 3% initially requested by President Carter. For many who inclined against the treaty, SALT II might be acceptable provided they could be sure it would not induce a period of complacency like that which they believed had followed SALT I, when Soviet strategic programmes accelerated while those of the United States slowed. Others embraced a notion of linkage different from that debated during 1978: trying to use SALT to punish specific Soviet actions might be unwise and unfruitful, but Moscow would be more likely to understand the general message of toughness conveyed by an increase in defence spending. For still others, the United States simply needed to do more, especially in the nuclear realm, quite apart from SALT.

Later in the year, the President took the unusual step of previewing his five-year defence plan for senators, as part of his effort to assure votes for SALT ratification. The plan called for average real increases in defence spending of 4.5% per year (although actual outlays – as opposed to appropriations – for Fiscal 1981 would go up by only 3%). The planned formation of a rapid-deployment force for use in third-world contingencies was a focus of the plan, and $9 billion was earmarked for equipment for it.

First Cuba and then, more importantly, Iran and Afghanistan demonstrated how thin support for SALT ratification was in the United States Senate. The curious episode of Soviet troops in Cuba, which occurred in September, demonstrated once again the inability of the Carter Administration to gain and retain the initiative in the SALT debate. During ratification of the Panama Canal treaties in March and April 1978, the President had made pledges to the Senate about Soviet activities in Cuba, thus ensuring that senators would be attentive to developments there. In September 1979 the continuing and apparently sincere debate within American intelligence about the precise purpose of Soviet troop deployments in Cuba led to the conclusion that there was in fact 'a combat brigade' there (see pp. 30–31). Senator Stone, who had a large number of Cuban refugee voters in his Florida constituency, brought the intelligence debate to the Senate's attention, and the chairman of the Senate Foreign Relations Committee, Frank Church, used the issue to prove his concern about the Soviet threat during a tough re-election campaign in Idaho. If the Cuban episode passed, although with some damage to the President's image as a competent foreign-policy manager and a loss of momentum towards the ratification of SALT, the taking of American hostages by Iran was much more serious. Again, the issue had little to do with SALT (even less than the Cuban episode in fact), since the USSR was mildly supportive of American efforts to secure the release of the hostages, at least after some initial broadcasts that seemed to encourage the terrorists. Yet the Iran crisis and, even more so, the Soviet-backed coup in Afghanistan underscored a growing domestic concern over the US position in the world, shifted attention from the control of arms to the need to increase American strength, and made it an unpropitious time to debate SALT II.

The Implications of Non-Ratification

As usual in foreign affairs, the non-ratification of SALT would probably confirm neither the worst fears of proponents nor the hopes of some opponents. But the effects would be serious, nonetheless. For the United States' friends and foes alike it would cast additional doubt on her ability to act in the world, and would seem, particularly to the Soviet Union, to be a manifestation of the general volatility of US foreign policies.

The Senate hearings produced few, if any, solid arguments against SALT and led to a broad consensus that the United States needed to do more in defence. President Carter responded to that pressure in ways which looked as though they should satisfy all but his sharpest critics.

There was never any chance that strategic programmes would lack funding, and still more dollars for MX mobile missiles or the new *Trident* long-range submarine-launched missiles could accelerate their deployment only marginally and at high cost. In those circumstances, it was difficult to understand why an agreement that served the useful purpose of regulating nuclear competition should be forced off the rails by a minor incident like Cuba, and even to push it down on the agenda because of the crisis in Iran seemed to indicate an inability on the part of the Administration and the Senate to act from a clear conception of American interests.

NATO's modernization of theatre nuclear forces (TNF) would be a specific test of arms control without SALT. European NATO members were prepared to take the December decisions approving TNF modernization even though SALT II had not been ratified, despite the fact that many of them had earlier argued that ratification was essential to approval of such modernization. NATO's December decisions compelled the Alliance to seek early negotiations over US and Soviet long-range TNF, and SALT III was the logical negotiating arena. Hence SALT II was necessary, in order that there could be a SALT III. But, without SALT II, NATO would be compelled to seek other forums for the discussions. The most obvious would be bilateral Soviet–American talks, whether or not they bore the SALT label.

Yet Soviet acquiescence in any such discussions was doubtful. In January 1980 the Soviet Union confirmed officially what Soviet press commentary had suggested earlier: that she would only be willing to discuss long-range TNF if NATO publicly reversed its December decisions. Moreover, without SALT II it would be difficult for President Carter to obtain Congressional backing for TNF talks. He would be accused of beginning the third round of SALT before being given constitutional authority to complete the second, and all aspects of the TNF talks would be scrutinized in terms of their effects on SALT II's ratification chances.

Without SALT, it was hard to imagine serious negotiations on theatre nuclear forces. That would certainly complicate the implementation of NATO's TNF decisions, especially by those countries where opposition was already strong – although the reaction to Afghanistan could help in holding the line, at least for a while. The first benchmark would be Belgian action, since Belgium went along with the December 1979 decision only with the proviso that she would review her participation in six months. The USSR seemed to regard her own interests as being best served by holding firm, at least until after the American Presidential election, hoping in the meantime to erode further the political support for the NATO decision. She would have every incentive to bring forward again her traditional proposals for a mutual undertaking not to be the first to use nuclear weapons, and for enlisting neutral and non-aligned European states in a campaign against NATO's 'destabilizing' plans, at the Madrid Conference on Security and Co-operation in Europe scheduled for October 1980. The most disturbing result of the delay in SALT II, however, would be if, over and above its specific effect on that agreement, it also discouraged strategic arms regulation itself.

The year 1980 was likely to be critical for SALT. So long as the ratification process had been moving along, however sluggishly, both sides had agreed to continue to abide by the provisions of the SALT I Interim Agreement, and to observe customary international law by not taking actions contrary to the intention of the new treaty. With SALT II delayed, it was not clear what, if any, rules would continue to govern the relationship between the US and USSR.

This was a novel situation in the history of strategic arms control, and it offered both a risk and an opportunity for the negotiating parties. The risk was that the entire SALT process would collapse, either because the two sides failed to agree on interim rules, or because one side or the other took actions which would unravel the SALT II package. A Soviet missile test with more than the SALT-prescribed number of warheads (or using coded telemetry), or the conversion of launchers for light missiles to accommodate heavy ones – any such action would contravene an agreed provision of SALT II and would require renegotiation of what was, for the United States in 1980, at best a marginally acceptable accord.

The opportunity was that the United States and Soviet Union could use the time to demonstrate their flexibility and continued interest in strategic arms control. An agreement, whether implicit or explicit, to continue to observe the Interim Agreement and to take no action inconsistent with the provisions of SALT II should not be impossible to negotiate. If this were not worked out, then the prospects for strategic arms control would be gloomy indeed.

What Next?

Even if SALT II was eventually ratified, the problem of what to do next in strategic arms control would remain. Technological development continued apace, complicating analysis of the role of arms control. Cruise missiles and other new systems confirmed what was true all along – that the designation 'strategic' was essentially arbitrary, and the attempt to fence off that category of weapons for SALT was bound to be increasingly difficult. More and more attributes of strategic weapons that arms controllers would like to restrain are difficult to verify. The development of multiple independently-targetable re-entry vehicles (MIRV) had created its own difficulties, although some progress had been made within SALT II to accommodate them, but cruise missiles would be far more difficult to verify. Not only are they small, highly mobile, and easily concealed, but even if one can count them it is almost impossible to tell what range or function they have, since the strategic and nuclear versions are indistinguishable from those that have tactical or conventional roles.

Similarly, in an era of MIRV, deep reductions in the aggregate strategic forces of the two super-powers might do little to limit the actual nuclear threat. Rather, it would increase concern about the surreptitious stockpiling of missiles and about how to handle the overlap of 'strategic' and 'theatre' systems. Limits on missile test flights were another example. They would be hard to implement and of dubious benefit if 'civilian' space programmes continued. And such limits, even if they were effective, would also limit the amount of information the West could gain about Soviet missile programmes through monitoring test firings.

If there was any consensus about the future of strategic arms control, that consensus was more negative than positive and related more to what should not be pursued than to what should. And yet analysts, if not political leaders, agreed that SALT III, when and if it came, should neither be comprehensive in form nor make deep reductions its central objective. The lesson of SALT II was that any comprehensive negotiation would take time, and by the time it was completed the strategic concerns of the two sides would bear little relation to those with which they entered the long, drawn-out process.

Yet the Senate Foreign Relations Committee passed (by 15 votes to none), and sent to the Senate with SALT II, the McGovern amendment calling on the President to seek 'continuous year-by-year reductions' in the SALT II ceilings during SALT III, along with qualitative restraints. The amendment would not bind the President, but it did record the broad agreement across the American political spectrum that real reductions should be the goal of the next phase of strategic arms control.

As a new decade began, there was more than a little sense that the specific SALT process was a relic of the 1970s. Many of the original hopes had proved unrealistic, and political developments at home and abroad had eroded support within the United States for the type of arms control that SALT represented. In the Soviet Union, too, a process of disenchantment had set in, as the invasion into Afghanistan demonstrated. For the Soviet leadership, pinning its faith on the declining likelihood of SALT II being ratified by the US Senate was not a sufficient incentive to justify risking the loss of the Soviet stake in a friendly government in Afghanistan by not intervening. All the same, it would appear short-sighted on both sides if disenchantment with SALT II were to lead to a general farewell to strategic arms control.

NEGOTIATING EUROPEAN SECURITY

The same divergence between political interest and technical analysis that was evident in connection with SALT also ran through European security discussions in 1979. One consequence of SALT II's travails was renewed interest in the Mutual and Balanced Force Reduction (MBFR) talks in Vienna. There were some signs of new life in these negotiations, but major obstacles remained. Similarly, with the approach of the October 1980 Madrid meeting of the Conference on Security and Co-operation in Europe (CSCE), there was no shortage of proposals for new measures and new arenas for negotiating European security, on which the non-ratification of SALT II was bound to focus political attention.

MBFR

Actions by both East and West seemed to give MBFR new impetus as 1979 ended. In his speech in East Berlin on 6 October, Soviet President

Brezhnev unilaterally announced a withdrawal of 20,000 men and 1,000 tanks from East Germany as a gesture of goodwill, a gesture which was subsequently given a measure of reality by the well-publicized entrainment for the USSR of various Soviet units from East Germany.

Since neither the Brezhnev speech nor subsequent Soviet statements linked these force reductions to MBFR, their only direct effect on these talks may be to reduce the overall numbers of Soviet troops which form the basis for comparison. However, the figure of 'up to' 20,000 men, the total complement of two tank divisions, was ominously close to the difference in aggregate numbers of forces in the area covered by MBFR that the Warsaw Pact negotiators had admitted in Vienna. A long-standing problem in Vienna had been the lack of agreement over data: the Western side was confident that the Warsaw Pact had about 150,000 more men than it admitted to, though Pact figures showed the difference as only some 15,000. By trimming off the latter figure unilaterally, the Warsaw Pact could argue that parity would be created and that subsequent concessions should be balanced.

At the instigation of West Germany, NATO made an MBFR move of its own as part of the arms-control package that accompanied its December decisions on modernizing theatre nuclear forces. Rather than a simple Phase I reduction of 29,000 American and 68,000 Soviet forces (together with some specified items of equipment on each side) as it had proposed in 1978, NATO suggested that this be reduced to sub-phases, with some 13,000 American and 30,000 Soviet troops withdrawn in the first of them – amounting to about 40% of the original first phase. It was not clear precisely how many tanks and infantry combat vehicles would be associated with the 30,000 Soviet troops in the NATO proposal, or even if equipment would be included at all, but 40% of the original Phase I figures would total 700 tanks and 100 infantry combat vehicles. Nor was it clear what other equipment would be included in the offer.

The idea of such an 'interim agreement' had most recently been proposed by Chancellor Schmidt to the SPD party congress in West Berlin. Given the TNF context, it must be seen almost exclusively in political terms, as a way of injecting some life into the protracted Vienna negotiations at a time when domestic political reasons made it important for the West to be seen to be taking arms control seriously.

NATO's unilateral announcement that it would withdraw 1,000 of the 7,000 or so American nuclear warheads in Europe as part of the TNF package did not appear directly in the MBFR context. However, it was likely to bear on these negotiations because the Western 'Option III' proposal of 1975 had offered the withdrawal of precisely this number of warheads and of 36 *Pershing* I missiles. The offer to scrap the latter had come to look increasingly meaningless as NATO moved to introduce 108 new *Pershing* II missiles as part of its theatre nuclear modernization. In effect, the TNF modernization plus the warhead offer amounted to withdrawing Option III from MBFR.

Much remained conjectural, especially how the East would react to these moves, but several points were clear. First, the new NATO initiative must be firmly linked to the subsequent phases of an MBFR agreement; otherwise an interim agreement, largely cosmetic in design, could be hailed as a major arms control achievement, which it clearly would not be, and the rest of the negotiations could slide into obscurity or remain in a state of deadlock. One suggestion was that the interim agreement should contain a clause to indicate that it would lapse if the next sub-phase were not concluded within a given period.

Second, the data issue would hardly cease to be a bone of contention, even though it may be a little easier to handle. If the major numbers in dispute concerned Polish forces and Soviet forces in Poland (the 'missing 150,000' were believed to be there), it might be relatively simple to agree Soviet and American data for forces deployed in East and West Germany only.

However, this led to the third important point. No Western government would be likely to endorse any MBFR agreement, however slight, unless an effective and reasonably comprehensive set of verification measures was in operation. In December, after long discussion, the West tabled a broad new set of measures, comprising both proposals for mutual verification and confidence building measures (CBM). Verification measures would include an exchange of observers, arrangements for ground inspection and reconnaissance over-flights, declared exit and entry points for the movement of men and equipment in and out of the designated area, and a mechanism for exchanging information on force levels. Two essential provisions would underpin these specific measures: a general agreement not to interfere with 'national technical' means of verification, and the establishment of a standing consultative commission in which to resolve disputes. Both would follow the precedent of SALT in their drafting and operation. In addition the West proposed some CBM similar to those already in effect as a result of the 1975 CSCE meeting in Helsinki, but with one very important difference: they would be obligatory and not voluntary. In order to lessen mutual fears of surprise attack, a group of CBM would be included in the associated measures to cover the prior notification of exercises and movements within the area (perhaps subsumed under a general heading of 'out-of-garrison activities') and the prior notification of troop movements into the area from outside. A further provision might place limits on the size of exercises and movements.

Because these proposals were only formally tabled just before the end of the year it was impossible to gauge Warsaw Pact reactions. MBFR negotiators on the Eastern side had eagerly awaited them for some time, and the East showed a growing commitment to the idea of CBM during the year. However, the Soviet interest in such measures had so far been clearest in CSCE, not MBFR. It was by no means impossible that two sets of CBM could co-exist – one mandatory set applying to the area covered by the MBFR talks, and another voluntary set which was widely applicable – but the grounds for confusion would be considerable.

With regard to any interim agreement, it was still unclear how the issue of collectivity would be handled. The East had always sought to negotiate, as part of Phase I, sub-ceilings framed in such a way that no country, and particularly not West Germany, would be able to increase its forces to make good withdrawals by any others. Prior to the idea of an interim agreement, the West agreed that Phase I would contain formal undertakings by all powers that they would stand by their commitments in Phase II. The sides were also reported to have reached a compromise in respect to sub-ceilings whereby no nation could have more than half of the deployed manpower of either bloc. In effect this would limit West German forces to 450,000 before reductions took place (the current declared figure was about 451,000), which is half the Western pre–reduction total for ground and air forces of 900,000. It was not clear at the end of the year whether the interim agreement would allude either to the principle of individual country limitation or to the commitment to reduce in subsequent phases — though there were hints that at least the latter point would be accepted.

Another outstanding issue was that of an immediate freeze on manpower at existing levels. This was primarily an Eastern proposal, although it was viewed quite sympathetically in some Western circles. The problem remained that a freeze sounded unconvincing in the absence of assured verification. On the other hand, the Eastern side appeared unlikely to be prepared to consider associated measures *before* discussion of reductions – arguing, fairly logically, that there is little point in discussing verification until you know what has to be verified.

CSCE

The approach of the Madrid meeting of the Conference on Security and Co-operation in Europe, scheduled for October 1980, was bound to direct attention to European security issues. Given the disappointment of many European states with the meagre results of the 1978 CSCE review conference in Belgrade, it had for some time been clear that security questions would loom larger in Madrid. The failure of SALT II and the uncertain state of East–West detente provided incentives to search for new forums and new means of filling the gap.

Expanding the CBM in the Helsinki Final Act would be a main task of the Madrid meeting. At the Belgrade conference NATO, the Warsaw Pact and European neutrals all made proposals for moving beyond the one mandatory CBM in the Helsinki Final Act (the requirement to notify manoeuvres exceeding 25,000 troops at least three weeks in advance), but no additional measures were agreed. In an effort to appear forthcoming, the Warsaw Pact on 6 December 1979 expressed its willingness to agree to reduce the threshold for mandatory notification to cover manoeuvres involving 20,000 troops and to increase prior notification from three weeks to one month. There were a number of other, very vague proposals concerning a willingness to notify 'big' air and naval manoeuvres as well.

Nevertheless, during 1979 the focus of attention was less substantive than procedural. France added detail to her 1978 proposal for a European Disarmament Conference, suggesting that it follow the Madrid CSCE Review Conference, that it be limited to conventional weapons, that its agreements be mandatory, and that it be applicable to all 'European' areas of the Soviet Union (presumably something more than the 250-km strip included in CSCE). Its first phase would focus on CBM, while a second phase would encompass manpower and equipment reduction. A parallel Eastern proposal, announced on 15 May, called for a European Conference on Military Detente, not formally linked to CSCE, which would discuss both conventional and nuclear issues, specifically including Soviet proposals for an agreement not to be the first to use force.

Interest in one form of post-Madrid European security conference or another increased for a number of reasons. Smaller European states still sought a standing forum in which to participate. West European states, especially West Germany, had been tempted by some extension of CSCE because of their interest in carrying force deployment limitations to Soviet territory. The USSR might attempt to mobilize European neutrals and non-aligned states in a campaign against NATO's December decisions to modernize its theatre nuclear forces and could be expected to emphasize her own no-first-use proposals.

From the perspective of West European countries in particular, in the light of SALT II's failure to be ratified and the consequently diminishing prospects of an early start on SALT III, there was likely to be growing interest in some new, perhaps multilateral, forum in which to discuss theatre nuclear weapons.

OTHER ARMS CONTROL NEGOTIATIONS

In arms-control matters outside the SALT and MBFR negotiations, 1979 passed without any real progress in areas that a year earlier might have appeared to be quite promising. The US-Soviet bilateral negotiations on conventional arms transfers and the talks on controlling chemical warfare both foundered, partly because of the general deterioration in the political climate between the two states, and partly because of seemingly intractable problems of definition and priority. On the question of regional arms-control measures, the creation of a nuclear-free zone in South Asia was again mooted by the United States, supported with reservations by Pakistan and rejected by India.

The venue chosen to announce the progress, or lack of it, of many of the negotiations (which were actually conducted at government-to-government level) was most often the reconvened United Nations Committee on Disarmament at Geneva. Membership of this organization had been expanded from 30 states to 40 in order to accommodate those UN members who felt that the 'nuclear club' had tended to dominate past meetings. The Committee faced an initial problem when China refused to take her allotted seat, but the situation was resolved in October, when China announced that she would end her boycott, having missed the entire 1979 session.

Control of Dangerous Weapons
Radiological Warfare
In July the Soviet Union and the United States submitted to the Committee a joint initiative towards a treaty banning the development, production and stockpiling of radiological weapons. These were defined as 'any device specifically designed to employ radioactive material by disseminating it to cause destruction, damage or injury by means of the radiation produced by the decay of such material, or any radioactive material specifically designed for such purpose'. This definition did not include the dissemination of radioactive material from a nuclear explosion.

First suggested by the United States in 1976, and taken up with the Soviet Union in 1977, the proposed treaty was confirmed by Presidents Carter and Brezhnev during their meeting in June 1979, with the provision that the final treaty (which it was hoped would be signed during 1980) would be of 'unlimited duration' and that its progress would be assessed by a conference convened ten years after the treaty's implementation. The initiative was well received by the Committee, probably because it forbade the development of devices that had excited little interest in the states that might possibly manufacture and use them. The proposed treaty represented the only major arms-control success placed before the Committee during the year, and was the result of bilateral negotiations rather than Committee action.

Chemical Weapons
After first rejecting a call by the Disarmament Committee to disclose details of their bilateral talks on the banning of chemical weapons, the United States and the Soviet Union announced in September that they had completed their tenth round of talks on the subject and hoped to

present a joint initiative to the Committee sometime in 1980. However, there were suggestions that the bilateral talks had reached deadlock over the issue of verification, especially in relation to on-site inspection. Britain hosted a 22-nation conference in March, aimed at testing the feasibility of the available verification methods, where it was noted that the Warsaw Pact states were extremely reluctant to discuss the matter of on-site inspection.

By the end of the year the United States Army was pressing for the inclusion in the Fiscal 1981 budget of funds for new chemical munitions, known as 'binary agents', which, by combining two chemical substances, achieve a greater toxicity than that of either substance individually. To counter the charge that the acquisition of such munitions would undermine the negotiations taking place between the US and the USSR, the Pentagon argued that, without the new weapons, the natural deterioration of the chemical weapons currently held by the US would reduce the USSR's incentive to reach an agreement. Early in 1980 the dichotomy was unresolved.

Nuclear Proliferation
Comprehensive Test Ban Treaty
Negotiations on this treaty continued to centre upon possible monitoring techniques and systems for the detection of underground nuclear tests. The placement and policing of 'black-box' seismic recorders became a matter of open contention in October, when the Soviet Union insisted that besides ten recorder stations in the USSR and the US there should be a further ten scattered throughout Britain, Hong Kong and the Falkland Islands. Britain objected to this suggestion, partly because of an unwillingness to put such stations in an area as small and sensitive as Hong Kong, and partly because of the cost of installing and maintaining them (it was estimated that each site would cost £3 million to build and a further £500,000 per year to maintain). The negotiating session ended in December with little discernible progress made.

Nuclear-Free Zones
In response to continuing apprehension about Pakistan's nuclear weapons development programme, the United States promoted the idea of a nuclear-free zone in South Asia that would be supported by security guarantees from the United States, the Soviet Union and China. The proposal put forward was that India and Pakistan should agree to renounce the acquisition of nuclear weapons and to accept safeguards on existing nuclear facilities. In exchange, the three guarantor states would agree not to threaten either of them with nuclear attack.

Pakistan had previously suggested such a zone and welcomed this initiative. In November she sponsored a resolution in the First Committee (Political and Security) of the UN General Assembly reaffirming support for the principle of a nuclear-free zone in South Asia and urging states of the region to do all they could to promote it, and to refrain from any action that might impede it. The resolution was approved by 86 votes to 3, but India – one of the three nations that opposed it – argued that such a zone could not be imposed from outside but must develop from an initiative in the region, thus nullifying the positive vote in the Committee.

On 22 September a US satellite detected a flash of light in the South Atlantic which was assumed to have been caused by the testing of a nuclear device by South Africa. In the ensuing furore this was for a while assumed to be proof that South Africa had achieved nuclear status, and in November the General Assembly's First Committee adopted a resolution sponsored by 26 African states calling for the establishment of a nuclear-free zone in Africa. However, the satellite's information was not immediately corroborated by other monitoring arrangements, and it remained an open question whether there had been a nuclear explosion, and, if so, what country had detonated it.

Conventional Arms Transfers
The control of conventional arms transfers (CAT) had been a major facet of President Carter's foreign-policy proposals both during his election campaign and in the early period of his Administration. As part of this policy, the United States and the Soviet Union had met four times between December 1977 and December 1978 to discuss limiting arms sales on a regional basis. The final meeting in Mexico City in December 1978 had collapsed over the issue of 'regions of application', with the US and Soviet negotiators completely at odds. Despite the personal commitment of the US President to CAT, the almost complete lack of any official pronouncement on future negotiations and the fact that the United States was once again using arms sales as a major element in her foreign policy seemed to indicate that the CAT talks were now moribund.

CHRONOLOGIES

NORTH AMERICA

January
8   White House officials say President Carter refused Pentagon request for another 90,000-ton *Nimitz*-class nuclear carrier in favour of smaller vessels.
13–14   US flies 14,000 troops to Europe to test her ability to reinforce NATO in a crisis.
22   Carter presents Congress with 1979–80 defence budget of $122.7bn (3.1% real increase over 1978–9), with 3% increase for NATO defence.
25   In first hearing on defence budget, Defense Secretary Brown notes a change in strategy: priority to military, rather than economic, targets.

February
10   Carter states 7th Fleet will continue to protect Taiwan against China.
25   Defense Secretary Brown says US will defend her interests in the Middle East with 'military force' if necessary.
27   Carter asks Congress to permit Defense Department to acquire 55 F-16 fighters, 2 destroyers and over 600 missiles originally intended for Iran.

March
5   Defense Department announces $99.8-m sale to Thailand of 18 F-5E/F fighters.
13   Nuclear Regulatory Commission (NRC) orders shut-down of five atomic power plants because cooling systems may be unable to withstand earthquakes.
13   Congress approves unofficial relations with Taiwan.
28   Radiation leak discovered at Three Mile Island nuclear plant, Pennsylvania.
29   House of Representatives refuses military aid to Jordan until she co-operates with Middle East peace efforts.

April
1   Carter inspects crippled Three Mile Island nuclear plant.
6   Administration approves $6.8-m computer sale to Soviet news agency Tass.
7   First US *Trident* missile submarine, *Ohio*, christened – to be operational in 1981.
10   First underwater launch of *Trident* missile fails.
26   Carter asks Congress for $50m extra aid for Turkey; final package to be $450m.
27   Two convicted Soviet spies, Vladik Enger and Rudolf Chermyayev to be exchanged for Alexander Ginsburg, Mark Dymshits, Edvard Kuznetsov, Valentin Moroz and Georgi Vins.

May
1   Canada concludes a financing agreement of up to $1bn with Romania for four 600 MW nuclear power plants.
2   NASA asks for $270–600m for Space Shuttle cost increases (from $6.6bn to $8bn).
3   NRC announces closure of 16 of 70 nuclear plants for safety reasons.
4   Senate approves $2.1-bn supplement to defence budget to acquire destroyers originally ordered for Iran.
7   US Navy announces decommissioning of 38 ships, including 3 cruisers, 20 destroyers, 1 submarine.
22   NRC institutes 3-month delay in licensing new nuclear plants.
23   In Canada, the Progressive Conservative Party led by Joe Clark elected; ends 11-year Trudeau premiership.

June
7   Carter announces US will not lift Rhodesian sanctions.
14   Senate approves Lt Gen. Edward Meyer as Army Chief of Staff, replacing Gen. Bernard Rogers, who becomes Supreme Allied Commander, Europe.

July
16   Carter announces US energy programme, imposing imported oil ceiling for 1979 of 8.2 million barrels a day and including $142-bn investment programme to reduce US oil import dependence.

NORTH AMERICA

17– At President's request, all US Cabinet members resign. Resignations of Attorney General Bell, Treasury, Health, Energy and Transportation Secretaries Blumenthal, Califano, Schlesinger and Adams accepted (19–20).

August
4 US suspends arms sales to Royal Ulster Constabulary.

September
3 Donald McHenry replaces Andrew Young as US representative at the UN.
6 US warns she will not 'tolerate' Soviet combat troops in Cuba.
7 Carter announces MX ICBM will be based in Western US in horizontal multiple protective shelters.

October
3 Carter abandons attempt to block another *Nimitz*-class carrier.
13 Cuban President Castro addresses UN General Assembly, asks for $300-bn investment over next 10 years in developing states.
13 Senate votes to cut foreign aid bill for 1981 by 3%.
18 US sends carrier *Midway* and 6 other ships to Indian Ocean in response to Middle East tension.
22 US announces she will sell armed reconnaissance aircraft, helicopter gunships to Morocco.
22 Shah of Iran arrives in US for surgery.
25 Carter promises $12m immediately to aid refugees from Kampuchea, part of $70 million total.

November
5 NRC announces moratorium on nuclear plant licences pending new safety regulations.
6 After two-year talks, US agrees to supply 34 lbs of plutonium to Britain next year for Anglo–American experiment on safety of fast breeders.
7 Senator Kennedy formally announces candidacy for 1980 Democratic nomination.
9 A computer error causes six-minute 'nuclear war' alert.
19 Senate approves military construction appropriations bill which includes $57 million for MX missile development and testing.
27 State Department advises Americans to avoid 11 Islamic countries and withdraws non-essential embassy staff from them.
28 Aircraft carrier *Forrestal* sails to Mediterranean to strengthen US presence in Middle East. *Kitty Hawk*, with 5 warships has joined *Midway* in Arabian Sea.

December
5 Five-year extension of US–British nuclear materials agreement signed; gives Britain access to *Trident* missile.
6 US Congress approves $131.7-bn military appropriations bill for FY 1980.
6 Eighth US cruise missile crashes during tests near Los Angeles.
12 Carter orders 183 of the 218 Iranian diplomats in US to leave.
12 Carter proposes $157-bn defence budget for 1981; represents 5% real increase.
13 US protests to the USSR about the recent build-up of Soviet troops near Kabul, Afghanistan.
13 Joe Clark's four-month-old Canadian government falls in no-confidence vote.
15 Deposed Shah of Iran leaves US for exile in Panama.
16 US lifts sanctions against Rhodesia.
17 US Defense Department team in Saudi Arabia to discuss possible American use of bases there. It will also visit Kenya, Oman and Somalia.
23 US accuses USSR of threatening Afghanistan by dispatch to Kabul of 1,500 combat troops, and build-up of three divisions on northern border.
26– Israeli Defence Minister Weizman makes unscheduled trip to Washington to discuss aid and defence issues; Carter announces additional $200m in aid, far short of Israeli request (31).
28 Carter condemns Soviet invasion of Afghanistan as 'blatant violation of accepted international rules of behaviour'.
30 National Security Adviser Brzezinski announces US will use armed force to defend Pakistan under 1959 defence agreement.
31 Defence treaty between US and Taiwan expires.

EUROPE

January
1 Hungary and Austria abolish need for visas between them.
3 Gen. Alexander Haig announces retirement from US Army and resignation as Supreme Allied Commander, Europe, effective 30 June.
4 Four-day US–British–French–German summit opens in Guadeloupe.
10 Greek- and Turkish-Cypriots accept UN formula for resumption of negotiations.
18 Turkey and US open talks in Ankara on a new defence agreement.
19 Spanish and Soviet Foreign Ministers conclude three-day talks in Moscow with cultural and scientific exchange agreement.
26 First F-16 fighter built under 5-nation co-production programme delivered to Belgian Air Force.
31 Italian Prime Minister Andreotti resigns when Communist Party withdraws support.

February
5 Spain formally opens negotiations to join the EEC.
10 Eduard Kardelj, Tito's heir-apparent, dies.
13 Turkey refuses to allow US marines at NATO base near Adana to help evacuate Americans from Iran.

February
22 Britain publishes defence white paper, estimating an £8,558-m budget for 1979–80.
25 Turkish Parliament extends martial law for additional 2 months.

March
2 International Energy Agency nations agree to cut oil consumption by 5% each.
5 Belgium's King Baudouin asks acting Premier van den Boeynants to try to form government; country has been without a government for 78 days.
7 France lifts her 3-month veto on start of European Monetary System.
15 Turkey announces withdrawal from CENTO thus joining Iran and Pakistan.
19 New Session of 158-nation Law of the Sea Conference opens in Geneva.
27 Britain announces Royal Navy will acquire new £50-m Type 42 destroyer.
30 USSR delivers 440,000-kW nuclear reactor to Czechoslovakia.

April
1 British Navy relinquishes its base on Malta.
10 Swiss Parliament presents defence budget of 1.7bn S.fr. (£470m), largest since Korean War.
15 Belgian Police and Israeli guards thwart hijack of El Al plane at Brussels.
24 NATO Nuclear Planning Group, meeting in Florida, agrees to strengthen nuclear forces.
24 Turkey again extends martial law.

May
1 Turkey withdraws some troops from Cyprus to improve climate for Summit talks with Greece later in month.
14 Warsaw Pact Foreign Ministers meet in Hungary to discuss Soviet views on SALT II and East–West relations.
15 Romania refuses, as she has for 10 years, to join Warsaw Pact annual manoeuvres.
15 NATO Defence Ministers agree to defence expenditure increase of 3% p.a. till 1986.
16 Tito's heir-apparent, Stane Dolanc, removed as Secretary of the Communist Party Presidium in party shake-up, seen as move to assure collective leadership when Tito dies.
16 NATO Defence Ministers express support for SALT II.
18 Greek- and Turkish-Cypriot leaders Kyprianou and Denktash meet to resolve differences; agree on 10-point plan.
21 Romania's President Ceausescu begins four-day visit to Spain – first by East European leader.
22 Soviet Premier Kosygin visits Prague to discuss Czech energy crisis.
23 USSR agrees to aid Turkey in oil exploration.
27 Turkey's Prime Minister Bulent Ecevit re-elected.
28 Greece becomes 10th member of the EEC.

June

3–4 Communist Party loses 26 seats in elections to the Italian Chamber of Deputies; Social Democrats gain 5, Liberals 4, Republicans 2 and Radicals 14.

5–15 Pope John Paul II meets tumultuous welcome on visit to Poland.

5 West German Chancellor Schmidt holds wide-ranging talks with Carter in Washington before Vienna Summit.

7 Premier Carlos da Mota Pinto, head of Portugal's 10th government since 1974 revolution resigns; 3rd government crisis in one year.

9 First direct election to European Parliament; centre-right parties win majority of the 410 seats.

12 Portugal agrees to continued US use of Azores air base.

24 Turkey refuses to allow US to stage SALT verification flights over USSR from Turkey.

July

15 Czech authorities arrest 10 leading members of Charter 77 human-rights group.

17 French delegate Simone Veil elected President of the European Parliament.

24 French government approves sale of 16 *Mirage* 50 aircraft to Chile.

August

2 President Giscard d'Estaing announces 15% increase in 1980 French defence budget.

11 Francesco Cossiga, head of a 3-party coalition, becomes Italian Prime Minister, ending 6-month hiatus in government.

15 Spanish parliament approves Catalonian self-rule, to be ratified by a referendum.

20 Turkey and US re-open negotiations on future of US bases in Turkey, 3 weeks before old agreement expires.

27 IRA murder Lord Mountbatten; on same day kill 18 British soldiers in ambush.

September

12 US offers Turkey $30m in aid to develop arms industry.

20 Non-Socialist alliance wins one-seat majority in Swedish general election.

October

3 After 2-day Franco–German talks, Schmidt and Giscard call for speedy ratification of SALT.

4 France begins biggest manoeuvres since World War II – 900 tanks, 200 planes, 120 helicopters, 17,000 men. Soviet and Warsaw Pact observers present.

5 Soviet President Brezhnev arrives in East Berlin for 30th anniversary of East German state; Romanian President Ceausescu only Warsaw Pact leader absent.

17– Turkish premier Ecevit submits resignation after defeat in mid-term elections; Justice Party leader Demirel invited to form a government (24).

27 Voters in Catalonia and Basque country approve autonomy statutes.

November

1 British defence white paper states defence spending will rise 3% in real terms next year.

8 Dutch government gives qualified support to deployment of new nuclear weapons in Western Europe.

8 Combined US–Spanish manoeuvres, largest since 1976 US Treaty of Friendship and Co-operation, take place in Spain.

12 Suleyman Demirel becomes Turkish Prime Minister for the sixth time in 14 years.

19 First Romanian Party Congress since 1974 opens in Bucharest. China sends her first delegation to a party congress outside China since 1960s.

19– Soviet Foreign Minister Gromyko, in Madrid, warns Spain against joining NATO; in Bonn, warns new nuclear missiles in Europe could seriously undermine East–West detente (22).

29 NATO's Council of Permanent Representatives reject Danish proposals for a 6-month moratorium on nuclear modernization.

29–30 At EEC summit in Dublin Prime Minister Thatcher unsuccessfully requests £1,000-m cut in Britain's budget contributions.

December

3 In Portuguese elections, the Democratic Alliance (coalition of four right-wing parties) wins 125 of 250 parliamentary seats.

4	European Justice Ministers sign new convention on terrorism, easing extradition regulations.
5–	Irish Prime Minister Jack Lynch resigns; Charles Haughey succeeds (11).
5	First Soviet troop withdrawal from East Germany (18 T-62 tanks and 100 soldiers) begins.
12	NATO meeting in Brussels agrees to deploy 572 new intermediate-range nuclear missiles in West Germany, Britain, Italy and Belgium by 1983.
13	European Parliament rejects the first EEC budget presented to it.
15–	Western Europe's space launcher *Ariane* fails in its first test flight attempt in French Guiana; third try succeeds (24).
18	British Energy Secretary Howell announces nuclear power expansion programme that will cost £10–12 bn.
18	EEC formally recognizes the Association of South-East Asian Nations (ASEAN) as a political body.

THE SOVIET UNION

January

12	US government sources report a third major Soviet aircraft carrier is completing construction, to be ready Spring 1979.
20	USSR releases her 1978 economic figures, showing falls in production of key commodities, including oil, coal, steel and cement.

February

1	US Administration officials say USSR has begun to test her own version of the long-range cruise missile.
7	Five-day manoeuvres involving 6,000 Czech and Soviet troops in Western Bohemia end.
9	*Tokyo Shimbun* newspaper reports that the USSR is building 3 air bases and five runways in the Northern Islands.
25	USSR launches *Soyuz-32* with 2 cosmonauts to check possible future use of *Salyut-6* space laboratory.

March

13	US officials say Soviet SS-18 ICBM has been adapted to carry 14 warheads, though only 10 are permitted under SALT II.
28	US defence sources report Soviet warships have anchored for the first time in Cam Ranh Bay, former US installation on Vietnamese coast.

April

10–	*Soyuz-33* launch with Soviet and Bulgarian cosmonauts, in attempt to link up with an orbiting laboratory; mission aborted (12).
25–	French President Giscard d'Estaing arrives in Moscow for 10th Franco–Russian Summit; joint communiqué pledges renewed efforts on detente and French support of new industrial projects (28).

June

5	USSR proposes talks with China, to be held in Moscow in July or August.
5	After 6-day meeting of Turkish–Soviet Commission on Economic Co-operation, USSR pledges construction of nuclear plant in Turkey, guarantees 20-year uranium fuel supply and $8bn for construction of 20 other projects.
10	US Department of Agriculture forecasts sharp drop in Soviet grain production from 237.2 to 190 million tons.

August

2	Leonid Brezhnev and President Ceausescu of Romania, in the Crimea, discuss foreign-policy differences.

September

19	Soviet request for visits to Philippine ports by Soviet warships refused.
24	Chinese delegation arrives in Moscow for talks on Sino–Soviet relations.

October
22   US Joint Economic Committee of Congress reports Soviet defence spending rose to 137% of amount spent by US in 1977.
25   USSR and South Yemen (PDRY) sign 20-year friendship treaty in Moscow.

November
12   *Pravda* editorial admits USSR faces energy shortage, calls for 'strict economy' this winter.
26–   EEC and COMECON begin talks in Moscow on framework agreement between them; talks end with suggestion that co-operation agreement may be signed in 1980 (29).
29   *Izvestia* publishes statistics showing Soviet national income growth to be lowest since World War II.
30   Month-long talks between China and Moscow end with no progress.
30   24th Soviet underground nuclear explosion this year.

December
5   First official Soviet comment on Iranian crisis charges US with blackmailing Iran 'by massing forces on its frontiers'.
28   USSR claims her airlift of troops to Afghanistan justified response to urgent request for military aid from Kabul government in accordance with 20-year-old treaty of friendship.

ASIA AND AUSTRALASIA

January
1   Formal diplomatic ties established between China and USA.
2–   Kampuchea asks UN for support against Vietnamese and Soviet aggression. Vietnam-backed Cambodian rebels claim to have seized two provincial capitals, Stung Treng on the Mekong River and Lomphat (3). Vice-Premier Deng Xiaoping tells US journalists China will not send advisers to help Kampuchea against Vietnam (5). Vietnam-backed Kampuchean National United Front claims to have taken Phnom Penh; US intelligence reports China has moved major military forces towards border with Vietnam (7). France reaffirms support for an independent Kampuchea (8). Eight-man revolutionary council formed in Kampuchea under Heng Samrin (8); recognized by USSR and Vietnam as legal government of Kampuchea (9). USSR vetoes Security Council resolution calling for withdrawal of all foreign forces from Kampuchea (15). Sources in Hong Kong and Bangkok report China has marched two divisions to within striking distance of Vietnam (26).
5   Prime Minister Callaghan announces Britain will sell *Harrier* jump jets to China if Peking agrees to increase purchases of British goods by £400m.
7   Britain and Brunei sign agreement for Brunei independence in 1985 and end agreement by which Britain handles Brunei's external relations and defence.
25   South Korea accepts North Korean proposal for preliminary unification talks.
28–   Deng Xiaoping begins official visit to US; he and President Carter sign agreements on science and technology, cultural exchanges and establishment of consulates (31).
30   Philippines President Marcos cancels plans for local elections this year, warns he may resume power to legislate by decree.

February
3–   Pakistan's military government orders arrest of hundreds of officials of the Pakistan People's Party, including former senators and National Assembly members. Supreme court upholds the death sentence passed on deposed premier Z. A. Bhutto (6).
10   President Carter halts US troop withdrawals from S. Korea until recent developments, including build-up of N. Korean forces, are reviewed.
12   Indian Foreign Minister Vajpayee arrives in China for talks, the first visit since 1962.
14   US Ambassador to Afghanistan Adolph Dubs killed when security forces storm the Kabul hotel where he is held hostage by Muslim dissidents.
15   Taiwan announces establishment of Co-ordinations Council for North American Affairs to handle relations with the US.
17   N. and S. Korea meet for first time in 6 years, agree to meet again in 3 weeks.

17–	Chinese troops cross 450-mile border and invade Vietnam. Vietnam accuses China of 'war of aggression' and asks UN action to force withdrawal (18). Chinese troops capture border city of Lao Cai (20). Western analysts report USSR has begun major airlift of military supplies to Vietnam (22). China calls for Hanoi to join in negotiations to end the border war (27).
26	US–Chinese negotiations begin in Peking on freeing assets frozen since Korean war, involving $197m of US claims against China and $80m of Chinese assets in the US.
27	US Senate confirms the appointment of Leonard Woodcock as Ambassador to China.

March

1	US embassy is formally opened in Peking.
5–	China announces the beginning of withdrawal from Vietnam, saying all her goals have been attained; Vietnam orders general mobilization. Vietnam claims Chinese troops still fighting inside Vietnam (7). Western analysts report Chinese troops beginning to withdraw, destroying bridges, rail and roads as they go (8). Chinese Premier Hua Guofeng announces all Chinese troops have left Vietnam (15).
11	China announces that Laos has asked her to withdraw her experts and end projects there.
12–	National Liberation Front, a Muslim group, declares holy war against the Socialist regime of Afghan premier Taraki. New clashes between army units and rebel Muslims reported in Paktia province (14). USSR admits Marxist Afghan regime faces strong Muslim opposition and attacks Pakistan, China and Egypt for aiding the opposition (19). Afghan army leave cancelled amid reports of fighting with Muslim rebels in at least 5 provinces (21). Carter Administration cautions USSR against military interference in Afghanistan as Soviet arms build-up is reported; rejects Soviet allegation of US intervention (23). Afghan foreign minister, Hafizullah Amin, named prime minister. (27)
12	Pakistan announces withdrawal from CENTO.
16	US intelligence says USSR conducting large-scale military manoeuvres near Sino-Soviet border.
27	Pakistan signs $330-m contract to buy 32 *Mirage* III and *Mirage* 5 fighters from France.

April

3	China announces she will not renew Treaty of Friendship, Alliance and Mutual Assistance with USSR, due to expire in 1980.
4–	Former Pakistani prime minister Bhutto executed in Rawalpindi. President Zia declares an end to martial law, in force since 1975 (6). Anti-government demonstrators clash with police in Karachi in protest at Bhutto hanging (6). Zia announces formation of 15-man caretaker cabinet, schedules elections for 17 November (22).
6	China accepts Vietnam's invitation to talks on border situation.
26	US completes military withdrawal from Taiwan.

May

2	Japanese premier Ohira, in US, signs agreement to reduce Japan's trading surplus.
3	China reveals 20,000 troops injured or killed in month-long campaign against Vietnam.
14	Soviet Deputy Foreign Minister Firyubin confirms Soviet ships are using US-built naval base at Cam Ranh Bay under friendship treaty with Vietnam.
18	China breaks off peace talks with Vietnam after fifth meeting; Vietnam accuses China of massing 500,000 troops on border.

June

8	Thailand forces 7–10,000 Kampuchean refugees back across border.

July

2–	ASEAN States announce they will accept no more Indochinese refugees and reserve right to send back those who have already arrived. At UN Conference on refugees, Vietnam government announces it will halve refugee exodus. (23)
15–	Indian Prime Minister Morarji Desai resigns. Charan Singh asked by President to form a new government (27).
30	In Cabinet reshuffle, Afghan President Taraki takes over foreign affairs portfolio from Prime Minister Amin, as well as defence portfolio.

ASIA AND AUSTRALASIA

August
5   Afghan army units revolt in Kabul; loyal troops using Soviet helicopter gunships, MiG-21s, tanks, crush revolt.
21 After 24 days in office, Indian government of Charan Singh falls when Indira Gandhi's party withdraws from coalition.

September
16 Afghan President Taraki overthrown by Hafizullah Amin. Taraki's death announced later.
25 Vietnamese-led offensive launched against Pol Pot forces north and north-east of Phnom Penh.
28 CENTO terminated with close-down of offices in Ankara, Turkey.

October
3   S. Korean government announces an increase of 32.3% for defence.
9   China announces talks with USSR have reached impasse on bilateral issues, especially border problems.
15– Chinese premier Hua Guofeng visits France, W. Germany (21–27), Britain (28 Oct–5 Nov) and Italy (6 Nov); pronounces tour 'a complete success'.
17 Pakistani President Zia-ul Haq cancels general election planned for 17 November, introduces press censorship, bans all political parties.
22– President Park of S. Korea puts army in charge of industrial cities of Nasan and Chongwon after student demonstration. Park killed by Kim Jae Kyu, head of Korean CIA; Prime Minister Choi Kyu Hah takes over as acting president (27). Defense Secretary Brown says US has sent 2 AWACS aircraft to S. Korea and ordered an aircraft carrier nearer to area (29).

November
4   Afghan President Amin declines invitation to visit Moscow to discuss the Muslim rebellion.
15 UN General Assembly vote 91 to 21, with 29 abstentions, demands Vietnam withdraw her troops from Kampuchea.
21 Muslim students attack and burn US Embassy in Islamabad. 100 US citizens rescued by Pakistani troops after a 6-hour siege; 1 US marine killed.

December
6– Choi Kyu Hah, elected S. Korean President, revokes emergency decree which outlaws all forms of political dissent; Shin Hyon Hwack, named Prime Minister (10). Group of generals seize military power and take command of key buildings in Seoul (13). Shin announces new Cabinet, with new military leaders as ministers of defence, justice and foreign affairs (14). Kim Jae Kyu sentenced to death for murder of Park (20).
25– USSR begins airlift of troops to Kabul. President Amin executed in Soviet-backed coup, replaced by pro-Soviet Babrak Karmal (27). Soviet strength in Afghanistan estimated at 25,000 as troops and equipment continue to arrive (30).

MIDDLE EAST AND NORTH AFRICA

January
3– Shahpur Bakhtiar becomes new civilian premier of Iran. Exiled Ayatollah Khomeini says Shah 'must be tried' for his crimes. Street violence erupts (7). Bakhtiar says Iran will revise all military contracts, estimated to be worth $10 bn (8). President Carter orders 12 unarmed F-15 fighters to Saudi Arabia to demonstrate US support and show concern over Iranian situation (10). Khomeini establishes Provisional Revolutionary Islamic Council to replace 'illegal' government in Iran (13). The Shah appoints Regency Council to represent him when he leaves for Egypt (16). Iranian military authorities ban all demonstrations (26).
13 US announces she is to give Lebanon extra arms worth $42.5 m.
14 Israel announces decision to build 3 settlements in West Bank and Gaza Strip.
30 Syria and Iraq conclude mutual defence pact and plan to create a unified state.
31 Col. Bendjedid Chadli, acting chief of armed forces, named Algerian President by congress of ruling National Liberation Front.

February

1– Khomeini returns to Iran after 14 years and threatens to arrest Bakhtiar government if it refuses to resign; names Medhi Bazargan premier of new Islamic republic (5). Bakhtiar government collapses, the army abandons its support, and Khomeini's forces take over (11). Khomeini installs Bazargan as Premier (12). Bakhtiar arrested (13).

7– President Carter invites Egypt and Israel to resume ministerial-level peace talks at Camp David. Egypt and Israel accept (8 and 10). Talks open with meetings between Foreign Ministers Vance, Khalil and Dayan (21).

22 Over 100 killed on the Iran–Iraq border in clashes between Kurds and supporters of new Tehran government.

25– Border fighting breaks out between N. and S. Yemen; US announces she is accelerating arms supplies to N. Yemen. Saudi Arabia cancels all military leave (28).

March

1– S. Yemeni troops reported deep inside North Yemen; Saudi Arabia orders a partial mobilization. After mediation by Syria and Iraq, N. and S. Yemen agree to cease-fire (2). S. Yemeni planes raid N. Yemen despite ceasefire; Secretary-General Mahmoud Riad announces plans for Arab League mediation committee to visit both countries (6). N. and S. Yemen begin to disengage under the terms negotiated by the Arab League, agree to complete withdrawals within 10 days (13).

1– Carter and Begin meet in Washington after failing to break Middle East deadlock. US presents new proposals (4). Carter arrives in Cairo for talks with Sadat (8). Carter and Begin hold talks in Jerusalem (11). Sadat agrees to US proposals; Carter returns to Washington (13). The Israeli Cabinet approves compromise proposals for Middle East peace treaty, paving the way for ratification by Knesset (14). Palestinian guerrilla leader Yasser Arafat calls for an Arab oil embargo against Egypt if she signs a peace treaty with Israel (14). Egyptian cabinet unanimously approves draft peace treaty (15). Begin and Sadat sign treaty in Washington (26). Israeli forces begin evacuating Sinai within 36 hours of signing (28).

19 Cease-fire reached between Kurds and Tehran government.

19 In United Arab Emirates, 3,000 demonstrators call for abolition of borders in the emirates, unification of armed forces and effective immigration policy.

April

1 Khomeini announces an Islamic Republic after 18 million vote for it in referendum.

22– Syrian-Christian fighting in Lebanon. Israel shells Lebanon, UNIFIL arranges truce (25).

29 First Israeli ship for 25 years sails through Suez Canal.

29 Joint Israeli-Egyptian Military Committee holds first meeting, discusses programme for Israeli withdrawal from Sinai.

May

4 Israel informs Egypt that Camp David accords do not oblige her to withdraw from West Bank, Gaza Strip or Golan Heights.

16 Lebanon's Cabinet resigns; Salim al-Hoss remains as caretaker premier.

25– El Arish, capital of the Sinai, restored to Egypt after 12 years as first step in Sinai withdrawal. Egypt and Israel open their border (27).

27 Iran decides against elections for a constituent Assembly, instead will hold national referendum to approve a new constitution.

June

5 Egypt announces arms agreement with China; no details given, but may include supply of 60 MiG-19 fighters to Egypt.

18– Lebanon sends army units into Beirut to calm fighting in Christian suburbs. Israeli jets engage Syrian jets in air battle over Lebanon (27).

July

16 President Bakr of Iraq resigns, replaced by Saddam Hussein, Vice-Chairman of Revolutionary Command Council.

20 UN Security Council vote condemns new Israeli settlements, asks for halt in construction.

25 Israel evacuates 2,500 square miles of Sinai along Gulf of Suez, hands land back to Egypt.

August

6– Mauritania signs peace agreement with Polisario and renounces all claims to former Spanish Sahara. Morocco says she will withdraw troops from Mauritania (10); announces West Sahara is 'new Moroccan province' (15).

17– Kurdish rebels reported to have overrun town of Paveh on Iraqi border. Iranian armed forces and Kurds involved in heavy fighting (27).

24– UN Security Council begins debate on resolution calling for creation of independent Palestine. Arab states agree not to push it to a vote (27).

September

3 Sadat offers military aid to Morocco for her fight against Polisario.

4 Syria sends 1,400 troops to port of Latakia to put down sectarian violence.

6– Sadat and Begin agree on joint Israeli-Egyptian patrols in Sinai as temporary measure on withdrawal of UNEF. Israel hands over further segment of Sinai to Egypt (25).

October

5 US supplies of helicopter and military aircraft spares to Iran resumed after 8 month pause.

10– Iran announces reinforcements to fight Kurds near Iraqi border. W. Azerbaijan provincial governor states government forces no longer control Mehabad (15). Kurds reported fighting for control of Mehabad (22).

20 Syrian President Assad ends visit to Moscow; USSR pledges substantial military aid to Syria.

24 France sending token force of 150 men to Mauritania to warn Morocco and Polisario not to violate Mauritanian territory.

27 Egypt, Israel and US agree Palestinians in West Bank and Gaza Strip can participate in organizing and conducting elections for self-governing authority.

November

4– Muslim students demanding return of Shah to Iran seize US Embassy in Tehran and take 63 hostages. Bazargan resigns (5). Khomeini replaces government with Revolutionary Council (6). UN Security Council orders release of hostages (9). President Carter orders Justice Department to deport all Iranian students illegally in US (10). US suspends oil imports from Iran (12); freezes Iranian assets (14). UN General Assembly adopts resolution condemning taking of hostages (17). Iranian students release 5 women and 8 black hostages on Khomeini's orders (19–20). UN Secretary-General calls for urgent meeting of Security Council (25).

20 Fanatical Moslem sect takes over the Grand Mosque in Mecca.

25 In fourth phase of Sinai withdrawal, Israel evacuates Alma oil field in Gulf of Suez, a major source of her oil supplies.

25 USSR reported to have concluded arms deal with N. Yemen, involving MiG-21 aircraft, anti-tank missiles and tanks, without any payment.

28 Serious disturbances in Saudi Arabia's Eastern province, the area of her richest oilfields; 20,000 troops break up pro-Iranian demonstration led by Shi'ite minority.

December

2 Mob of 2,000, including Libyan troops, burns US Embassy in Tripoli; no Americans injured.

3– First results of 2-day referendum confirm Khomeini's position as ruler of Iran. Unanimous UN Security Council resolution calls for immediate release of US hostages (4). US carrier *Kitty Hawk* joins *Midway* in Arabian Sea (5). Largest American presence since 1945 – 21 warships – reported in Arabian Sea (6). Iran's leading opposition figure, Ayatollah Shariat-Madari warns that if revolt in Azerbaijan (Turkish-speaking area of north-west Iran) is mishandled 'civil war will take place' (11); several hundred thousand march through Tabriz to support him (13). International Court of Justice unanimously orders Iran to release US hostages immediately (16). UN Security Council votes 11-0 to give Iran one week to release hostages, USSR and three others abstain (31).

11– Colonel Gaddafi, the Libyan leader, announces the suspension of all Libyan contributions to the PLO; withdraws recognition of PLO and closes PLO offices in Libya (21).

16 Saudi troops finally regain complete control of the Grand Mosque in Mecca.

30 Sadat announces Egypt will provide military facilities for American troops to defend Arab countries in the Gulf.

SUB-SAHARAN AFRICA

January

4   Internal wing of SWAPO agrees to participate in UN-supervised elections in Namibia and accepts Waldheim proposals on condition no changes are made.

10–   In first call-up of Black Rhodesians for military service, only 300 of 1,544 drafted report for duty. Rhodesia extends military draft to include men in 50–59 age group (12).

15   Judge Marthinus Steyn and UN representative Ahtisaari begin talks on plans for UN-supervised elections in Namibia.

20–   Uganda accuses Tanzania of invading her. Tanzania admits her troops entered Uganda (26).

27   The two main Eritrean liberation fronts, ELF and EPLF, announce formation of joint political leadership and joint delegation to negotiate settlement of the war in Eritrea.

February

7   Congo Defence Minister Sasson-Nguesso replaces President Opango in bloodless coup.

12–   Fighting breaks out in Chad's capital between forces of President Malloum and Premier Habre. Malloum takes refuge at French military base in N'Djamena, handing over power to chief of national police (15). Malloum and Habre sign a cease-fire agreement as the first step to national reconciliation (19).

12–   59 killed when Air Rhodesia *Viscount* shot down with 2 SAM-7 missiles by ZIPRA guerrillas. Joshua Nkomo claims responsibility (13). ZAPU guerrillas shell Salisbury airport, first attack there since 1972 (19). Rhodesian planes attack nationalist guerrilla camp and military base close to Zambian capital (23).

25   Tanzanian forces and Ugandan rebels take Masaka in southern Uganda; Uganda admits her forces being overwhelmed, appeals to friendly countries for military aid.

26   UN Secretary-General Waldheim proposes 15 March date for a cease-fire in Namibia and start of UN preparations for pre-independence elections.

March

4–   Fresh clashes in Chad violate cease-fire and cause over 800 deaths. Nigerian peace-keeping force arrives to police cease-fire in N'Djamena (6). After 6-day talks, accord to end civil strife signed in Kano, Nigeria, by rival Chad leaders and Nigeria, Libya, Cameroon, Sudan and Niger: calls for general cease-fire, Nigerian peace-keeping force and establishment of a transitional 'government of national union' (16).

4   Iran severs relations with S. Africa and confirms that she will not resume oil sales to her.

7   Ghana announces end to military rule; Presidential and Parliamentary elections to be held on 18 June.

8   UN Security Council adopts resolution condemning forthcoming Rhodesian elections and declaring results will not be recognized.

17   Warrant issued for arrest of Eschel Rhoodie, former S. African propaganda chief, who threatens to expose the full extent of 'Muldergate' scandal.

26–   Ugandan President Amin says he is besieged by Tanzanian troops and tanks at his Entebbe residence. Libyan leader Gaddafi threatens war on Tanzania unless she halts invasion of Uganda (27).

April

1   Sasson-Nguesso elected Congo's new president; former President Opango to be tried for treason.

6   Dr Connie Mulder expelled from S. Africa's ruling National Party for his part in 'Muldergate' scandal.

10   Rhodesian planes bomb Joshua Nkomo's military HQ near Lusaka.

11–   Kampala falls to Tanzanian troops. Yusefu Lule becomes President of Uganda (13). Britain restores diplomatic relations with Uganda (16).

17–   Rhodesia holds elections for first majority black parliament. Bishop Muzorewa's United African National Congress wins majority (24).

22–   In Uganda, Jinja falls to Tanzanian troops. Amin's former Vice President, Mustafa Adrisi, arrested (25). Kenya turns back 1,000 fleeing Amin troops at border with Uganda (25). Amin troops gun down people in Tororo after posing as Tanzanian liberation forces (27).

26	Presidents Kaunda of Zambia and Machel of Mozambique meet in Maputo to seek unity between Rhodesian Patriotic Front groups; condemn the Rhodesian election.
27	President Mobutu of Zaire orders OTRAG (W. German rocket company) to halt tests on site leased in Shaba province.
30	In Chad, Mohamed Shawa forms new provisional government to replace provisional State Council.

May

1–	UN Security Council condemns Rhodesian elections and describes result as null and void; Muzorewa appeals to guerrillas opposed to government to accept unconditional amnesty and stop fighting (15). US Senate votes 75-19 for US economic sanctions against Rhodesia to be lifted (15). Vance and Carrington meet in London to discuss new strategy for Rhodesia (21).
14	S. Africa sets up Namibian National Assembly, with considerable legislative and fiscal powers.
15	Libya agrees to pay $40m to ransom troops captured by the Tanzanians in Uganda.
15	In Ghana attempted coup led by air force Maj. Jerry Rawlings is defeated.
22	Central African Empire ambassador to France confirms reports of massacre of children by Bokassa regime.
29–	Bishop Muzorewa sworn in as first black Prime Minister of Rhodesia. Appoints himself minister of defence (30).

June

1	UN General Assembly resolution calls on Security Council to impose economic sanctions on S. Africa to enforce compliance with UN independence plan for Namibia.
3–4	Tanzanian and Ugandan liberation troops complete takeover of Uganda from Amin forces.
4	S. African President Vorster resigns as investigation into 'Muldergate' scandal continues.
4–	Ghanaian air force coup deposes President Akuffo, releases Rawlings from jail. First general election since 1969 held (18).
20	Ugandan President Lule resigns and is succeeded by Godfrey Binaisa.

July

11	Dr Hilla Limann's People's National Party wins run-off vote in Ghanaian election.
13	Tanzania requests $375m from 9 Western states to help defray cost of Ugandan war.

August

1	Nigeria nationalizes British Petroleum production and refining interests; warning to Britain not to lift sanctions against Rhodesia or recognize the internal settlement.
1–	Commonwealth Conference begins in Lusaka, Zambia. Britain agrees to oversee elections in Rhodesia after constitutional agreement. Six-point plan (Lusaka Agreement) put forward to resolve Rhodesian problem (6); Muzorewa's Rhodesian government agrees to attend constitutional conference in London (16). Patriotic Front also agrees (21).
2	S. Africa appoints Gerrit Viljoen Administrator General for Namibia, replacing Judge Steyn.
5	President Macias of Equatorial Guinea overthrown in coup led by Minister of Defence Obiang.
18	France cuts off aid to Central African Empire after report implicates President Bokassa in massacre of schoolchildren in August.
22	Rival Chad leaders reported to have reached agreement on ending 16-year civil war.

September

7	Rhodesian troops raid 50 miles into Mozambique (withdraw after 3 days).
10	Rhodesian constitutional conference opens in London.
10–	President Neto of Angola dies in Moscow. Jose Eduardo dos Santos announced as acting president (20).
11	Presidents Arap Moi of Kenya and Siad Barre of Somalia meet in Saudi Arabia to draw up defence and friendship treaty.
21–	Emperor Bokassa of Central African Empire overthrown by David Dacko, with French help; country's name changed to Central African Republic. Refused entry into France, Bokassa takes refuge in Ivory Coast (25).
24	In Ghana, Armed Forces Revolutionary Council hands over power to civilian government of President Hilla Limann, as promised 3 weeks earlier by Council head Jerry Rawlings.

October

8– At Rhodesia conference in London Britain gives ultimatum to Patriotic Front: accept new constitution or face breakdown of talks. Patriotic Front agree to new constitution put forward by UK (19). Britain proposes a British governor with executive power and control of security forces to supervise new Rhodesian elections (23). Patriotic Front insist UN and Commonwealth forces supervise elections and preceding cease-fire (27). Muzorewa accepts British proposals for transition of power in Rhodesia (29).

9 Dr Eschel Rhoodie, former secretary of S. African Department of Information, sentenced to 6 years for fraud.

27 US announces evidence of low-yield nuclear explosion on 22 September in Indian Ocean near Southern Africa. S. Africa's prime minister denies she has exploded nuclear device.

November

4 Rhodesian troops report 22 soldiers, 60 guerrillas killed in 2-day raid into Zambia.

5– Rhodesia halts rail shipments of maize to Zambia to pressure Kaunda to stop guerrilla attacks. Kaunda says he will not yield (6). Rhodesian troops blow up three bridges east of Lusaka, cutting main links to Southern Zambia (18). Kaunda announces Zambia is on a full-scale war alert (20). UN Security Council resolution condemns Rhodesian raids, calls for damages to be paid to Zambia (23). Rhodesian planes bomb guerrilla camp near Lusaka (25).

7– Britain announces Rhodesian sanctions will be allowed to lapse on 15 November, when due for renewal. President Kaunda of Zambia arrives in London for discussions with Britain and Patriotic Front to try to break deadlock in talks (8). Parliament passes bill enabling Britain to send British governor to Salisbury to supervise transition to new elections (13). Agreement reached on the transition to independence: guerrilla forces to have equal status with Rhodesian army under the British governor during transition, and Britain will feed and house guerrillas at agreed assembly points (15). Muzorewa government accepts cease-fire plan (26).

8 In a by-election, S. African National Party loses first parliamentary seat since coming to power in 1948.

12– UN talks on Namibia open in Geneva; all parties in principle accept a demilitarized zone (16).

December

1 S. Yemen and Ethiopia sign a treaty of friendship and co-operation.

2– Maj. Gen. John Acland appointed commander of Commonwealth monitoring force for Rhodesia. Patriotic Front agrees to cease-fire plan (5). US Senate agrees to lift Rhodesian sanctions as soon as British governor arrives in Salisbury (6). Lord Soames appointed Governor of Rhodesia for pre-election interim period (7), arrives in Salisbury (12). Rhodesian settlement agreements signed in London by the leaders of the three delegations (15). UN lifts economic and diplomatic sanctions imposed on Rhodesia 13 years ago (21). Zambia opens border with Rhodesia, closed since 1973 (23). Lord Soames announces election dates: 14 February 1980 for the 20 white seats, 27–29 February for the 80 black seats (28). Soames sends Rhodesian troops to Mozambique border area to stop guerrillas infiltrating in violation of cease-fire (30).

3 The Eritrean People's Liberation Movement reports it is engaged in an 'all-out offensive' against Ethiopian troops in north-west Eritrea.

5 S. Africa informs UN she accepts a demilitarized zone between Namibia and Angola.

8 A 35-member Soviet Military mission arrives in Angola.

12 Due to shortage of pilots, the S. African air force is now open to blacks.

13 2-year agreement signed for Tanzania to train Ugandan military and police.

LATIN AMERICA

January

6 Peru's military government calls state of emergency to prevent 72-hour general strike; at least 120 union leaders arrested in Lima within 24 hours.

7 Cuban President Castro proposes that US partially lift her trade embargo to improve relations.

8– Argentina and Chile agree to ask Pope to mediate Beagle Channel conflict. Pope agrees (24).

10– Over 10,000 Nicaraguans peacefully protest against government, calling for opposition unity and fall of President Somoza. Somoza rejects proposals by US, Dominica and Guatemala for internationally supervised plebiscite (18).

February

7– USSR delivers diesel-powered *Foxtrot*-class attack submarine to Cuba, also 2 high-speed *Tanya*-class torpedo boats (9).
8– US recalls 47 officials from Nicaragua, ends all military aid and freezes further economic assistance. Sandinista guerrillas open offensive against Somoza regime (20).
12 Argentine government approves plans for 4 more atomic reactors by 1997, costing $14.5 bn.
16 Presidents Carter and Lopez Portillo, in 3-day talks in Mexico agree to reopen stalled negotiations on US purchases of Mexican oil and gas.

March

9 Chile's military regime extends for six months the state of emergency in effect since 1973, citing renewed terrorist activity.
13 Bloodless coup in Grenada replaces Prime Minister Sir Eric Gairy with Maurice Bishop, head of the New Revolutionary Government.
14 Sandinista guerrillas attack Nicaraguan National Guard outposts at Grenada, Ticuantepe and Chichigalpa.
25 Manuel Colom Argueta, leader of the Opposition United Front of the Revolution Party of Guatemala, killed by unidentified gunman.
29 Hugo Banzer, former president, and five generals retired from duty after allegedly conspiring to thwart Bolivia's return to civilian rule.

April

6 Peruvian government extends the state of emergency for fourth month.
8 Jamaican Premier Manley flies to USSR for talks on closer trading links with Eastern bloc.
13– Sandinistas capture Esteli; Nicaraguan National Guard recapture town (15). After further fighting near Costa Rican borders (20), moderate and left-wing opposition meet to unite in overthrowing Somoza regime (24). Sandinistas attack Leon (30).

May

1 Nicaraguan National Guard re-establish control over Leon.
4– Rebels in El Salvador seize French and Costa Rican embassies and San Salvador cathedral. Hostages escape from Costa Rican embassy (8). National Guard kill 19 and injure 38 outside cathedral (9). Rebels seize Venezuelan embassy (11); kill Education Minister (23). President Romero imposes 30-day state of siege (24). Occupation of French and Venezuelan embassies ends (1 June).
14 IMF approves $66-m loan to Nicaragua.
15 US withdraws ambassador from Chile in protest at the Chilean refusal to permit extradition of 3 secret police officers wanted in US for murder.
16 Castro visits Mexico, for first time since 1956, for talks on economic ties; three Mexican ministers resign in protest.
22 Dominica and St Lucia admitted to OAS, bringing membership to 28.

June

1– Heavy fighting in Nicaragua. Two-day general strike closes down Managua; Sandinistas gain control of Leon, (5-6). Somoza declares 'state of siege' as government's position weakens (6). US calls for talks on political settlement in Nicaragua (18). OAS calls for 'replacement' of Somoza (23).

July

3– Israel announces suspension of weapon sales to Nicaragua. Sandinistas advance on Managua (11); name 18-member provisional junta (16). President Somoza flees country (17); Francisco Urcuyo, named by Nicaraguan Congress as replacement, announces he will not hand power to Sandinistas (18). Urcuyo flees Nicaragua; National Guard surrenders and Sandinistas enter Managua (19). Sandinista junta announces nationalization of banks (27).
12 Grenada signs 2-year technical assistance pact with Cuba.

August

6 Inter-American Development Bank promises Nicaragua $225m for reconstruction.
8 Walter Guevara designated temporary Bolivian president for one year.
11 In Ecuador, Jaime Roldos sworn in as first constitutionally-elected president in 9 years.

September

1– US Intelligence confirms 2–3,000 Soviet 'combat troops' are in Cuba. USSR denies she has sent any combat troops to Cuba (11). President Carter asks her to withdraw at least some of the combat troops US insists are there (22). US and Soviet Foreign Ministers end talks on Soviet troops in Cuba (28). Soviet press attacks US threat to take action over the issue (29).

4– Castro opens 6th Summit of Non-Aligned Movement. President Tito appeals for movement's continued independence (5). Conference ends with moderates prevailing on most issues (10).

30 France sells 16 *Mirage* aircraft to Chile.

October

2 Seventeen US ships arrive in the Caribbean for an exercise.

2 US hands Canal Zone to Panama after 76 years of control.

3– To counter Soviet presence in Cuba, Carter announces increased surveillance of Cuba, diplomatic assurances to Latin nations, establishment of a permanent Caribbean Joint Task Force at Key West, expanded military manoeuvres in region, increase in US aid to Caribbean. Soviet Union accuses US of 'gunboat diplomacy'. US stages 1,850-man Marine exercise at her base at Guantanamo, Cuba (19).

17– Romero government overthrown by army coup in El Salvador. Junta cracks down on opposition (18), lifts martial law and ends curfew (24). Clashes with police cause 24 deaths (31).

28 Island of St Vincent gains independence from Britain.

November

1– Col. Alberto Natusch seizes power in Bolivia; declares himself President. US suspends all military and economic aid; general strike paralyses country (2). After demonstrations and shooting in La Paz, Natusch institutes martial law (4). To break general strike, the military arrest trade union leaders (6). General strike continues; Natusch lifts martial law and reinstates Congress (7). Strike is called off (8). Military reaffirms support for Natusch (14), continued opposition forces Natusch to give up Presidency (16); Senora Lydia Gueiler, first woman head of state in Bolivia, elected interim President (17), swears in cabinet (19), appoints new commander-in-chief (21). Deposed C-in-C leads revolt, seizes army barracks in La Paz (23); another new C-in-C appointed and revolt ends (25).

11 After 2-day visit to Venezuela, Brazil's President Baptista signs new trade and energy pact.

28 El Salvador breaks diplomatic relations with S. Africa in protest at her racialist policies.

30 Carter imposes sanctions on Chile for refusing to extradite 3 men wanted for murder in US.

December

4 Nicaragua's revolutionary government cabinet resigns at request of ruling junta.

5 US ambassador returns to Chile after nearly 7 months.

EAST–WEST ARMS CONTROL

January

23 USA and USSR begin a new series of anti-satellite weapons talks in Berne.

24 UN Committee on Disarmament opens 13-week session in Geneva, with France participating for the first time in a standing UN body on disarmament.

February

7 USSR announces willingness to allow some on-site inspection of nuclear blasts, provided it is voluntary and under national control.

23 White House announces US will abide by terms of SALT II treaty even if Senate rejects it.

March

6 US and USSR begin talks in Geneva on limiting chemical weapons; USSR refuses to allow on-site inspection.

15 A 22-nation conference of chemical warfare experts begins in Britain with visit to disused nerve gas establishment to test the feasibility of on-site inspection and verification methods for proposed UN treaty.

April
20 US and USSR Foreign Ministers meet for 5th time in a fortnight to negotiate final SALT II agreement.
23 USSR and US resume talks in Vienna on banning anti-satellite weapons.

May
2   US and USSR agree to complete SALT treaty before Carter-Brezhnev summit in June (contentious points were to have been discussed there).
10 USSR announces agreement to SALT II; minor points still to be clarified.

June
18 Presidents Carter and Brezhnev sign SALT II agreement at Vienna Summit meeting.

August
31 Soviet Premier Kosygin, meeting US senators in Moscow, gives assurance that capability and production rate of *Backfire* bomber will not be increased and notes willingness to accept other Senate reservations on SALT II.

September
27 Ex-President Ford urges US not to approve SALT II Treaty.

October
6– At ceremony to mark thirtieth anniversary of GDR, Brezhnev announces USSR will withdraw 20,000 troops and 1,000 tanks from GDR. NATO reacts coolly; US announces she will continue plans to deploy new theatre nuclear weapons in Europe (8). Soviet Defence Minister Ustinov pledges the 20,000 troops will be withdrawn behind Soviet borders (26).
18– In a series of votes on amendments to SALT II, Senate Foreign Relations Committee: rejects inclusion of *Backfire* in weapons permitted under treaty, rejects proposed inclusion of diesel-powered Soviet subs (20); votes unanimously to attach to treaty 'understanding' asserting US rights to supply nuclear weapons to NATO (23); rejects 2 amendments requiring USSR to dismantle 308 SS-18s (25); approves reservation asserting US claims that MX missile is compatible with treaty (31).

November
9   US Senate Foreign Relations Committee approves SALT II Treaty by 9-6 vote; sends it to Senate for debate.
11 Brezhnev calls for immediate negotiations on NATO's plans to station new medium-range nuclear missiles in Western Europe.

December
6   US Senate announces there will be no debate on SALT II Treaty before 1980.
12 NATO Foreign and Defence Ministers, meeting in Brussels, agree British and French nuclear forces will not be included in SALT III talks.
17 At MBFR conference, NATO presents new proposal for withdrawal of 13,000 US troops from W. Germany if USSR withdraws 30,000 men from Eastern Europe.
17 Comprehensive Test Ban Talks between US, USSR and Britain adjourn till February 1980.

ADELPHI PAPERS

The following is a selection of those available. They may be ordered from the Institute at a current price of £1.50 ($3.50) per copy, post free (by Accelerated Surface Post or Bulk Air Mail to non-UK destinations).

No. 108. THE ALLIANCE AND EUROPE: PART III: WEAPONS PROCUREMENT IN EUROPE — CAPABILITIES AND CHOICES by Roger Facer. Winter 1974/75.
No. 109. THE ALLIANCE AND EUROPE: PART IV: MILITARY DOCTRINE AND TECHNOLOGY by Steven Canby. Winter 1974/75.
No. 111. THE ARAB-ISRAEL WAR, OCTOBER 1973 — BACKGROUND AND EVENTS by Elizabeth Monroe and A. H. Farrar-Hockley. Winter 1974/75.
No. 112. DEFENCE BUDGETING: THE BRITISH AND AMERICAN CASES by Richard Burt. Winter 1974/75.
No. 113. PROSPECTS FOR NUCLEAR PROLIFERATION by John Maddox. Spring 1975.
No. 114. THE MIDDLE EAST AND THE INTERNATIONAL SYSTEM: PART I: THE IMPACT OF THE 1973 WAR. Papers from the IISS 16th Annual Conference. Spring 1975.
No. 115. THE MIDDLE EAST AND THE INTERNATIONAL SYSTEM: PART II: SECURITY AND THE ENERGY CRISIS. Papers from the IISS 16th Annual Conference. Spring 1975.
No. 117. OIL AND INFLUENCE: THE OIL WEAPON EXAMINED by Hans Maull. Summer 1975.
No. 118. PRECISION-GUIDED WEAPONS by James F. Digby. Summer 1975.
No. 119. MILITARY POWER AND POLITICAL INFLUENCE: THE SOVIET UNION AND WESTERN EUROPE by R. J. Vincent. Autumn 1975.
No. 120. THE ALLIANCE AND EUROPE: PART V: NUCLEAR WEAPONS AND EAST-WEST NEGOTIATION by Uwe Nerlich. Winter 1975/76.
No. 122. POWER AT SEA: PART I: THE NEW ENVIRONMENT. Papers from the IISS 17th Annual Conference. Spring 1976.
No. 123. POWER AT SEA: PART II: SUPER-POWERS AND NAVIES. Papers from the IISS 17th Annual Conference. Spring 1976.
No. 124. POWER AT SEA: PART III: COMPETITION AND CONFLICT. Papers from the IISS 17th Annual Conference. Spring 1976.
No. 125. INDIA'S SECURITY IN THE 1980s by G. S. Bhargava. Summer 1976.
No. 126. NEW WEAPONS TECHNOLOGIES: DEBATE AND DIRECTIONS by Richard Burt. Summer 1976.
No. 127. DEFENDING THE CENTRAL FRONT: THE BALANCE OF FORCES by Robert Lucas Fischer. Autumn 1976.
No. 128. THE ARAB-ISRAEL DISPUTE: GREAT POWER BEHAVIOUR by Lawrence L. Whetten. Winter 1976/77.
No. 129. THE ALLIANCE AND EUROPE: PART VI: THE EUROPEAN PROGRAMME GROUP by D. C. R. Heyhoe. Winter 1976/77.
No. 130. NUCLEAR POWER AND WEAPONS PROLIFERATION by Ted Greenwood, George W. Rathjens and Jack Ruina. Winter 1976/77.
No. 131. THE SOVIET UNION AND THE PLO by Galia Golan. Winter 1976.
No. 132. AMERICAN SECURITY POLICY IN ASIA by Leslie H. Brown. Spring 1977.
No. 133. THE DIFFUSION OF POWER: PART I: PROLIFERATION OF FORCE. Papers from the IISS 18th Annual Conference. Spring 1977.
No. 134. THE DIFFUSION OF POWER: PART II: CONFLICT AND ITS CONTROL. Papers from the IISS 18th Annual Conference. Spring 1977.
No. 135. BALKAN SECURITY by F. Stephen Larrabee. Spring 1977.
No. 136. OIL AND SECURITY: PROBLEMS AND PROSPECTS OF IMPORTING COUNTRIES by Edward N. Krapels. Summer 1977.
No. 137. LATIN AMERICA IN WORLD POLITICS: THE NEXT DECADE by Gregory F. Treverton. Summer 1977.
No. 138. THE ROLE OF ARMS CONTROL IN THE MIDDLE EAST by Yair Evron. Autumn 1977.
No. 139. SEA POWER AND WESTERN SECURITY: THE NEXT DECADE by Worth H. Bagley. Winter 1977.
No. 140. THE FUTURE OF LAND-BASED MISSILE FORCES by Colin Gray. Winter 1977.
No. 141. THE FUTURE OF ARMS CONTROL: PART I: BEYOND SALT II. Edited by Christoph Bertram. Spring 1978.
No. 143. A SEA OF TROUBLES? SOURCES OF DISPUTE IN THE NEW OCEAN REGIME by Barry Buzan. Spring 1978.
No. 144. NEW CONVENTIONAL WEAPONS AND EAST-WEST SECURITY: PART I: Papers from the IISS 19th Annual Conference. Spring 1978.
No. 145. NEW CONVENTIONAL WEAPONS AND EAST-WEST SECURITY: PART II: Papers from the IISS 19th Annual Conference. Spring 1978.
No. 146. THE FUTURE OF ARMS CONTROL: PART II: ARMS CONTROL AND TECHNOLOGICAL CHANGE: ELEMENTS OF A NEW APPROACH by Christoph Bertram. Summer 1978.
No. 147/8. DECISION-MAKING IN SOVIET WEAPONS PROCUREMENT by Arthur J. Alexander. Winter 1978/79. *This title is a special double issue: price £3.00 ($7.00).*
No. 149. THE FUTURE OF ARMS CONTROL: PART III: CONFIDENCE-BUILDING MEASURES. Edited by Jonathan Alford. Spring 1979.
No. 150. SOVIET PERSPECTIVES ON SECURITY by Helmut Sonnenfeldt and William G. Hyland. Spring 1979.
No. 151. PROSPECTS OF SOVIET POWER IN THE 1980s: PART I: Papers from the IISS 20th Annual Conference. Summer 1979.
No. 152. PROSPECTS OF SOVIET POWER IN THE 1980s: PART II: Papers from the IISS 20th Annual Conference. Summer 1979.
No. 153. CONGRESSIONAL POWER: IMPLICATIONS FOR AMERICAN SECURITY POLICY by Richard Haass. Summer 1979.
No. 154. GLOBALISM OR REGIONALISM? UNITED STATES POLICY TOWARDS SOUTHERN AFRICA by Garrick Utley. Winter 1979/80.
No. 155. THE AEGEAN DISPUTE by Andrew Wilson. Winter 1979/80.
No. 156. THE FUTURE OF BRITAIN'S DETERRENT FORCE by Peter Nailor and Jonathan Alford. Spring 1980.
No. 157. SOVIET POLICY TOWARDS IRAN AND THE GULF by Shahram Chubin. Spring 1980.
No. 158. SAUDI ARABIA'S SEARCH FOR SECURITY by Adeed Dawisha. Spring 1980.
No. 159. SOUTH AFRICA'S NARROWING SECURITY OPTIONS by Robert S. Jaster. Spring 1980.

Discount rates are available for bulk orders of 11 or more Adelphi Papers of the same title.

IISS PUBLICATIONS

The Military Balance

This highly regarded annual survey of military forces around the world is indispensable for accurate information on their armaments, manpower and budgets. Published in September.

Strategic Survey

An analytical review of the past year's security-related events and trends, including arms-limitations efforts. It is of constant value in interpreting subsequent events. Published each Spring

Adelphi Papers

Monographs analysing current and future problems of international security affairs, written by experts from many nations. Eight to ten published each year (for titles available, see opposite).

Survival

The Institute's Journal, containing original articles, reprint articles and documentation on matters of current concern, is both a forum for debate and a digest for those who cannot follow all the journals in the field. Published in alternate months (six issues a year).

Available from: Publications Department, IISS, 23 Tavistock Street, London WC2E 7NQ
(See card between pages 60 and 61 for subscription terms.)

IISS BOOKS

Published in the United Kingdom by The Macmillan Press Ltd and in the United States by Praeger Publishers Inc.

Recent titles include:

South Asian Crisis: India — Pakistan — Bangladesh. Robert Jackson £7.50.
Nations in Arms: Theory and Practice of Territorial Defence. Adam Roberts. £7.50.
Arms Control and European Security: A Guide to East-West Negotiations. J. I. Coffey. £10.00.
New Conventional Weapons and East-West Security. Christoph Bertram (ed.). £12.00.

Order through your bookseller

Price
£3.00
$6.50